"Chandran Nair asks difficult questions and offers bold, provocative answers. One may disagree with his answers but has to admire his willingness to tackle thorny problems. These pages open our eyes to some of the most urgent problems facing humanity. A must-read."
—**Moisés Naím, Distinguished Fellow, Carnegie Endowment for International Peace, and author of *The End of Power***

"Nair shows that more than ever, state capacity matters for sustainable prosperity, and this is precisely the Achilles' heel of most of the developing world."
—**Gurcharan Das, author of *India Unbound*, *The Difficulty of Being Good*, and *India Grows at Night***

"Chandran Nair is an incisive and visionary thinker with a properly sober take on our 'crowded and resource-constrained' future. He is totally right in *The Sustainable State* that the emerging economies' adoption of the consumption-driven model of growth that has characterized the wealthy West would exhaust our planet's capacity. As he also rightly argues, what is needed is both a cultural shift from an aspiration of well-having to one of well-being and a shift from the free rein of the market's invisible hand to intelligent governance through the guiding hand of the state."
—**Nathan Gardels, cofounder of the Berggruen Institute and Editor-in-Chief, *The WorldPost***

"Most development models, including those concerning sustainability, are based on Western experiences and ideology. Problems have arisen therefrom and they have proven inadequate or inappropriate for current challenges and socio-economic realities of the developing world. In *The Sustainable State*, Chandran Nair draws upon the Asian experience—including China and its successes—to suggest a more fitting approach for the 'global majority.' His arguments are persuasive but extremely 'disruptive.'"
—**Ronnie C. Chan, Chairman, Hang Lung Properties, and Chairman Emeritus, Asia Society**

"Much of our current understanding of the nature of the state and its role comes from Western experience, e.g., Westphalia, the Industrial Revolution, the Cold War, the internet. But this is not what government and good governance means to most people outside of the West. Chandran Nair's groundbreaking book tries to explain from a non-Western perspective what governments can and must do for the global majority in an era of resource constraints."
—**Professor Kiyoshi Kurokawa, Chairman, Fukushima Nuclear Accident Investigation Commission, and Science Advisor to the Cabinet of Japan**

"In this brilliant new book, Chandran Nair takes on the elephant in the room: how could a genetically and culturally small-group animal reorganize itself to live in groups of millions and billions without finishing the job of destroying its life-support systems? Can huge poor nations create governance systems that will allow all their people to enjoy decent lives, and how can huge rich states modify theirs to make this possible? Everyone with an interest in the human predicament will want to read *The Sustainable State*."

—**Paul R. Ehrlich, author of *The Population Bomb* and coauthor of *The Annihilation of Nature***

"First with *Consumptionomics*, now with *The Sustainable State*, Chandran Nair describes an alternative path and meaning of progress: governance, when good, is an essential antidote to irresponsible, injurious capitalism and individual license. This is a book for our times."

—**Zoher Abdoolcarim, former Asia Editor, *Time***

"The role of the state has withered. Chandran Nair is one of the few people to understand that the pendulum has swung too far and that more and better government will be needed to address our global challenges successfully. His arguments are persuasive and powerful."

—**Graeme Maxton, Secretary-General, Club of Rome, and coauthor of *Reinventing Prosperity***

"Nair is saying it when others are shying away. Liberal democracies and capitalist markets have not helped mankind achieve sustainable development. These are the rich countries of the world—the biggest of which don't believe in too much regulation. In developing economies, competing thoughts have emerged that argue for the necessity of comprehensive state intervention. Nair gives us a fulsome narrative to consider this crucial debate that has finally dawned."

—**Christine Loh, Chief Development Strategist, Institute for the Environment, Hong Kong University of Science and Technology, and former Undersecretary for the Environment, Hong Kong**

"Chandran Nair's commendable new book, *The Sustainable State*, provides an inspirational new way of thinking about developing the type of state that can do the most good for the largest number of people. His propositions are especially useful for the governance of crowded, resource-constrained countries such as mine, Nigeria. He offers great insights on how developing a strong pro-people state can steer people and resources along the path of genuine sustainable development that serves the interest of the masses."

—**Jibrin Ibrahim, Professor of Political Science and Senior Fellow, Centre for Democracy and Development**

THE SUSTAINABLE STATE

The Future of Government, Economy, and Society

Chandran Nair

Berrett–Koehler Publishers, Inc.
a BK Currents book

Berrett-Koehler Publishers, Inc.
1333 Broadway, Suite 1000
Oakland, CA 94612-1921
Tel: (510) 817-2277
Fax: (510) 817-2278
www.bkconnection.com

ORDERING INFORMATION
Quantity sales. Special discounts are available on quantity purchases by corporations, associations, and others. For details, contact the "Special Sales Department" at the Berrett-Koehler address above.

Individual sales. Berrett-Koehler publications are available through most bookstores. They can also be ordered directly from Berrett-Koehler: Tel: (800) 929-2929; Fax: (802) 864-7626; www.bkconnection.com.

Orders for college textbook / course adoption use. Please contact Berrett-Koehler: Tel: (800) 929-2929; Fax: (802) 864-7626.

Distributed to the U.S. trade and internationally by Penguin Random House Publisher Services.

Berrett-Koehler and the BK logo are registered trademarks of Berrett-Koehler Publishers, Inc.

Printed in the United States of America

Berrett-Koehler books are printed on long-lasting acid-free paper. When it is available, we choose paper that has been manufactured by environmentally responsible processes. These may include using trees grown in sustainable forests, incorporating recycled paper, minimizing chlorine in bleaching, or recycling the energy produced at the paper mill.

Library of Congress Cataloging-in-Publication Data
Names: Nair, Chandran, author.
Title: The sustainable state : the future of government, economy, and society / Chandran Nair.
Description: First edition. | Oakland, CA : Berrett-Koehler Publishers, [2018] | Includes bibliographical references and index.
Identifiers: LCCN 2018019439 | ISBN 9781523095148 (pbk.)
Subjects: LCSH: Sustainable development—Developing countries. | Economic development—Developing countries. | Developing countries—Economic policy. | Institution building—Developing countries. | Developing countries—Politics and government. | State, The.
Classification: LCC HC59.72.E5 N35 2018 | DDC 338.9/27091724—dc23
LC record available at https://lccn.loc.gov/2018019439

First Edition
25 24 23 22 21 20 19 18   10 9 8 7 6 5 4 3 2 1

Project manager: Susan Geraghty
Cover designer: Mimi Heft Design
Text designer: Paula Goldstein
Compositor: Westchester Publishing Services
Copyeditor: Michele Jones
Proofreader: Sophia Ho
Indexer: Sylvia Coates

This book is dedicated to my late brother Venu Nair.

It is also dedicated to the global majority, who are subject to the harsh realities of an unsustainable path to growth and prosperity, the fruits of which are enjoyed by a minority.

All proceeds from direct sales of the book by the Global Institute for Tomorrow and from worldwide royalties will be directed toward furthering the debate on the nature of the sustainable state. This will be done by organizing workshops, conferences, and debates across the world.

CONTENTS

• • •

T he seeds of this book were planted soon after my first book, *Con-sumptionomics: Asia's Role in Reshaping Capitalism and Saving the Planet,* was published. One idea I outlined in the book was the need for the state to take a more active role in resource allocation to avoid a catastrophe in the developing world. Another was for their societies to be organized such that collective welfare took precedence over individual rights. As one might expect, I was often attacked as a Communist, an anticapitalist, or, most annoyingly, a poor misguided Asian environmentalist.

This led me to connect the dots among everything I had read, seen, heard, and experienced in thirty years of traveling and working around the world on development, environmental, and sustainability issues. I wanted to explore the role of the state in a constrained and overcrowded planet. This drew on project work in almost all the major countries in Asia and five years in Africa, and professional engagements and visits to the Middle East, Europe, Australia, and the US. I used every opportunity to immerse myself in local knowledge and conditions, which continues through my work with the Global Institute for Tomorrow.

I used international forums on sustainability to test the waters on an idea that was becoming clearer to me each day: that only a strong state can help the world's large developing nations navigate the twenty-first century's sustainability challenge.

More often than not, I was labeled as an extremist and a pessimist who did not believe in human ingenuity and progress. Nothing could be further from the truth. But after listening carefully to the arguments of many who spoke to me and what was presented as fact at global events, I increasingly believed that the arguments at the core of most current approaches were weak. I concluded that most of the approaches widely accepted as received wisdom—based on free markets, technological advances, and the spread of democracy—were simply wrong. In fact, the working title for this book was *The Indispensable State.*

Interestingly, I did not get much pushback from Asians, Africans, and others in the developing world. It was the growing support I received from many in Asia that convinced me of the need to write this book.

This book is an attempt to contribute to a new narrative of sustainable development. This narrative must come from parts of the world that are confronted with the real sustainability challenge at a scale and level of impact the West has never experienced and never will. Yet leadership on this issue has only been provided by the West.

This book will attempt to broaden the discussion in the hope that leaders in the developing world will rethink their approaches and expectations regarding development, growth, and sustainability. It will ask more fundamental questions about the reach of our rights and freedoms in the face of an existential threat. It is also my hope that Western economic, development, and academic institutions, as well as thought leaders, will consider these arguments and pause before they provide advice to the developing world on the challenges of sustainability.

The book hopes to get the world's non-Western elites, who are comfortable with Western ideas, to think again regarding the future of their countries, for which much is at stake in the face of the global sustainability challenge. They have usually attended Western colleges and graduate schools, and likely spent part of their lives in Western cities. They may even have worked for Western multinationals. They may have close connections with important and prominent people in the West. Thus, when it comes to sustainability challenges, they rely on Western ideas rather than radical new ones, even though they live at the front line. Rather than go to Yangon, Dacca, or Chennai, they would rather go to the comfortable surroundings of Harvard, MIT, or Cambridge. This book is for them.

This book is also for the next generation of young leaders who have ambitions to make a difference and "be the change." There are many examples of how these young elites deemed to be leaders of the future can be stuck in groupthink on key global issues. To belong to such prestigious groups requires some acquiescence to the feel-good approaches as defined by "the great and the good." Thus, on cue, they march to the same drumbeat. They say they want to make the world a better place, but don't ask the hard questions. They are young, but seeking legitimacy means avoiding radicalism. They align themselves to "do-good" causes, often the usual-suspect topics and linked to philanthropy. They seek business solutions and try to build a social enterprise; if it involves technology and venture capital, all the better.

I have spoken to such groups on many occasions and am surprised at how difficult and discomforting it is for them—mainly those from the developing world—to open their minds to a new conversation and particularly to a new historical perspective. What they find most difficult is the challenge posed to them about how they are the victim of Westernization yet perpetuate it without trying to take the best from both worlds. It is often emotionally difficult for them to process. Yet they are meant to be the next generation of leaders, where so much hope is placed. They openly express support for sustainability and other such causes, and say they seek change. But the change they seek is skin deep, as they are unwilling to accept the core challenge in the sustainability crisis: that Asia (and the rest of the developing world) will need to take a very different path than the West and must reject the West's unsustainable economic and political systems. This is book for them too.

Finally, this book is for those who are working on these issues but feel that current approaches are weak and do not relate to the conditions and realities they experience. They have been searching for something new, a different narrative that speaks to their appreciation of the issues and realities. In the absence of this, they have succumbed to the tired narratives, lost their radicalism, become cynical, or given up. I hope this book captures some of "their narrative" and that they will help mainstream it for those who will come after them. This book is for them too.

INTRODUCTION

The Indispensable State, Sustaining Our Future

In 2012, I traveled to Youyu County, nestled in the northwestern corner of China's Shanxi Province. It can be easy to assume and expect that Youyu County, like large parts of central China, is a dusty, arid semidesert—especially after you learn that almost 90 percent of the local economy is driven by coal mining. But Youyu County isn't brown; it's green. Forests and grasslands blanket the landscape, holding back the nearby deserts.

This wasn't always the case. The county is close to the Ordos Desert, which had steadily expanded into the region due to soil erosion and drought. In 1949, over three-quarters of the region's land had been affected by desertification. This was clearly bad on its own terms, but the desertification also had serious effects on the county's development. Agriculture was difficult, which kept incomes low and kept people in poverty. Those who could leave often did.

An old rhyme from Youyu puts the issue more plainly:

It was so dark that people needed lamps during the day,
At night the sand will bury your door which won't open in the morning
Once windy there was a sandstorm,
Once rainy there was a flood
The hills were bare like the head of a monk,
Nine out of ten years there was no harvest
Most men left in search of better lives,
The ladies left behind dug wild herbs to feed themselves.

Nowadays, desertification is one of China's major national environmental priorities. The country's expanding deserts are blamed both for swallowing up large tracts of arable land and for worsening the air pollution crisis in Beijing and other major cities. China has launched many programs to combat desertification, from tree-planting campaigns to moving communities away from overgrazed and overfarmed regions. The Chinese government is now starting to plant forests—a "Green Necklace"—along the Hebei-Beijing border to help combat creeping desertification and large-scale pollution from the manufacturing-driven Hebei Province.

But, in Youyu, the fight against desertification started much earlier. The county's first party chief, upon taking office in 1949, reportedly stated that the county's development guideline should be: "To be rich, stop the sandstorm. To stop the sandstorm, plant more trees." Over the decades, this approach made the county a national leader in reforestation. Government officials took pride in their work, even as China's opening to the rest of the world and subsequent rapid growth highlighted flashier symbols of development. When I was there, I was told that when the county mayor was promoted to a new position elsewhere in the country, the only souvenir he took from his office was the beat-up shovel he used during his twelve years in Youyu.

Today Youyu is called a "Green Pearl"—far from the barren desert landscape of decades past. The numbers are truly staggering. At the founding of the People's Republic of China in October 1949, only about 0.3 percent of Youyu County was covered in forest. By 2016, this number had risen to 54 percent, higher than both the national average (21.36 percent) and the world average (32 percent). Water and soil erosion during the rainy season have been reduced by as much as 60 percent. The number of sandstorm days has been halved. Desertification has been effectively halted in its tracks, and the planting of trees has become a revered activity for all age groups in this rural population.[1]

Controlling the sandstorms unlocked Youyu's economic potential. The county has replaced traditional subsistence farming with "high-quality, high efficiency ecological agriculture."[2] The forests have also encouraged tourism, with over seven hundred thousand visitors to the county in 2010.

Youyu is a shining example of not just environmental protection but also environmental regeneration and achieving long-term sustainability objectives. But it took heavy government intervention and unusual leadership over a period of decades to hold back the desert. The government devised a strict blueprint for reforestation that was followed for over half a century, spanning two generations. Party cadres became "Forest Directors," responsible for tree planting. Finally, the government organized the people into a mass reforestation movement, which supported the efforts of the state, thereby also gaining legitimacy at the same time.

It is hard to think of another country that has actively reforested its countryside in this way over two generations in such extreme conditions, and certainly none can be found in the developing world. Youyu's officials had a great deal of authority, but they were passionate about governance and improving the lives of society as a whole. And, in turn, the people trusted their leaders' judgment and worked over several decades to support their objectives.

It is worth asking a potentially bold question: Could the Indian government reforest one of its states in this way? Would Indonesia's government be able to reforest vast parts of Kalimantan (Borneo), where, very fortunately, the climate would easily support such an effort? Or could the US launch such a large-scale program of reforestation? To ask an even more bold question about the role of the state in attaining sustainability goals: Would the US be able to build a network of high-speed trains across the country and thus reduce the carbon footprint of the transportation sector as China has done? Are these countries capable of turning the tools of the state toward sustainability, resource protection, environmental regeneration, and survival?

• • •

Throughout my career, both as the former chairman of Asia's largest environmental management consultancy and currently as the founder of a pan-Asian think tank focused on economic development and sustainability, I've come away from countless conferences and meetings about sustainable development with business leaders, government officials, and NGOs with the same nagging thought.

Very few people seem—from what they say and write—to have truly grappled with the multidimensional and global scale of the sustainability challenge and confronted the realities and the brutally honest nature of the solutions needed, apart from actions (untested in policy to date) against global climate change—an important part of the sustainability challenge, but only a part.

This is not to say that people do not grasp the severity of the problem, nor that they are not passionate in trying to find solutions. Instead, it would appear that the current conversation about sustainable development is based on several flawed premises that distract us from coming up with real solutions that will require painful adjustments, especially by the global "haves," and redefining our ideas about prosperity.

The idea of sustainable development has become confused with pollution reduction, being environmentally friendly, or even just being environmentally conscious. This has allowed many organizations across the world, especially businesses, to paint their actions as improving their sustainability and tackling the global challenge. Actions as small as an office lowering the temperature setting of its air conditioning and as indirect as Coca-Cola's sponsorship of a water-use reduction conference are placed under the umbrella of "sustainability"—in spite of the fact that both entities either engage in massively unsustainable practices themselves or encourage them in others. Organizations such as the UN have, in my view, muddied the waters by not taking a clear position and instead creating platforms such as the Global Compact, where multinational corporations can showcase their all-too-often superficial attempts at sustainability while allowing the UN to promote its engagement business, and thus claim it is being fair and inclusive to all stakeholders. Even worse, these platforms have become respected institutions, thus not even allowing well-informed UN officials to be intellectually honest, for fear of upsetting corporate members of the Global Compact and the numerous other Business Advisory Councils it has created.

Here is why environmental awareness is not the same as being "sustainable": "being green" is about reducing the environmental costs of economic activity and other human impacts, such as proper disposal of human waste. In this day and age, one could even say that taking action about the environmental impacts associated with economic activity is simply doing the "decent" thing, which should be no badge of honor. Sustainability goes deeper than harm reduction. It concerns the management of common and public resources to ensure they are not overused or abused, so that all people have fair and equal access to them.

Perhaps it would be best to start from first principles. *Sustainability* is the ability of a system to survive indefinitely, by not using or abusing resources faster than its ability to replenish itself. A more sustainable economy, therefore, is one with a smaller gap between its use/abuse of resources and the Earth's ability to renew them. Some green techniques, though good on their own merits, do not reduce this gap. In other words: all sustainable systems are green, but not all green systems are sustainable.

Development, by contrast, refers to the provision of basic needs and standards of living to a population that constitutes an improved quality of life. A developed economy is one that largely provides basic needs universally among its entire population; by contrast, a developing country has yet to achieve this. The basic needs include, but are certainly not limited to, safe and secure food supply systems, clean water, safe and sturdy shelter, basic energy systems, sanitation, and high-quality health care and education.

Like sustainability, development has become a broad term. Some use it to refer to high economic growth, even if fundamental living standards have not improved for a large part of the population. Some tie it to modernization, especially along Western lines. This often links development with flashy symbols of modernity: skyscrapers in Shanghai, Kuala Lumpur, or Manila are seen as proof of development, even as poverty continues to exist not far from the city center and targets the majority. The newest development fad is the internet, with exaggerated claims that connectivity is a must to address issues of poverty alleviation and will also help the cause of sustainable development. The new development paradigm seems to have more to do with fiber optics and satellites to connect everyone than with toilets, sewers, water supply networks, and proper roofs.

There is also a bad habit of deeming unfamiliar systems as "undeveloped" even if they get better results. The West can be particularly guilty of this, calling countries that follow Western models of economics and politics to be more developed, even if the results are growing inequality, and even if non-Western models have had better results.

This return to first principles leads us to the idea of *sustainable development*: the improvement of living standards and provision of basic needs in a manner that does not consume or abuse resources at a faster rate than they are replenished and that also preserves the right of future generations.

My first book, *Consumptionomics,* was a critique of the increasingly common economic approach in Asia to ape the Western model of consumption-led growth. I argued that by focusing on consumption, high rates of economic growth, and Western-style development, Asia was putting itself on the road to ruin. Massive overconsumption would greatly strain the region's already fragile environment and worsen the consequences for the very poor suffering from the effects of scarcity, pollution, and climate change. It would ultimately have catastrophic global impacts due to the fact the region is home to 60 percent of the world's population.

Consumptionomics highlighted a problem in how we understand economics and economic development. But that leads us to the next question: If the world should not use relentless consumption based on the underpricing of externalities as its engine for further development, what should governments use instead? In a world of hard resource constraints, what would "Constrainomics" look like? That in turn raises more difficult questions about rights and freedom in a resource-constrained planet. Is car ownership a human right?

If the world, and especially Asia, are to get through a hot and crowded twenty-first century, they need a new model for economic development and new definitions of *prosperity* and *freedoms*. They need a new political philosophy and uplifting vocabulary about human progress in an era of constraints, beyond simplified slogans that conflate rights and freedom of choice. There is little in past economic history that matches the scale of the coming challenge; in fact, past models have likely served to make the problem worse. There is no template for this challenge, and for the global majority in Asia, Africa, and South America to look to the West and its institutions for solutions is the height of folly.

Something new is needed, and this book is an attempt to figure out what that might be. The book aims to ask some highly inconvenient questions, expose some of the fallacies at the heart of the sustainability discourse from the viewpoint of a developing world "reality check," and postulate some solutions. But it is not going to arrogantly suggest that these solutions are the blueprint for addressing all the challenges we face.

This will not be an attempt to devise a solution for the world as a whole. Developed economies cannot run away from the fact that they have a disproportionately large footprint per capita, without the added challenge of achieving basic living standards for their people. But the world's majority, with a much smaller footprint per capita, lives in China, India, Indonesia, Nigeria, Brazil, and the rest of the developing world. Their footprints will—and must—increase. These countries still need to achieve a basic standard of living for all their people, as the majority continue to be mired in poverty, yet the only development models available to them are unsustainable and borrowed from the West.

There is, as of now, no answer to what I will call the "India question": How can India, a country of 1.2 billion (peaking at 1.5 billion in 2050), lift hundreds of millions, and perhaps as much as half a billion, out of poverty in the next thirty years, yet also curtail its emissions and resource use at the same time? All the economic development models available to India would release huge amounts of emissions, produce mountains of waste, overuse resources and create even more pollution, and would thus worsen the global sustainability challenge. However, India, with some justification, argues that it would be unfair to deny better living standards to its hundreds of millions of people and so should strive to standards attained by Europeans and Americans by employing the same approach to development. In a perfect world, India would be absolutely right. But as the book will argue, this will not be possible, and this problem encapsulates the sustainable development challenge for the developing world.

India is not alone in needing to pursue sustainability and development at the same time. Despite huge progress in alleviating poverty globally (mainly in China), many in the global majority are still not provided with basic needs. According to the World Bank, 700 million people still live on less than US$2 a day. One in ten people lack access to clean water. One in three does not have a proper toilet despite having a mobile phone. Then you have the hundreds of millions who, although not living in abject poverty, still do not have a reasonably comfortable living standard, with access to good education, a safe home, and health care for themselves and their families.

However, the current attempts by developing countries to improve the livelihood of their people, while successful in alleviating abject poverty, have also had huge repercussions in terms of environmental degradation and resource depletion, not to mention social costs. Cramped cities with inadequate housing are choked by smog and poor waste disposal, which create huge public health risks for residents. Ancient forests, reservoirs of biodiversity, are cut down to make room for plantations. Groundwater and waterways are contaminated by trash, industrial and agricultural chemicals, and human waste. Then add the carbon emissions that are likely to be added by the construction of new power plants, the massive growth in car ownership levels, and the expansion of agriculture (among other activities), and one can see how this quickly becomes a global issue even if impacts are most felt at the local level.

Developing countries like India are thus currently stuck in a dilemma. Do they develop using the models available to them, and risk damaging, if not destroying, their environments and impoverishing their people further? Do they lie and promise Western living standards to their people, despite the fact that this will lead to ruin? The harsh truth is that they can't. But without an alternative understanding of prosperity and development, this admission is tantamount to dooming their people to perpetual poverty—a morally and politically difficult argument. This is a dilemma not addressed by Western experts and institutions, as it would raise some fundamental questions about the economic and political models being promoted and result in all sorts of accusations that liberals are unwilling to confront. The resource footprints of countries like China, India, Indonesia, Nigeria, and Brazil will—and must—increase if they are to achieve a basic standard of living for all their people. Yet the only development models available to them are unsustainable and borrowed from Western economic and political orthodoxy.

How can the developing world provide the most basic living standards for their whole population, without destroying the planet in the process? This is the real challenge of sustainable development.

The Sustainable State focuses on how the world's poorer nations—particularly the larger ones—address the particular conundrum of uplifting hundreds of millions of people from drudgery while avoiding the worst aspects of an economic model at war with the planet and its people. However, its core argument about the indispensable role of the state is also relevant to more advanced economies, such as the US, Europe, Japan, and South Korea.

But the scale and nature of the challenge are different in these richer economies. The need to share with "the rest" has unsettled several wealthy, modern, and democratic countries, especially as the rest begin to take their rightful place in the world after centuries of domination by the West. It has resulted in a battle between so-called globalists and populists in democratic countries, each reacting to the prospect of sharing with the rest.

I have come to the conclusion that the drastic shifts and sacrifices needed in these advanced economies are unlikely to come to pass. The evidence suggests that their democratic institutions, as currently constituted, will not facilitate such changes. It is difficult to ask a population accustomed to a certain standard of living and privilege to downgrade in the interest of greater global sustainability.

I certainly hope that there will be change in the rich world, but it will only happen when truly enlightened leaders emerge who are bold enough to change the narrative and create a new political philosophy that addresses the issue of collective welfare over individual rights, critiques the idea of unconstrained individual choice, and reinterprets the definition of prosperity in a constrained world. No Western leader has yet shown any appetite to do these things. Almost all, despite lofty rhetoric, seek to preserve the old order and their dominant role.

One can look at France to see how the promise of radical change affects political popularity. An initially popular President Macron with fresh ideas and a desire to take the mantle of European and global leadership has seen his approval ratings plummet upon trying to reform France's old labor laws. The French population has gotten used to privileges, and so resists the wider structural changes needed. Ironically, democracy allows this denial, as the state remains too weak to take bold policy action.

This is not to let these countries off the hook. Advanced democracies will have an important role to play as partners of the global majority when facing the challenges of the twenty-first century. In fact it is in their interest.

How can mature democracies become strong and thus more effective states? One can think of a few general prescriptions: more effective governance, rewriting of constitutional structures that are no longer suited to current needs and challenges, an ability to move past political gridlock, greater responsiveness to what majority public opinion actually asks for, and a more active intervention in the economy.

It will also require coming to terms politically with the rise of the rest and the inevitably of sharing with others. Thus Western economies have to stop thinking they can impose their approaches on the rest, and that means examining the role of Western-dominated international organizations, most of which were created in a different era and are now past their sell-by date, but are still hung on to in order to retain past privileges and prestige. They will also have to address their own problems, which are only likely to get more severe as their populations feel the discomfort of a more globalized world. This will require addressing the issue of why they are becoming weaker and apparently failing and why the panacea of democracy is unable to serve their populations.

I will not pretend that *The Sustainable State* provides an answer to this question, but I hope it raises enough questions to spur a robust debate in the West—and the rest of the world—on the subject of sustainability and the role of the strong and effective state to resolve it.

• • •

There is a school of thought that essentially argues that "everything will be fine." It denies that there could be a trade-off between development and sustainability, as the free market, operating within democratic systems, will eventually self-correct. Technology would provide a panacea to social problems. As resources become scarcer, resource prices will increase, and companies will be encouraged to create more energy- and resource-efficient products. Inventors may even develop entirely new technology that allows everyone to live a lifestyle that is both American and sustainable.

This can be a comforting argument, as the policy prescriptions can be quite lucrative. What better win-win strategy than one that allows for going green while making money? Regulations would be discouraged, as they would interfere in the proper functioning of the market. Governments would take a step back and let the market innovate; at most, a government could subsidize tech companies in the hope that they will invent something that will allow the world to live like Americans.

There may be, in the distant future, technologies that make a high level of consumption possible without the external environmental costs, though they would have to overcome many laws of nature and are thus highly improbable. Such technologies certainly do not exist today, and may never exist in a form affordable for the developing world. Climate change and environmental devastation are happening now, and the world cannot afford to places its hopes on a deus ex machina. And this is not to even ask the question of what unrestrained consumption does to human societies, and whether it is even desirable.

Most people—Western and non-Western—understand that the developing world needs an economic model that keeps a path to continued development open while using resources in a sustainable manner. They know that the expectations of the developing world must be managed, moving them away from expecting a Western standard of living but still providing them with what I will be describing as a "moderate prosperity," allowing them to live well and comfortably within limits. However, pressing for details often leads to sheepish shrugs and an admission that the problem seems unsolvable. Why?

The difficulty comes from an unwillingness (mainly for ideological reasons) to jettison our current ideas about how to organize our economies, societies, and states. There is also the difficulty of articulating the politically incorrect but honest idea that the world's majority cannot and should not aspire to live like the West. And there is the troubling thought of coming to terms with the idea of unconstrained individual rights and freedoms. This will be discussed further, but a condition for navigating the challenge in developing countries will be to create political and economic systems where collective welfare overrides individual rights. For example, many Asian cities need more cars like I need a hole in the head, and the solution is not more technology but restrictions on car ownership and/or usage and investments in public transport. That will infringe on individual rights, but the collective majority will benefit. The ability of individuals to exercise their right to a car in these crowded cites has created a collective nightmare.

Further, there is the challenge of dispelling the well-established answer to all of this: that multinational corporations, given their immense economic power and reach, are in this struggle together with people of the world and that together with technology will be the key to success. This is a lie, and a goal of this book is to make it clear that although corporations will play a part—often not voluntary—the challenge of sustainability is one of protecting public good, and this is neither the business nor the role of companies. After all, sustainability is about the notion of "less," and corporations do not do "less"; they do "more." To paraphrase business language, it is in the DNA of a company to innovate and do more, not less. Mainstream (and Western) economic and business models have put developing countries in a box where creating solutions to sustainable development is extremely difficult. A new paradigm is needed.

The free market has long been the centerpiece of orthodox models of international development. Sustainable development too must now be achieved through the instruments of the free markets and with the private sector taking the lead. Almost all mainstream economists would argue that the free market allocates the world's scarce resources in a way that allows them to be used most efficiently and in a way that does the most good. Assuming everything is working properly, the market would optimize society's use of resources. By extension, any move to interfere in the market's operations would lead to a worse and more inefficient outcome.

But the underlying problem with the free-market doctrine of development is that it puts continuous high growth as its aim, driven by consumption as its engine. Barring the development of a whole range of radical new technologies and plans to facilitate their constructive use, infinite growth is impossible. Ask any eminent scientist. We already consume more resources than the Earth's ability to restore them, so we will eventually hit the hard boundaries of what our planet can provide. As long as we value growth above everything else, we will never have truly sustainable development: governments would too often choose to boost growth in the short term by unsustainably consuming resources. In the developing world, where the majority are still disenfranchised, the growth at any cost model can only lead to a bleak future.

If the developing world is to truly have sustainable development, it needs to radically rethink the development consensus. It needs to change its focus on free markets; on Western versions of economics, politics, and modernity; on the free flow of capital; and other "truths" of development. These rules have been written by Western countries and institutions: even though I am sure many are sincere in their wish to improve the lives of the less fortunate, the bureaucrats that operate them still live and work in a Western context far removed from realities on the ground. They can push outdated doctrines long past when empirical evidence has proven their failure.

This problem is compounded by the fact that many in the developing world accept ideas from the West unthinkingly and uncritically. One example is how Asia understands "prosperity." Asians currently model prosperity after an American lifestyle: two cars, a sizable two-story house in the suburbs, a large TV, air-conditioning, fast internet, and meat with every meal. Asia urgently needs to redefine what it means to be prosperous. In a more constrained era, what does it mean to live the "good life"?

Asia also needs to redefine its attitude toward consumption. Too many societies have unthinkingly and rapidly abandoned well-established norms of frugality and now function and even thrive on the notion that all of us have a right to our own consumption. To borrow a metaphor, consumption is often perceived as innocent until proven guilty. It is deemed acceptable unless it presents clear harms to the consumer and to others, and even then any actions must be of a light touch.

But our understanding of "harm" does not go far enough. Instead, consumption where externalities are not priced in (i.e., almost everything we consume in goods and services) needs to be guilty until proven innocent. We should be aware that all consumption places costs on the resource base and also other members of society, and that it should only be approved once those costs have been recognized and accounted for. This is not to call for a utopian pricing regime for all forms of consumption, because that would not be feasible. Human survival depends on careful resource/commons usage and rent, and there are always externalities and limits involved. The challenge is to determine which ones to price appropriately—to allow for responsible levels of consumption—so as to reduce negative impacts, and which ones to tolerate where impacts are not too significant or intolerable. That is ultimately the biggest role of the state, and this book will give examples of this critical balancing act the state must play in developing countries. These examples will make the point that this role cannot be abdicated by the state in the false hope that it will be fulfilled by the workings of markets and innovations by tech firms or multinationals, especially those dependent on natural resources either as feedstock or sinks. In this regard, the state has an obligation and much to do to ensure that one person's consumption is not an absolute violation of another person's basic human rights.

Someone—or something—needs to make these decisions on how to manage resources, economies, and expectations. The same can be said about redefining what prosperity will look like in the twenty-first century. What goods can a society afford to let people strive for? What standard of living is too extravagant given hard resource constraints?

It should be obvious that these questions cannot be the remit of the private sector or NGOs. The private sector has no real interest in pricing in the externalities of the consumption of their goods and services, as their business models often rely on *not* paying for them—carbon dioxide is just the tip of the iceberg. And why would they pay for externalities voluntarily? Thus, the private sector seeks to demonstrate care by initiatives such as corporate social responsibility and others with regard to the environment and sustainability issues. All of these have their value, and many companies do take it seriously, but, as most of the specialists within the corporations know, this does not address the "less" versus "more" issue at the heart of the challenge on how societies become more sustainable.

Systemic market failures, such as the gap between the private benefits and the external costs of consumption, mean that the market does not allocate resources toward long-term sustainability. The lack of a mechanism to properly price and manage public and common goods means that they are perpetually overused, leading to overproduction and, in turn, overconsumption. We need governance of the economy in order to overcome these market failures.

Nor can governance be successfully exerted at the global level. Global agreements still require states to implement their directives. If states are unable or unwilling to do so, then global governance fails. "Bottom-up governance"—a common and romantic refrain of liberals from the West on how to manage sustainability in the developing world—would be nice to have, but is also not a viable alternative, due to the reality of the erosion of village authority in relation to both the state and the global market, not to mention the need for consolidation rather than fragmentation to serve organizational purposes in developing countries. Granting authority to villages too early would likely end up worsening the problem, as weak local governments are captured by vested interests.

In a perfect world, sustainability would be driven by a combination of global, state, and local governments. But we do not live in such a world. Rather than living in a world marked by the demise of the state, we instead live in a world driven by it: the only governing entity with the legitimacy, accountability, and actual ability to make the necessary political choices about the economy and the use of resources.

I will readily admit that few states are perfect. Many, especially in the developing world, have serious problems with efficiency, corruption, weak institutions, incompetence, and an unwillingness both to recognize sustainability issues as central to their legitimacy and to think outside the box. Some rely too heavily on force and oppression to mask their internal weaknesses and mismanagement of their economies. However, even with spreading globalization across the world, the state is still the only governing body that a population sees as the most legitimate wielder of authority and protector of their interests.

In his book *India Grows at Night*, the Indian author and former business leader Gurcharan Das says, "I celebrated the heroic idea that India was rising despite the state. Two decades later, I have realised that I might have been wrong. I am now convinced that the state is of first-order importance. It can either allow human beings to flourish or it can become the biggest obstacle to their realisation of their potential. To rise without the state is courageous but it cannot be a long term virtue."[3]

• • •

This book argues that the sustainability challenge is what will define this century, and for the people in the large poorer nations of the world to have a chance to flourish—not the same as living some American dystopian dream—then the state will need to be actively involved in the economy and particularly in how the majority have access to basic resources.

If states are to fulfill their role and responsibilities and provide for societies in a hot and crowded twenty-first century, they need to be strong. They need to be able to intervene effectively and consistently in the economy to support sustainability goals. They need to be able to resist the influence of the vested interests that currently thrive on and benefit from overconsumption, allowing "others" to pay the price for their buy-one-get-one-free business models. And they need to be able to decide fairly and justly what their vision of limited prosperity should look like.

Allow me to make a brief, but important, aside about how I understand the state. The state is often seen purely as the body that governs a society. Society and the state that governs it are thus two separate entities. It is quite easy to see how state strength can be seen as risky: state power can be turned against the people. But I believe this is distorting. States that use force and violence against their own people can seem strong at first glance, but this repression often masks deeper instability and internal weakness.

I instead believe the state to be a combination of the people and the government, constituted in the relationship between them. When the people feel that they are included in governance, which responds to their needs and wants, then the relationship is strong, leading to a strong state. When this relationship is broken, then the state is weak. This is why oppression and violent coercion are not symbols of state strength: if the state were truly strong, there would be no reason for the government to resort to force in the first place. And, as I will discuss in chapter 6, the strong state as I define it is not necessarily a condition to be found only in democracies as defined by the West, and the book will highlight examples.

• • •

I think it is important to understand state strength independently of how democratic a state is. A poorly designed and weak democratic system will be as incapable of addressing the challenges of sustainable development as a poorly designed nondemocratic system. The point is that strong democratic and nondemocratic states will be better placed to make necessary decisions about constraining consumption and spreading access to basic needs.

An often-used comparison is between authoritarian China and democratic India. Objectively speaking, China has had far more success than India in reducing poverty and providing basic needs for its very poor. China also seems more capable of long-term strategic thinking, from its infrastructure program to its new sustainability agenda. By contrast, India still struggles to provide basic sanitation to its population, and necessary projects, such as cleaning the Ganges River, have idled for decades. India can make grand sweeping policy gestures, but its priorities are sometimes misplaced.

This is not to say that India should emulate China's one-party authoritarian system. Nor does this imply that China's performance has been perfect: widespread environmental degradation clearly shows that China has made several mistakes in its drive to develop. But it is true that China's performance in poverty reduction and almost all spheres of development is far more successful than India's, despite the latter being a democracy.

The idea that state management of the economy can be used to achieve a social goal, despite the orthodoxy of free markets, is not a new one in the literature. The success of such countries as Japan, South Korea, and China in the latter half of the twentieth century gave rise to the concept of the "developmental state." These governments used state investment and protection of the economy to drive modernization, mechanization, and urbanization. These models were especially suited for an increasingly global economy, as protection allowed these countries to develop globally competitive manufacturing sectors. Bucking the Western-derived orthodoxy was also helpful in insulating them from global economic and financial contagion, as shown by the different reactions to the 1997 Asian financial crisis, during which countries such as Malaysia that ignored the IMF did better than those that followed its prescriptions.

However, the developmental states, even as they drifted from Western orthodoxy in their methods, did not stray from it in their goals. Their aim was to eventually become a Western-style economy, one with high growth, driven by consumption as the engine of growth. This extended to their populations as well, who aspired to Western standards of living and levels of consumption. This desire to ape the West and even do better—a perverse form of revenge—is deeply rooted in the psyche and culture of societies that were colonized by the West for centuries. This neurotic subservience is poorly understood by Western intellectuals or is conveniently ignored, as it reinforces the superiority of Western ideas and offers many privileges to Western businesses and politicians.

The developing world needs to instead take the lessons of the developmental state to build the "sustainable state": a state that uses the tools of state management to build a twenty-first-century economy based on providing a shared prosperity for their large populations through the management of constrained resources, containing the runaway impacts of consumption-driven economic growth and the associated externalities, yet avoiding the need to be authoritarian. That is the challenge of sustainability in the twenty-first century for the developing world, and this book seeks to open that debate.

• • •

Some of the ideas in this book are not new. They are based on economic concepts that have been accepted for over half a century, if not longer. Many have argued about the value of state strength in solving social goals.

But few books, if any, have tackled the fundamental misconceptions that have long limited the discussion of sustainable development by failing to factor in the critical role of the state. We have neglected a discussion of a whole set of options that may prove more suited to the challenges of the twenty-first century. The following is an overview of the contents of this book.

Chapter 1 will examine the current debate surrounding sustainable development, the free market, and the role of the state. It will study how development theory has shifted away from state management and toward free-market theories, and how the Western historical and political experience began to dominate the discussion.

Chapter 2 will argue that the problem of sustainable development must be tackled by governments, rather than by markets or technology. The free market is plagued by several systemic failures that encourage overconsumption and underpricing. Finally, the chapter will argue that technological development is unlikely to be the panacea it is often hoped to be.

Chapter 3 will discuss the major element of the free-market model that makes it impossible to reconcile with true sustainability: its focus on making economic growth as high as possible, fueled by overconsumption and underpriced resources. This focus ignores the hard resource constraints of natural systems, and also explains why corporations are poor vehicles for sustainability, as their raison d'être is revenue and profit growth. Sustainability would force them to decide, of their own volition, to produce less. This would be unrealistic.

Chapter 4 will focus on the state—as opposed to the globe or the local community—as the locus of governance. Although global and community governance would, in an ideal world, be part of the overall solution to the sustainability challenge, they are poorly placed to solve the issue in today's world. Global governance still relies on the authority of states to exercise its demands, whereas community governance has been too eroded by decades of centralization to act as an effective tool of resource management. States—even flawed ones—are still the governing entity best suited to govern sustainable development. Flawed ones need to be strengthened, not ignored.

Chapter 5 will detail the book's solution to the sustainability crisis: "the sustainable state," which will use state strength to place resource management at the heart of economic planning, rather than treating it as an afterthought to economic growth. This state will seek to provide universal access to basic needs by providing fair and equal access to common and public resources. It will intervene in the economy, through regulations, investments, subsidies, and other government tools, to constrain the top end of the consumption scale and to provide alternatives to unsustainable economic activity.

Chapters 6 and 7 will counter the fear that state strength and a greater state presence in the economy would create a slippery slope to authoritarianism. As noted earlier, the state is more than just the body that governs a society; it is the relationship between the people and those who govern them. A strong state is one where the people feel they are included in governance. Whether this relationship is founded on democratic mechanisms or not is beside the point: the chapter will discuss "strong" non-democracies and "weak" democracies to show how good governance should be separated from the question of whether a state is democratic. Chapter 7 will take this idea further by looking at checks and balances, not just on the strong state but also what it can do to "check" and "balance" the market.

Chapter 8 will challenge how the concepts of prosperity, rights, and freedom should be understood in the twenty-first century, and offer its own definitions more suited to a hot and crowded era. Rights correspond to the "basic rights of life": what is the standard of living that all people deserve to have? Prosperity, by contrast, concerns a standard of living that people can reasonably aspire to have in an era of hard constraints. What would a "moderate prosperity" look like, and how should we understand it?

Chapters 9, 10, and 11 will examine three case studies that highlight the need for strong state governance.

Chapter 9 will look at the causes behind an annual catastrophe in Southeast Asia: the haze that blankets Indonesia, Singapore, and Malaysia, which causes thousands of preventable deaths every year from lung and respiratory conditions. The haze is caused by slash-and-burn agriculture on the island of Borneo, driven by the expansion of palm oil plantations. Weak governance means that the forests are de facto unprotected. This chapter will propose how a strong state could develop a solution: using state management of the sector to restrict damaging palm oil production while also supporting high-value, small-scale farming through investment, subsidies, and price supports.

Chapter 10 will examine the tropical city in an age when millions of migrants are moving to urban areas. Cities across the region have been unable to cope with this massive wave, leading to overcrowded, overtaxed, and overheated communities. Rather than let unmanaged urbanization continue, the state needs to intervene. It needs to direct urban planning to provide efficient, safe, and dense housing (as opposed to sprawling suburbs and slums) and pursue a policy of broad-based economic planning centered on multiple cities and regions, rather than on purely the commercial capital.

Chapter 11 will examine one of the best examples of a strong state: China. The country's success in economic development and poverty alleviation already challenges traditional economic and political theories. Unlike Russia, which aggressively liberalized its state-driven economy, and India, whose weak democracy has been unable to solve the country's pressing issues, China's more state-managed economy has lifted almost half a billion out of poverty. China has even started to move toward a more sustainable economic structure by investing in alternative energy and environmental protection, which may push it into a global leadership role when it comes to sustainable development. However, it remains restricted by its primary goal: a consumption-driven, high-growth economy. Until it decides on a different model as its objective, its ability to be truly sustainable will be limited.

Chapter 12 will outline the ideal transition path for a state trying to implement stronger governance for sustainability. It will focus on key sustainability "pillars": policy fundamentals that developing states should consider as they start to implement a true sustainability agenda so as to avoid some of the worst consequences of current models.

DEBUNKING "SUSTAINABILITY"
Moving beyond "Feel-Good" Slogans

A few years ago, I was invited to sit on a panel for a major European forum on sustainability. Apart from myself, the panel was made up of Western corporate leaders, each there to talk about his company's commitment to sustainability. One speaker stood out to me: the CEO of a global beer company. He talked about his company's "sustainability" efforts: some water conservation, some energy management in factories, some recycling programs. But no one at the time—not he, not the other panelists, not the moderator, not the audience—seemed to grasp the irony of a CEO whose company's express objective was to get as many people to drink his product as possible talking about resource sustainability. Nothing he spoke of tackled the core issue when it came to his company's sustainability record: that to truly embrace the ethos of sustainability— less is more—his company would need to sell less beer.

That was a turning point for me. I began to notice that most conferences treated the sustainability question in a muddled way. Conferences were dominated, if not sponsored, by corporations and businesses. Real discussions were left at the door, replaced with public relations exercises. Non-Western business leaders were often unaware of what was happening right in their own countries: the business leader in Kuala Lumpur knew more about New York or London than the surrounding Malaysian countryside.

Sustainability should include an all-encompassing discussion of our long-term use of economic resources throughout the entire economic system. It needs an honest evaluation of our economic model and our destructive lifestyles, and of what must be changed so that resources can be both more equally shared for current populations and preserved for future generations. We need a candid discussion instead of one that papers over the real issues in favor of a misleading feel-good outcome.

Yet the conversation around sustainability often ends at the environmental impact of production lines and supply chains—an important concern, but a tiny bandage over a toxic wound. We talk about how to make our increasing production and consumption more resource efficient when we should actually talk about how a global population of ten billion by 2050 must produce and consume *less*.

Before this whole chapter is interpreted as anticorporate, I know plenty of business leaders who are concerned about climate change, diminishing resources, and global sustainability. But many know that their business models are still rooted in unsustainable practices, unless one wants to mask environmental improvement measures as sustainability initiatives. Even the beer company CEO, when I privately challenged him after our panel together, admitted that he also found his presence on the panel strange and that he found it difficult to say anything serious about sustainability.

Why did he turn up? The answer is simple: this is how sustainability is showcased at media events to promote corporations. A business leader expressing support for climate action or implementing a few risk and harm minimization initiatives is in keeping with the ethos of many sustainability conferences: that businesses and markets should take the lead on tackling sustainability, as opposed to the government and tough public policy.

• • •

Why has the idea of sustainability—and sustainable development—strayed so far from what is needed?

The main culprit is our understanding of development, which is too tied to free markets, business-friendly policies, and the Western historical narrative. We do not understand that the developing world faces a different sustainability problem than the developed world. There are actually two different sustainability challenges: one for richer countries and one for poorer ones. Whereas richer countries can focus purely on resource efficiency, the developing world needs not only to protect its environment and preserve its resource base for future generations but also to improve the lives of its poor majority and offer a path to a prosperous yet still sustainable lifestyle. By understanding development along market-based, probusiness lines, we make it difficult to achieve sustainability and development at the same time. When the two are put into conflict, it is often development that wins out.

Sustainable development as an idea grew out of the environmental movement in the 1960s and 1970s. There was a growing concern that the world could not support an expanding (and increasingly wealthy) global population relying on a resource- and energy-intensive economic growth model. One of the earliest discussions of sustainability (before the term *sustainable development* was conceived) was *The Limits to Growth,* commissioned by the Club of Rome in 1972. The book modeled a world where world population, industrialization, pollution, food production, and resource depletion would grow exponentially, while technological development would progress linearly; previous models had held resource use constant. The book projected "overshoot and collapse" of the global system by the mid-to-late twenty-first century if then-current trends continued. The book gave a dire conclusion:

> If the present growth trends in world population, industrialisation, pollution, food production, and resource depletion continue unchanged, the limits to growth on this planet will be reached sometime within the next one hundred years. The most probable result will be a rather sudden and uncontrollable decline in both population and industrial capacity.[1]

The book proved controversial, and was called neo-Malthusian by its often defensive, progrowth, profreedom critics. It has been lumped in with books like *The Population Bomb,* whose dire predictions have not yet come to pass in the short amount of time since they were made. Even US president Ronald Reagan made fun of *The Limits to Growth,* stating that the title offended his sensibilities, telling an audience at the University of South Carolina that "in this vast and wonderful world that God has given us, it's not what's inside the Earth that counts, but what's inside your minds and hearts, because that's the stuff that dreams are made of, and America's future is in your dreams."[2]

Commentary referred to the failed predictions of Thomas Malthus, the eighteenth-century economist who was concerned that a growing population, driven by increased living standards, would outpace the ability of a country's agricultural sector to feed it. The country would eventually run out of farmland; this "limit" would have eventually led to mass starvation. Commentators argued that this prediction never came to pass due to new developments in agricultural productivity and that later pessimistic predictions about limits should therefore be treated just as skeptically.

Of course, Malthus was writing in a wholly different time and place. Malthus's predictions were argued to have been proven wrong due to a technological transformation, the Industrial Revolution. It was argued that this got countries out of the Malthusian Trap; ironically, however, it laid the seeds for today's current sustainability crisis. Our economy relies on far more inputs than it did in Malthus's day, and now systems for food, fresh water, energy, and raw materials are all under threat. The world population is also seven times larger.

Some new transformative technology could be invented to get us out of today's trap, but none seem to be forthcoming at the moment. Chapter 2 will tackle this almost religious faith in technology in more detail.

(It should be noted that a retrospective forty years after the publication of *The Limits to Growth* found that population, birth rates, food per capita, industrial output per capita, resources, and pollution were all following the general trends predicted by the Club of Rome's model.[3])

In 1983, the United Nations launched the World Commission on Environment and Development, commonly named the Brundtland Commission after its chairperson, Norwegian prime minister Gro Harlem Brundtland. The commission released *Our Common Future*—commonly known as the *Brundtland Report*—which offered one of the first definitions of sustainable development: "a process of change in which the exploitation of resources, the direction of investment, the orientation of technological development, and institutional change are all in harmony and enhance both current and future potential to meet human needs and aspirations."[4]

Although the report was well intentioned, it did not address what the "process of change" would require, and was steeped in Western liberal ideas about the role of technology and institutional change. It was an important first step, but (perhaps understandably at this early stage) relied on platitudes and politically correct sentiments.

Sustainable development quickly became a central concept in development discussions, often led by Western experts who rarely confronted the unsustainable means by which their economies had grown. Several UN conferences enshrined certain principles of environmental protection and sustainability, such as the 1992 Rio Declaration and the 2000 Earth

Charter. In 2000, "environmental sustainability" was one of the UN's Millennium Development Goals. UN member states were asked to integrate sustainable development principles into their economic policies, reduce the loss of biodiversity, and halve the share of their population that lacked access to clean water and sanitation.

With the release of the Sustainable Development Goals (SDGs) in 2015, sustainable development moved to become the central priority of international development. The seventeen goals (see Figure 1.1), meant to be achieved by 2030, run the gamut of environmental, social, and economic issues, from "no poverty" and "zero hunger" (Goals 1 and 2), to "gender equality" and "peace, justice and strong institutions" (Goals 5 and 16). The process of developing the goals faced many criticisms: that it focused too much on high economic growth as the vehicle for development, that it set too many targets, and that some of its various goals strayed too far from sustainability or development. But the unanimous promulgation of the SDGs seemed to be a victory in itself, and today politicians and business leaders cite the SDGs at every opportunity.

However, the SDGs and similar efforts by other international institutions are merely guidelines and targets, rather than firm policy platforms. Although all UN member nations have agreed to commit to these goals, there are no enforcement mechanisms to ensure that they do so. (Chapter 4 will go into more detail as to why global governance may be ill-suited to solving the problem of sustainable development.)

It is not clear whether achieving the SDGs is correlated with reducing the environmental and resource footprint of national economies. Researchers from the Global Footprint Network found that countries that scored highly on Bertelsmann Stiftung's SDG index also had large resource footprints. Countries that scored poorly had small footprints. They concluded that the SDGs were far more weighted toward development than sustainability, which would be "anti-poor because lowest-income people exposed to resource insecurity will lack the financial means to shield themselves from the consequences."[5]

Sustainability and sustainable development have since been adopted by global business and corporations, though their adherence to sustainability principles can vary significantly. Business is often invited to attend conferences on sustainable development to ensure their cooperation and to help bring about a "broader consensus." Some of the first business initiatives in sustainable development date to 1992, when Stephan Schmidheiny (a Swiss industrialist who produced asbestos and asbestos-replacement

1 NO POVERTY

2 ZERO HUNGER

3 GOOD HEALTH AND WELL-BEING

4 QUALITY EDUCATION

5 GENDER EQUALITY

6 CLEAN WATER AND SANITATION

7 AFFORDABLE AND CLEAN ENERGY

8 DECENT WORK AND ECONOMIC GROWTH

9 INDUSTRY, INNOVATION AND INFRASTRUCTURE

10 REDUCED INEQUALITIES

11 SUSTAINABLE CITIES AND COMMUNITIES

12 RESPONSIBLE CONSUMPTION AND PRODUCTION

13 CLIMATE ACTION

14 LIFE BELOW WATER

15 LIFE ON LAND

16 PEACE, JUSTICE AND STRONG INSTITUTIONS

17 PARTNERSHIPS FOR THE GOALS

THE GLOBAL GOALS
For Sustainable Development

Figure 1.1 The United Nations Sustainable Development Goals. Although many of these are laudable in themselves, some have little to do with sustainability specifically.

products) was appointed the chief advisor for business and industry. Schmidheiny founded the Business Council for Sustainable Development, later renamed the World Business Council for Sustainable Development, or the WBCSD.

The WBCSD today has two hundred members, 67 percent of which are from Europe and North America. It has been criticized for including companies with a heavy environmental impact. The current executive committee includes directors and executives from oil producers Sinopec Corp and Royal Dutch Shell, packaged food producer Nestlé, chemical companies Solvay and Yara International, and motor company Toyota. Each of these companies follows a business model with significant environmental costs, either through its production lines or through the consumption of its products (or both). Many of these companies are also guilty of diminishing the world's stock of raw materials and common resources despite their more recent efforts on the environmental/pollution front.

In 2011, the environmental NGO Greenpeace, in a blistering report titled *Who's Holding Us Back?*, blamed industry involvement in climate change and sustainability for the lack of effective climate legislation. In announcing the report, then executive director Kumi Naidoo stated, "Our research shows beyond a shadow of a doubt that there are a handful of powerful polluting corporations who are exerting undue influence on the political process to protect their vested interests," and specifically highlighted the WBCSD's executive committee as a "Who's Who of the world's largest carbon-intensive companies who continue to profit from continued inaction on climate change."[6]

• • •

There is definitional slippage among the terms *corporate sustainability, corporate social responsibility* (CSR), and *greening* a company; they may overlap in certain areas, but they are not the same thing. CSR is defined as a company's "giving back" to the wider community; there is no requirement that a company's CSR actions have anything to do with its business operations.

"Greening" a company is also used interchangeably with "corporate sustainability," but refers to something different. Greening is harm amelioration and risk minimization: reducing the environmental impact of a company's production. This may be reducing waste or pollution, or extracting resources more cleanly. But it is not the same as corporate sustainability, which entails reducing the level of resources a company uses or impacts when its goods are produced or consumed. "Greening" is still a worthwhile objective, and some policies can achieve that and sustainability at the same time. But a company can be green and environmentally friendly without affecting its overall (over)use of resources (See Table 1.1).

Why do we have this definitional confusion? One cynical answer is that it is convenient. Cutting deep with unambiguous definitions can

Table 1.1   Sustainable development is not environmental protection (greening).

Issues	Environmental Protection (Examples)	Sustainable Development (Examples)
Mobility	• Cleaner fuel • Emissions standards • Noise barriers	• Road pricing • Taxes on car ownership • Investment in public transportation • Bans, reducing car parks
Energy	• Environmental standards for extraction • Gas cleaning systems at power plants • Use of renewables (to reduce emissions and carbon footprint)	• Demand-side management • Caps on consumption • Use of renewables (to reduce resource consumption)
Housing	• Green building standards • Construction waste recycling • Indoor air quality	• Smaller homes for all, lawn restriction in water-stressed areas • Passive design to reduce energy needs (no AC) • Compost toilet to reduce water needs
Water	• Cleaner production and process efficiency • Higher discharge standards • New water treatment technology	• Reduction of consumption through pricing • Caps on per capita consumption • Water catchment area protection and bans on access • Bans on golf courses in arid areas
Food and Agriculture	• Reduction of chemical footprint • Reduction of chemical run-off • Ban on certain pesticides and herbicides • Certification	• Reduction of industrial food production • Investment in rural agriculture infrastructure • Fair pricing for farmers and ecosystem services • Promotion of circular farming
Biodiversity	• Targeted conservation areas • Listing of endangered species • Quotas on hunting	• Development no-go zones—zero tolerance • Conservation of native seeds • Pricing ecosystem services
Fisheries	• Fishing quotas	• Total ban to prevent collapse of certain threatened species • Strict licensing on fishing vessels • Pricing consumption of certain threatened species

Note: Although sustainable development is not environmental protection, they are not mutually exclusive.

expose festering wounds and create great discomfort. They can disrupt existing business models and devalue sunk costs overnight.

I also believe it's because sustainable development is understood from the perspective of advanced economies rather than developing ones, which must confront the past, deal with current challenges, and in the process not bankrupt the future—sustainability in a nutshell.

The standard development narrative is straightforward: the West's growth comes from the cultivation of markets, which in turn led to capitalism, industrialization, and consumerism. This was an economic and manufacturing engine that increased the wealth and power of Europe and North America versus the non-Western world, which only started to develop once these countries too embraced free markets, open trade, and modern capitalism. This led to the Washington Consensus on what is best for a country's economic development and growth: market liberalization, deregulation, and free trade. There is no mention of why and how the division between the so-called developed and developing worlds was created over the last two to three centuries, nor how the seeds of unsustainable growth were sewn through the plunder and pillage of people and resources in distant lands. Many of these lands are today's "developing countries."

The free-market mainstream argues that markets best allocate resources to create the maximum level of benefit. Any attempt to interfere with the economy, whether through regulation, intervention, or direct support, would lead to a suboptimal, if not an objectively worse, outcome. This has been extended to a political argument: that markets are good from a moral standpoint as the best way to resolve social (not just economic) problems—and if the market does not or cannot solve them, then the cure of state intervention would be worse than the disease.

I admit this is an extreme characterization. Apart from those on the hard right of Western politics, many politicians will accept some level of state intervention in the economy. But it remains true that, all along the Western political spectrum, market-based solutions are seen as the first option for solving social problems. Sadly, most elites of the developing world, such as Pakistan's Shaukat Aziz, Thailand's Abhisit Vejjajiva, or India's Rahul Gandhi, either educated in the West or who don't know better, simply accepted this as natural law, never appreciating how it was at war with natural systems and their people.

But the fact is that most of the world's economies had a very different experience than the advanced economies of Europe and North

America. For one, many of the West's largest economies never suffered the indignities of colonization and resource plunder. Colonial powers destroyed centuries-old cultural and governing institutions, replacing them with structures purely focused on extracting resources for the colonial center and with a local elite that followed Western ideologies. From Spanish Latin America through the British Raj in India[7] to the Scramble for Africa,[8] imperial powers tried to exploit the natural resources of the non-Western world to fuel their economies. Even non-Western powers—namely imperial Japan—tried to launch their own empires for the same reason.

Colonialism and imperialism were pervasive. Even countries that never formally became colonies, such as China, still suffered interference from foreign governments. At best, these countries were held back from developing at the same rate as their Western counterparts. At worst, newly independent colonies, often damaged by violent independence and post-independence struggles, had to build governing and economic institutions entirely from scratch. Many failed due to bitter internal struggles and a lack of competence.

The Indian environmentalist Claude Alvares explained the effect that Western-imposed systems had on postcolonial countries:

> Scholars in several societies outside Europe, schooled in an educational system imposed on their societies through the colonial establishment, readily incorporated similar ideas about their own histories. The colonisation project succeeded in convincing many of our intellectuals and scholars that only the West was active. . . . The new global knowledge system therefore merely required competent, hired disciples to diffuse its truths to those ignorant of them. This has become the dreary function of our educational systems. Whether it is geography or economics or sociology or psychology, the expansion of the West's intellectual discourse has been seen in terms of a diffusion of knowledge from the centre to the peripheries. The main issues and controversies are debated in the centre; they are then transferred to the peripheries through texts and authors and subject to onward diffusion. No creativity flows backward from the periphery since it is assumed none exists there at all.[9]

There have been attempts to challenge these mainstream arguments. Theorists in the 1970s—Fernando Cardoso, Walter Rodney, and others—started to argue that economies on the "periphery" (namely, in the developing world) were locked into an economic structure that made them dependent on the West. As weaker members of the world economy, these countries needed different policies, as opposed to copying the West's. "Dependency theory" now has a poor reputation among mainstream economists: Latin America's protectionist policies did not bring growth, and Cardoso himself (when he was president of Brazil) was forced to accept the Washington Consensus in exchange for debt relief from the International Monetary Fund (IMF). However, Cardoso and other dependency theorists' fundamental point still stands: the experience of developing countries, growing in an already developed global economy with several powerful economic players, will be different than that of countries that came before.

The Washington Consensus remains orthodoxy even as several other countries succeeded by following a different path. China, in particular, has not fully embraced the free market, preserving state management throughout the economy, yet it now has the best record of poverty alleviation in human history. This is why China's rise has been treated with such skepticism in the West, even though the developing world sees China's path to development as an increasingly viable model.

Japan, South Korea, Taiwan, and Singapore also used state support, intervention, and protection to help grow their economies, which fostered the creation of a new concept: the *developmental state*. Economist Chalmers Johnson noticed the difference between the US and Japan as early as 1982, in noting that Japan had a much stronger industrial policy apportioning state support. The idea was soon applied to describe South Korea and China. The varied experiences within Asia led Joe Studwell to create an "Asian model" based on three elements: export-focused, state-led manufacturing; land reform that split large feudal farms into tightly packed smallholder farms; and a managed financial system that would subsidize manufacturing without causing a financial crisis.[10] Despite often being hailed as a "free-market utopia" by conservative economists in the West, Singapore, economist Kalim Siddiqui notes, "regulates land, labour and capital resources . . . [and] sets prices on these very resources on which private investors largely rely [for] their future business calculations and investment decisions."[11] Singapore controls both the health and housing sectors of the economy, which has led to near universal health care and public housing.[12]

Most important, the current understanding of development is a poor fit for the challenges of the twenty-first century. The touchstones of free-market economics were written under very different political and economic conditions. Adam Smith, writing in the eighteenth century, wrote *The Wealth of Nations* to criticize the state-chartered monopoly in the Western world. Friedrich Hayek wrote *The Road to Serfdom* when he was worried about the rise of totalitarianism in Europe—an important concern, to be sure, but less relevant to today's challenges, and especially in the developing world.

One new challenge is climate change. Climate change is here and yet the developing countries have an obligation to lift their majorities out of poverty and reduce the drudgery of life. This will not be achieved in a pristine, carbon-neutral or "green" way no matter how we try to fudge the definitions.

Another coming challenge is the increasing scarcity of global resources, driven both by overconsumption and increasing population. Increasing global incomes and an expanding population have led to greater consumption, production, and thus resource use, and resource stocks around the world have felt the strain. These are not just the resources directly involved in production; other "common" resources feel the strain too—from increased car use affecting our stocks of clean air and open road space to runoff from industrial farming creating massive algae blooms in water bodies.

The final challenge comes from global modernity: globalization, digitalization, mechanization, and the loss of local traditions, cultures, wisdom, and knowledge. Changing economic models and technological development have made certain development paths obsolete. Automation, digitalization, and open borders have led to "premature deindustrialization," whereby developing countries lose their manufacturing sector to countries with even lower labor costs.

• • •

When looking at sustainable development from the perspective of advanced economies, we assume that development has already been achieved. These economies largely provide universal access to basic needs and offer expansive social services. If continued poverty exists, it is due to a lack of political will to deal with vested interests and inequalities. These countries thus have more ability to smooth the economic and political transformations that come with sustainability, keeping living standards steady, or even reducing them, as they try to better manage resources.

However, developing countries still have sizable parts of their population living in poverty and near-poverty. Average living standards, even in success stories like China, remain largely low when compared to the Western world. China's GDP per capita at PPP (a crude proxy for living standards) stands at US$15,399, just below the world average of US$16,318, and far below the OECD average of US$42,051 and that of the US at US$57,436. The irony is that China's increasing GDP per capita comes at a high price for the planet.

Experts argue that extreme poverty levels have been reduced, but they seem to be unaware of the wide spectrum of poverty that affects the majority. A hotter, crowded, and resource-constrained world is a slap in the face for those at the bottom of the pyramid. Moving people out of extreme poverty is critically important, but using such data to argue that the world is better off is a form of arrogance. The world is also being compelled to embrace robots and AI to replace labor in the name of progress—a silly idea that still fits the orthodoxy of our current economic model and its narrow definition of productivity. Any development program for these countries must continue to provide an upward path for those who still live in poverty and drudgery. However, all the current models available to them are environmentally damaging and unsustainable.

Developing countries need to pursue sustainability and development at the same time. They need to aim for a standard of living that allows people to live well "within limits." They must consume fewer resources than a Western lifestyle yet provide people the chance to live a "prosperous" life (defined in a twenty-first-century context). There is no recipe for this, and progress has been thwarted by the religious fervor for neoliberal development across the world.

Why have we been unable to resolve the dilemma between sustainability and development, and formulate a truly sustainable understanding of development?

The answer is that we are still too tied to a free-market understanding of economic development and the neoliberal idea that we can have it all. The truth is that the majority of the citizens of the developing world cannot have it all, and will have to settle with "just enough for all." This is a moral dilemma for the "haves." The focus on free markets as the best vehicle for social progress puts development and sustainability objectives at odds, and development usually wins out. The only way to resolve the conflict is to hope that either market allocation or technological development allows both to be achieved simultaneously. We need a different understanding of economic development that does not rely on free markets and that allows both the moderate improvement of living standards and the management of resources to ensure their preservation for future generations to meet the most basic human "rights of life."

Despite the failures and missteps of a Western-derived, free-market model, and the insights that could be drawn from taking an alternate approach, the developing world has not created its own view of what sustainable development would look like. Even the "developmental states" noted earlier have a Western objective: an economy driven by high domestic consumption with a Western standard of living as the ultimate objective. These countries may use different economic means to get there, and they may not emulate the West's liberal democratic political structures, but the end goal—the high level of resource consumption—is the same.

One reason we may not have seen many non-Western alternatives is the dominance of Western ideas in the literature and in global multilateral organizations. There are thousands upon thousands of books written on Western history, politics, and business practices. Western corporations dominate global media, and global academia is centered around a few premier Western universities. We live in a world shaped and dominated by the thoughts of the minority and its elites, which has stifled new thinking and made elites in the developing world subservient. We desperately need new narratives, and this book is an attempt to contribute.

Many developing countries have politicians or leaders, groomed by Western education and business, who strive to implement the most "efficient" set of economic policies for a country (regardless of popular opinion). They are generally probusiness and promarket, and come in to "fix" an economy by slashing benefits, privatizing social services, and lowering regulation to encourage domestic and foreign investment. They can be found in both democratic and nondemocratic states (though both can be equally dismissive of their policies' effects on the population). They are also not universally successful—many technocrats have been dismissed as mediocre by both constituents and observers—yet are still invited to conferences and speaking engagements around the world.

These elites operate from the fundamental assumption that the status quo as defined by the West is largely acceptable, and that tweaks could fix whatever problems exist. When faced with a challenge that threatens the foundations of society, be it economic, political, or, in our case, environmental, they tend to be left floundering, and look to the West for "thought leadership." The need for a sustainable economic model that is not at war with the planet is one such challenge.

• • •

In 2016, the research firm Trucost estimated the scale of the external costs of major industries around the globe. They found that for the most polluting industries, the scale of their impact on the natural world was often as great as, if not several times greater than, the sector's total revenue. None of these industries would be profitable if they were forced to consider external costs in their business models.[13]

The industry with the greatest impact overall was coal power generation, with an estimated impact of over a trillion US dollars across the entire world. For scale, that is the same size as Mexico's entire economy. Just about half of that impact comes from coal power plants in East and South Asia.

Other industries have an impact that is several times higher than their total revenue. One example is the South American cattle ranching and farming industry. The total revenue for this sector is about US$16 billion. However, the total impact of the industry, expressed through land use and the release of greenhouse gases, totals US$350 billion (equal to the total amount the US spends on beer each year). If beef were priced properly, a hamburger made from Brazilian beef would be an extremely rare luxury, rather than a staple of the Western diet.

This data reveals the underlying issue at the heart of many of the world's industries: that an honest accounting for their overuse of resources would almost certainly put most of them out of business. And, for us as consumers, that many things we treat as standard goods should instead be priced as if they were expensive extravagances. This immediate change to our current economic system is not going to happen overnight, but we can't continue to reject the evidence. When confronted with the dilemma between sustainability and development, many who subscribe to a more market-based version of sustainable development tend to point to two possible escape mechanisms. These are the easy and safe options, bereft of intellectual honesty and diverse opinions.

The first is to double down on the free market as the best way to allocate the Earth's resources. The second is to hope that some new technology will be invented that will render the dilemma between sustainability and development obsolete. Technological development would allow the world to consume on the level of Americans without using an American level of resources.

Neither of these options are viable alternatives to a true platform of sustainable development: one that tries to create an economic system that can sustainably manage resources for future generations. Chapter 2 will explain why.

CHAPTER | 2

SUSTAINABILITY BY THE STATE, NOT MARKETS OR TECHNOLOGY

November 11 is not a traditional Chinese holiday. Singles Day (a reference to its date of 11/11) was originally a time for China's youth to "celebrate" their singlehood. They would gather in cafés and restaurants and have a day for themselves, without obligations to partners or family.

Singles Day ballooned from these humble beginnings into something unrecognizable. It is now the largest shopping day in the entire world, thanks to the efforts of Chinese e-commerce companies like Alibaba. In 2017, Alibaba alone sold US$25.3 billion worth of merchandise—a lot of it probably unneeded—in just twenty-four hours, beating last year's record by 40 percent.[1] Alibaba launched the day with a huge midnight celebration in Shanghai with appearances by Western celebrities such as Nicole Kidman and Pharrell Williams. Singles Day is now vastly larger than Black Friday in the US, which in the same year had a relatively piddling US$5 billion worth of online sales.[2] China now sells more in a single day than all of Brazil sells in an entire year.

A few months later, Jack Ma, along with several other global business tycoons, contributed to a US$1 billion fund for new, low-carbon investments.[3] This was hailed as further proof that the business community was taking the problems of climate change and sustainability seriously (especially as politicians, especially in the US, were looking as though they were wavering on the issue). The irony is that the narcissistic shopping frenzy of Singles Day is probably the biggest single organized mass-shopping contributor to carbon dioxide emissions the world has ever known. To be clear: US$1 billion is a lot of money, and one hopes the money is put to good use. But the amount pledged by multiple billion-aires pales in comparison to the mammoth sales of Singles Day—just one of the many e-commerce sales days that happens globally each year.

Think about how many products were sold on Singles Day. Then think about how many resources and how much labor was used to make all those goods. Then, finally, think about how many of those goods were truly needed by those buying them; after all, these shoppers were not will-ing to buy them under normal circumstances and were instead taken up in the consumerist frenzy of a nationwide shopping spree. Then think about the carbon footprint of delivery and all that waste packaging— hundreds of tons of it. Finally, there is the untold cost of disposal of un-used or wasted products. All these costs are not paid for because the whole attraction of Singles Day is that prices are at their lowest, seducing buyers by externalizing cost. Yet people do not criticize these practices.

● ● ●

The introduction described the choice faced by developing countries: pur-sue "sustainability" or pursue "development," as defined by our economic theories of the day. Developing countries need to improve living stan-dards for their people, many of whom are still poor. However, all cur-rent models for development are unsustainable, in that they overconsume resources. Without thinking of an alternate economic model, forcing sus-tainability on developing countries would doom people to perpetual pov-erty while not tackling the unrealistic aspirations they are led to believe they can have.

However, many commentators—especially those operating in the Western media—largely deny or are ignorant of this dilemma. Instead, they argue that countries can pursue sustainability and Western-style living standards at the same time. These commentators point to the free market and technology as the ways that plenty can be provided to the world's entire population, without risking the Earth's scarce resources or creating intolerable living conditions. Our current lifestyles, even if they are massively unsustainable now, will be sustainable in the future, due to the development of new technology, and mostly from investments by Western corporations.

This is not just an argument made by antienvironmentalists; even those who sincerely support sustainability efforts buy into it. They argue that new technologies have already brought down the emissions of ad-vanced countries and note that investment in renewable energy has

already increased tremendously without widespread government interference or intervention, proving that a stronger state presence in the
economy is not necessary. Minor tweaks and subsidies are all that are
needed.

This hope in the free market can be seen even among proponents of
renewable energy, especially during the antienvironment, pro-fossil-fuel
Trump administration. Blogs and newspapers across the world have tried
to present the view that, even if President Trump supported American
coal, oil, and natural gas, the world would still be fine. *HuffPost* published
a piece with the headline "The March of Renewable Energy Is Unstoppable Even by President Trump."[4] The *New York Times* reported that the
"American energy market has already shifted away from the most polluting fossil fuels, driven more by investors and economics than by federal
regulations."[5] The *Financial Times* released a long feature piece soon after
President Trump withdrew from the Paris Climate Accord, titled "The
Big Green Bang: How Renewable Energy Became Unstoppable."[6]

This was echoed in the highest offices in the land: former president
Barack Obama, writing in *Science,* hoped that "putting near-term politics aside, the mounting economic and scientific evidence leaves me confident that trends toward a clean-energy economy that have emerged
during my presidency will continue. . . . The economic opportunity for our
country to harness that trend will only grow."[7]

Prosustainability policies are wrapped in the rhetoric of "green jobs"
or "the renewable energy industry": an assertion that sustainability is not
good on its own terms but rather in terms of what it can provide for a
country's continued economic growth. Until very recently, sustainability
policies had to be hidden within platforms for "resource- and energy-
independence," implying that overusing resources was acceptable so long
as those resources didn't come from abroad.

In this view, if sustainability efforts close off some economic opportunities, shave off a percentage point of economic growth, increase unemployment by a point, or disrupt certain key industries, then they are a
failure. These groups want to tackle sustainability without sacrificing economic growth, intervening in the business practices of global companies
and the global economy, or even considering all possibilities.

This approach is a mistake, and serves to distract people from the
economic, social, and political transformations needed if the developing
world is to survive. The mainstream is fixated on growth, prosperity, and
progress. Rather than hoping that market dynamics or technological

innovation will save the world and alleviate poverty, developing countries need to take matters into their own hands: their states must pursue
sustainability as the key pillar of their political philosophy and shape it
without the baggage of the flawed narrative of today (as addressed in chapter 1). This requires a true paradigm shift delivered through a new political philosophy.

This chapter will discuss why a faith in free markets and technology
as panaceas is ill-suited to tackle the thorny and complex issues of sustainable development, especially in large developing nations. The key institution of society—the state—has to take the lead and not abdicate its
ideas, born out of a different context, to the rich nations of the world or,
even worse, to mainstream economists and business schools.

• • •

According to the market-based view of sustainable development, as
the world economy continues to grow, resource consumption will increase. This will both make resources scarcer and increase prices, thereby
achieving an equilibrium between supply and demand. Commentators
argue that market forces would thus contribute to a less resource-intense
economy:

1. Increased input prices would carry through to the final product, in-
    creasing their price. This would lower demand and thus the level of
    resources consumed.
2. Increased input prices would also "unlock" resource stocks that are
    normally uneconomical to exploit. This would lead to an increase in
    the supply of even nonrenewable resources. For example, oil that is
    too expensive to extract at $40 a barrel is suddenly economical at $80
    a barrel, "increasing" the available supply of oil. It may make "cleaner"
    nonrenewables, such as natural gas and nuclear power, more com-
    petitive, leading to a more diverse energy base.
3. Increased input prices would open a business opportunity for more
    resource-efficient production. Whether through new technologies or
    new business models, this would allow consumers to live more extra-
    vagant lifestyles without using as many (now-pricy) resources.

Thus the market-based approach would argue that the properly functioning free market would automatically resolve the problems associated
with diminishing resources. Government intervention and management

are thus unwarranted, as the market would automatically resolve these social problems. In fact, state action could hinder the development of these
new opportunities, by diverting resources toward areas that are less efficient and optimal.

This approach is based on a great deal of faith in market forces—"the
invisible hand"—to correct human behavior in the economy. Market forces
would, by themselves, lead to a better equilibrium, due to each of us acting in our own self-interest. This is hubris.

A related approach relies on the hope that some new technological
invention would allow the world to keep consumption high while using
far fewer resources. Thus people in the developing world would not need
to moderate their expectations: technology would allow all of them to live
a life of high consumption.

These approaches reinforce each other. Increasing resource prices
(through market forces) would encourage the development of energy- and
resource-efficient technology. This technology might also make it easier
to extract difficult resources, increasing supply. Thus the combination of
market forces and technological innovation would lead to a new equilibrium of high consumption and low resource use.

The market-based approach has the benefit of not requiring anyone
to make a difficult choice about how to best allocate resources, as the market would magically handle things on its own. It is a convenient way to
shift responsibility elsewhere. That can be appealing to governments that
rely on business or corporate support, as what is ultimately best for these
businesses would end up being best for wider society (not to mention
the government and the politicians who run them). It can also be a relief for
governments worried about the short-term political effects of sustainability
policies: states, democratic or nondemocratic, may be wary of restricting
the consumption of scarce resources (or those with severe associated
externalities, such as fossil fuels or carbon dioxide) by their populations,
who may be likely to exert political pressure against any controls.

•••

There are several reasons why the free and unregulated market cannot be
truly sustainable. None of these reasons are radical; they are all part of any
introductory economics course. Despite this, these ideas seem to have
been forgotten by those looking at market-based solutions to sustainable
development, who often do not take the insights from these concepts to
their logical conclusion.

The first concept to consider is external cost, or a cost placed on a third party. Almost every economic action places a cost on someone else. This cost may be incurred by the consumer directly, or may have been incurred at some point along the production chain, from extraction, through conversion and consumption, and finally to disposal. These costs are not reflected in the market price, which reflects a balance between private demand and supply. When private cost (i.e., the price) is low, market demand is high. This means that the market equilibrium—where private benefit equals private cost—have a higher level of consumption than the social equilibrium—where social benefit equals social cost.

The standard example of an externality is pollution. Waste from industry, power plants, or vehicles has numerous negative effects—be they respiratory illness; increased toxicity in the air, water, and soil; and even lowered property values—on third parties. Even when the final product is ostensibly "clean," extracting the raw materials often creates pollution. Neither the producer nor the consumer pays these costs. As these costs do not figure into a private cost-benefit calculation, polluting products are thus overconsumed, and pollution is overproduced.

This externality is the economic justification for antipollution regulation: to reduce, if not remove, the gap between the private optimum and the social optimum. Regulation can aim to

- Increase the private cost of polluting production (e.g., taxation on pollutants)
- Reduce the social cost of production (e.g., mandating the use of clean production techniques)
- Directly reduce the amount of polluting production (e.g., closing polluting factories and stopping production)

Externalities are an accepted part of economic theory: they are the go-to justification for government regulation of the economy. However, we rarely grasp the full scale and extent of the external costs of consumption. For example, climate change was called the "greatest and widest-ranging market failure" by British economist Sir Nicholas Stern in the 2006 *Stern Review on the Economics of Climate Change,* in that carbon emissions (and the resulting climate change) were an external cost created by every economic action in the modern economy.[8]

The external costs of consumption emerge at every part of the production chain. Take our use of cars. Some obvious externalities are the external costs from vehicle exhaust, as well as the lost time and health effects from traffic congestion. But the manufacturing process also has environmental consequences, as does the mining of the metals and minerals needed, none of which are included in the final price. Shipping of parts and final products also has external costs. Auto manufacturing is increasingly located in areas with lax labor standards; the falling price of cars is paid for by illness and injury among auto workers in places as far afield as Bangladesh and Alabama. Mass adoption of cars worsens congestion in cities, which has effects on public health, the environment, and urban planning (due to the expansion of suburbs and roads). Finally, the use of petroleum and diesel in cars has its own social costs, sometimes going as far as triggering outright war.

The consumption of meat also has external costs. The environmental consequences of raising livestock is high: pollution from farming, carbon emissions from livestock, soil erosion from overgrazing, and deforestation from expanding pastures. But there are other external costs. The overuse of antibiotics as a cheap and easy way to control infection and encourage livestock growth have increased antibiotic resistance in bacteria, which have spread to humans. Industrial livestock farming has transformed other parts of agriculture, encouraging the growth of corn and soybeans for feed, rather than staple crops or fruits and vegetables. Finally, a meat-based diet can have significant health effects, such as increased rates of heart disease. An increasingly unhealthy population places costs on the whole society by burdening the public health system and losing productivity from sick workers.

One economic phenomenon whose external costs have not been accounted for is the rise of digital and internet technology. Again, this has environmental costs; smartphones and other digital products use minerals from mines that often have poor environmental controls and safety standards (see Figure 2.1). The drive for greater openness and connectivity has also led to a more unstable system, which can easily be toppled by an unruly algorithm, human error, or criminal intent. Digital connectivity is also transforming economies. The rise of e-commerce has cut out huge parts of the supply chain: although retail jobs do not necessarily pay well, they at least pay better than the low-skilled, low-paid, and insecure jobs in the massive "fulfillment centers" of the major e-commerce companies.

This is the reason why e-commerce deals are often so cheap: the costs of fulfillment and delivery are pushed downward and outward, to affect

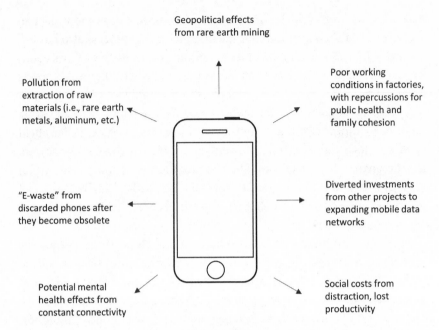

Geopolitical effects
from rare earth mining

Pollution from
extraction of raw
materials (i.e., rare earth
metals, aluminum, etc.)

Poor working
conditions in factories,
with repercussions for
public health and
family cohesion

"E-waste" from
discarded phones after
they become obsolete

Diverted investments
from other projects to
expanding mobile data
networks

Potential mental
health effects from
constant connectivity

Social costs from
distraction, lost
productivity

Figure 2.1 Some of the externalities that stem from the smartphone. These are merely some of the direct, first-order effects that come from the purchase of an individual phone. There are more disturbances and externalities that emerged when the smartphone became more widespread. Yet even with these, the business model can still be one where a consumer gets a phone for free.

workers, their families, and wider society. Yet it's something people do not consider when they order a product. This happens now hundreds of millions of times every day as some human "robot" is sent to pick, pack, and serve yet another craving by another mindless consumer who has not considered the ramifications of his or her decision, yet wants to have the results as soon as possible.

Evidence shows that much of the increase in consumption in recent years in advanced economies is not due to increasing incomes (which have stayed roughly constant, if not decreased, over the past several decades), but rather because goods are significantly cheaper and financing is more easily available. Buy things you do not need with money you do not have, to impress people you do not like. Much as how a fast-food chain needs consumers to consume ever-increasing amounts of junk food, the financial sector looks to provide easy money as a way to expand its reach and power. Going cashless also plays into this: no longer will people's consumption be restricted by whether or not they have enough cash in their wallet. Going without something, especially as goods become cheaper, will no longer be part of the purchasing dilemma. Swipe and it's yours.

But we rarely ask why these goods and services have become so much cheaper: low wages, poor working conditions, too-easy access to credit, cheaper commodities, and other economic changes have contributed to "lower" prices, larger quantities, more variety, and unsustainable overconsumption. This is taught in business schools to supposedly bright minds as the way to make money and build companies.

In 2010, the *Harvard Business Review* published a piece that asked companies and firms to internalize their externalities, as the public was becoming more aware of externalities, and the impact of externalities was becoming easier to measure.[9] This led to a spirited response by a fellow of MIT's Sloan School, who argued that an awareness of externalities "invites misinterpretation, misunderstanding and mischief": "If everything is increasingly interrelated—and it is!—then who won't be aggrieved? Who won't be wounded? Who won't be disadvantaged? Who won't be harmed—or see themselves as harmed—in some meaningful way? What won't be an externality to some third party?"[10]

In the eyes of this research fellow, it would be too difficult to sustain the free market if we accounted for externalities; given that the free market is prima facie good, then accounting for externalities *must* be bad. This view led him to some strange conclusions, such as his assertion that "'Pollution' enabled the most innovative product innovations of the time."

Although the MIT professor shied away from honestly confronting the failures of the free market, he did get at the core issues. Every economic activity in the marketplace does place some external cost on some third party. This would infer a much greater role for government intervention and management of the economy in order to alleviate the gap between private and external cost. Rather than shy away from that, we should accept the responsibility to transform our economies far more than we have been willing to thus far. It is the ultimate and arguable sole role of the government to protect the public good in the interest of the welfare of the collective.

• • •

The second reason that the free and unregulated market cannot be truly sustainable is that there is a mismatch between the private interest to consume as much as possible and the collective interest to sustainably manage common shared resources. This is also an old idea: the concept of the "tragedy of the commons" was first used by William Forster in 1833 to refer to unregulated grazing on the unowned, public commons. The idea was picked up over a century later by the ecologist Garrett Hardin in 1968, who popularized the term as applied to any public resource. Although the popular term refers to a modern (and Western) phenomenon, communities and societies across the world and across history have faced issues around resource management. Asia in particular has several examples both of societies that successfully managed public resources (such as the Thai preindustrial system for managing increasingly scarce forests or the Japanese management of fisheries) and of those that failed (the depletion of Korea's forests and the collapse of how Indian villages managed what was uncharitably called "the wastes" by colonial officials).[11]

In short, the tragedy of the commons describes how shared, unregulated, and unowned resources are often overexploited. Any one person's consumption has no significant effect on overall stocks, so people believe they can use as much as is personally feasible. However, this calculus is true for everyone else; everyone uses as much as they can, and so the resource stock is eventually depleted or exhausted. There are some common themes to "common" resources:

1. The resource stock, be it a forest, a fishery, or the atmosphere, needs to be large enough so that any one person's use of it will not have a significant effect on supply (and thus increase prices). Thus, the usual market forces from increased exploitation would not apply.
2. The resources are not "owned," formally or informally. Without an owner, no one has an interest in preserving the level or quality of the resources.
3. The fixed costs of exploiting the resource are low. Some unowned resources (such as undersea oil) require a large level of up-front capital, restricting the number of entities that can exploit it. "Common resources," such as fisheries and forests, are cheaper to exploit, thus allowing a large number of people to consume them.
4. It is difficult to enforce rules and regulations governing the resource. This makes it difficult for industries to collectively develop regimes that can sustainably manage resources on their own. Any agreement can fall apart due to lack of trust or fears of defection.

5.   The market does not send the proper signals that indicate when a resource stock is in danger of being exhausted. When these signals are sent, it is often too late to reverse course.

The tragedy of the commons can be seen with the collapse of the world's major fisheries. Each individual fisher has an incentive to fish as much as possible (and especially more than his or her competitors). The cost of launching a fishing boat is fixed; the more fish that are caught, the higher one's income. The problem is that every fisher is operating under the same calculus, leading to massive overfishing. Even as the fishing industry began to realize that fishing needed to be constrained in order to preserve fisheries, there was still a heavy incentive to "cheat": to illegally overfish in order to sell much more fish than anyone else.

For much of history, when demand for fish was relatively low and fishers fished locally with small vessels, fishery stocks were not under threat. However, as catches grew in size and as demand for fish increased, the total catch grew to unsustainable levels. Fishers could now catch enormous amounts of fish, spurred by new technologies: larger nets, longer-range boats, sonar and radar systems to track schools of fish, and cooling systems to preserve large catches.

It took the almost complete collapse of fisheries in the North Atlantic to encourage Europe and the US to start to implement regulations to manage fish stocks. Markets did not do much to avoid this major resource collapse. The industry also realized the threat that overfishing presented, and so tried to self-regulate the size of the catches. Although some fisheries have been able to recover, others, such as the fishery of the Atlantic Northwest cod, may be gone forever.

Another example of the commons are forests. Individual farmers and landowners clearing land or selling timber may not affect the size of the overall forest. However, if every farmer or landowner eats a small amount into the forest, it will rapidly shrink.

Forests are difficult to manage or control. For one, they cover a large area, making it difficult to monitor where illegal logging may be taking place. Indonesia has nine hundred thousand square kilometers of forest; Brazil has four million square kilometers of forest. If both these forests were countries, they would be the thirty-third and sixth largest countries, respectively. The equipment needed for logging is also relatively cheap and easy to move, meaning that illegal logging can take place at times and places that are difficult to monitor.

This has had dire effects on the world's forests. The Amazon rainforest has lost about 20 percent of its total forest cover; the WWF predicts that deforestation could severely damage up to 60 percent of the Amazon by 2030. In Southeast Asia, a third of the rainforest has been lost, with some countries (e.g., Thailand) losing as much as 43 percent of forest cover.[12] Chapter 9 will deal with one of the major repercussions of Southeast Asia's deforestation: the annual haze from forest fires, raging on the island of Borneo, which blankets Singapore, Indonesia, and Malaysia every year. It will argue that the only hope is strong government intervention, and that markets and technology can only play a peripheral role to save the world's oldest rainforests and its indigenous inhabitants as well as the iconic orangutan.

• • •

The third reason that the free and unregulated market cannot be truly sustainable is that it does not include the effects of power. Those who benefit from overconsumption tend to be wealthier, giving them more power in both the marketplace and the political process. They also tend to be fewer in number, which helps them organize and demand, as a collective, privileges and protections from the government.

By contrast, those who suffer the external costs of privileged consumption tend to be poorer, with fewer resources to pressure for change or to protect themselves from external costs. They also tend to be larger in number, which complicates their ability to organize as effectively and exert political pressure. They are sometimes more desperate, living in or close to poverty; they may therefore decide to suffer through external costs rather than risk what little income they have.

Without some way to resolve this power gap, overconsumption will continue, as those who benefit will fight to preserve their privileges and offload their costs on the wider population.

The effects of power are not unknown to economists. Power differences have been used to justify protections for organized labor, minimum-wage legislation, and collective bargaining, all of which serve to increase the power of the employee vis-à-vis the employer. Power has also been used to justify antitrust legislation, to prevent monopolies from abusing their market power to bully suppliers and customers.

However, in many cases, the free market orthodoxy ignores the impact of power on economic negotiations. It assumes that people (or even nations) go into transactions as equals and are fully capable of turning down an economic transaction if it places too heavy a burden. As we all know from the global supply chain, which provides everything from T-shirts to iPads, this is utter nonsense. The same applies to smaller and poorer countries signing trade deals, or even agreements like the Trans-Pacific Partnership, which purportedly had environmental protection as one of the positive objectives.

We have not expanded our definition of the "powerless" to match our new resource-constrained reality. Arguing that the poor are able to make a conscious economic decision from a position of power when it comes to scarce resources is to hide from the truth and neglect their real deprivation and desperation.

• • •

What about technological development? Why is a deus ex machina not a viable pathway for sustainable development?

To reiterate, a technological approach to sustainability would hold that increasingly scarce resources would drive up input prices. This would encourage innovators and inventors around the world to develop new technologies—either significant improvements in energy or resource efficiency (thus reducing supply costs) or an entirely new technology that does not rely on scarce resources—to keep costs low.

Thus there would need to be market signals that encourage the development of sustainability-supporting technology—namely, high resource/input prices. And that can only come from the state, as markets thrive on a free ride until it is too late to correct. If the market encourages business as usual—perhaps due to the significant upside and profits from the mass externalization of cost and the underpricing of resources—then the market signals and business opportunities that motivate technologies will not emerge.

The tribulations of the electric car show how market dynamics can hurt the development and adoption of more sustainable technologies. Although they wouldn't be the cure-all they are often claimed to be (electric cars have significant environmental externalities), they would alleviate some vehicle pollution and carbon emissions. In the first decade of the twenty-first century, environmentalists, policymakers, and even some car companies hoped that high oil prices would finally encourage drivers to ditch gas-guzzling cars for cleaner hybrid and electric cars. As the production of electric cars increased, economies of scale would bring prices down, allowing electric cars to compete with their gas-fueled brethren.

Almost ten years later, electric cars have yet to gather significant market share. Countries that made bold statements about bolstering electric car usage, such as the US in 2008 and Germany in 2016 (when chancellor Angela Merkel declared that all German cars would be electric by 2030), have seen no increase in demand. In Germany, for example, only 1.5 percent of the 3.4 million new car registrations in 2016 were electric or hybrid cars. By contrast, 20 percent of Germany's new car registrations were gas-guzzling SUVs.[13] And this is Germany, which is, by any reckoning, a leader both in automotive technology and the adoption of renewable energy through the preferential government treatment of green energy sources in the *Erneuerbare Energien Gesetz,* or Renewable Energy Act.[14]

The only cars with any mass appeal are gas-electric hybrids; the only fully electric cars are sold as luxuries. Demand for inefficient SUVs has recovered from its previous low. Car companies have pointed to the price of oil as the major reason why electric cars have failed to take off. The 2008 financial crisis caused oil prices to collapse—thus undercutting the consumer incentive to buy an electric car (perhaps showing that buyers are ultimately more concerned with price, prestige, and comfort than any "green" characteristics). Oil prices are extremely volatile, changing according to macroeconomic conditions, geopolitical tensions, collusion by oil-producing countries, new technologies, speculation, and even just the vagaries of the market. Thus the market signal for a more sustainable kind of car is nonexistent. If electric cars are to take hold (and, again, they are not the panacea they are sometimes claimed to be), strong government intervention is needed.

Some innovation does happen ex nihilo. However, if a technology that can greatly improve sustainability is created, there is no mechanism to get this technology into the hands of the developing world. The developing world generally does not have the resources to purchase expensive equipment and technology. Relying on technology means little if the developing world—where the sustainability challenge mostly lies—does not have the money to buy it, because the creators of this technology are driven not by social causes but invariably by power and greed (as opposed to making a decent and fair profit).

Recognition of this latter issue has been a major stumbling block in climate change negotiations. Developing countries understood that they lacked the resources to purchase expensive technology for power generation and renewable energy, and polluting and carbon-emitting options were relatively cheap. Thus, developing countries asked for help from richer, more advanced economies to purchase new technology: the Green Climate Fund (which became a sticking point for advanced economies, who largely did not want to pay).

Finally, the experience of developing countries shows that these economies often lack access to tried and tested technologies. Millions around the world lack access to basic sanitation, the technologies for which have been available for over a century. If through the free market the developing world can't even get basic toilets, let alone advanced collection, treatment, and disposal facilities, to the people who need them, how can we expect developing countries to get the newest, most innovative, and most expensive technologies?

This is not to say that technology will play no role in solving the sustainability crisis. I often work with technology companies to push their managers to think about how their technologies could be used to solve our most pressing social and environmental problems. But the creation of technology is, at best, merely one step in the process. Many of the technologies to solve some of the world's most persistent development problems already exist, but have yet to be adopted and implemented on the mass scale needed. For example, the technical solutions to clean the Ganges River are well known. However, the barriers to cleaning the Ganges are not technological but economic and political.

The same is true for any solution to the sustainability challenge. Technology is merely a tool—perhaps an essential or even necessary one, but not one that can be used without direction. That "direction" is provided by proper pricing and public policy, which are both the remit of the state.

On the national scale, we need something to provide direction. The free market is not exerting this role properly, encouraging technologies with unclear social applicability. The government would be far more capable of ensuring that technology is applied to the right kinds of problems.

• • •

The only sure way to reduce the external costs of consumption, which affect all aspects of a sustainable future, is to directly reduce unnecessary and wasteful consumption, which is currently hardwired into our economies. This will lead to a number of difficult choices. What do people deserve to have access to? What level of consumption is reasonable, and what level is unreasonable (and should therefore be subject to control)? What resource stocks are at risk of overexploitation, and how can their collapse be prevented by state intervention?

These issues boil down to a single question: In a more resource-constrained and environmentally stressed age, how should people's economic choices and actions be governed? These cannot be left to free markets or the self-serving motives of tech wizards. This governance requires someone, or something, to make decisions about society and the economy. That something is the institution of society: the state.

Market-based solutions are based on the belief that no one person or institution needs to make the tough choices about what is deserved and undeserved. However, the persistence of external costs and underpriced resources, and the subsequent growth of vested interests and overconsumption shows that unmanaged and unregulated markets lead to flawed outcomes and prevent societies from creating a more sustainable economy.

Relying on the market or hoping for some new technological development is not a delegation of responsibility, but an abrogation of it. Hope is not a plan for a planet that is being assaulted on all fronts. Instead, states in the developing world need to own up to their responsibility to manage their economies and societies to overcome the flaws of the free market, manage the expectations of their people, and provide a sustainable upward path for the hundreds of millions who still live in poverty and drudgery.

But there is yet another element of the free-market model that must be discussed, one that makes it impossible to reconcile with sustainability. This is the hyperfocus on growth at all costs, fueled by consumption and underpriced resources. Chapter 3 will examine this problem in greater detail, and why it restricts any move toward sustainability by governments and companies.

CHAPTER | 3

THE STATE OF GROWTH

Politicians running for high office in the developing world often put a bold promise about economic growth at the center of their campaigns. In his campaign, Joko Widodo promised that Indonesia would see 7 percent economic growth by 2018. India's Narendra Modi promised one million new manufacturing jobs and doubled farmers' incomes by 2022. Nondemocratic Vietnam promised to achieve 6.7 percent growth over 2017. Nor are developed countries immune from promising high economic growth. President Trump, upon his inauguration, promised 4 percent economic growth, to be achieved by deregulating the economy and cutting taxes.

Growth targets are central to any developing country's economic planning as a way to bolster its legitimacy. Targets are so central to our conception of how developing countries engage their economic planning that their absence makes news. When China's president Xi Jinping addressed the 19th National Party Congress, news headlines reported that the new president had dropped a promise made in 2010 by his predecessor Hu Jintao to double the size of China's economy by 2021. As analysts at the time noted, this was not due to an inability to achieve it, but rather that Beijing was paying "higher attention to tasks such as curbing pollution, taming financial risks and closing the income gap."[1]

The world's businesses are just as focused on growth. The primary goal of a corporation is to produce and sell more, grow revenues, and pursue greater profits. Public companies enshrine this responsibility further, with the goal of maximizing shareholder value, achieved by growing revenues and profits.

But our obsessive focus on economic growth, fueled by mindless consumption, as the centerpiece in our economic model has made it impossible to think clearly about sustainability and resource management issues. Governments pursue growth at any cost, ignoring the clear environmental and social consequences. Businesses find that they cannot simultaneously embrace corporate growth and focus on sustainability and thus get trapped in never-ending yet facile discussions about their commitment to sustainability challenges.

This chapter will suggest that we need to think about growth differently. Rather than pursue growth at any cost, we need to instead consider what growth is actually for, and what costs are worth bearing.

To be clear: this chapter is not "antigrowth." Economic growth—in the descriptive sense of a larger economy—will occur as the state focuses on basic needs and lifting its population out of poverty. Growing more food, building more homes, expanding energy access, and other development initiatives will expand the economy. This is growth that is linked to rights, and is thus needed. It has to be initiated and celebrated—but also managed.

But we must also accept that any economic growth—whether or not it reflects increased levels of development—has an impact on the environment, sustainability, common resources, and people. The questions for the sustainable state are how to ensure that these impacts are being borne only for the purpose of development, and which kinds of economic growth are too harmful to pursue.

In that vein, I suggest an idea of *developmental growth*—a version of economic growth that reflects increased access to basic needs across a population. This version of growth will be optimized (and not maximized) along with the effect on resources and sustainability. Such a version of growth would be better suited to and critically important for developing countries operating in a resource-constrained twenty-first century.

• • •

In the trickle-down narrative of economics, a growing economy means more economic opportunities: the unemployed find paying labor, save money, and are eventually able to sustain themselves. The rewards from growth eventually make their way into the hands of ordinary people.

There is some truth to this argument. For a poor developing country, a growing economy is better than a stagnant one. And if we hold resource use constant, higher economic growth is better than lower economic growth.

But in practice, much of our current economic growth does not come from "doing more with less" but from "doing more with more." Crudely put, it is doing more, cheaply, so that we can grow by consuming cheaply. High economic growth is fueled by consuming more and more resources, which worsens resource scarcity and levies external costs on the poor majority. Productivity may appear to increase, but only because much of the cost is not included in the calculation.

It is worth taking a step back and explaining why we are pursuing economic growth in the first place. It is possible we have confused economic growth as a descriptive measure with growth as a prescription. Growth is not the goal but merely an indicator of good work being done. However, many observers, including many national leaders, forget this point. Rather than pursuing good social policies and having economic growth statistics reflect that, countries, ranging from large ones such as the United States and India to smaller ones like Thailand and Vietnam, treat economic growth as the objective in itself, pursuing high growth for its own sake.

This can lead countries to pursue a version of economic growth that does not yield much, if any, social benefit. Some of the easiest ways to juice growth come from deregulation, tax cuts, and quick liberalization. These methods may lead to higher growth according to the statistics, but its benefits will be captured only by wealthier individuals rather than the rest of the population.

• • •

The most important problem within the free-market orthodoxy is that it sees perpetual growth as the success metric for the economy. Regardless of the final amount, you will never see a government or economist argue that a no-growth economy is desirable.

Perpetually high growth, given the world's finite resources, is impossible. As the economist Kenneth Boulding is commonly attributed to have said "Anyone who believes exponential growth can go on forever in a finite world is either a madman or an economist."

We will eventually hit a hard limit on what we can produce: we won't be able to grow the economy because there will be little left that we can easily use, and what is left will have such large external costs on the global majority as to be effectively impossible to exploit.

This was the argument in the Club of Rome's *The Limits of Growth*, discussed in chapter 1. The computer model that generated the book's results tried to compare the growth trends in the human economy with the limits of the natural system and found that the economy was predicted to overshoot these limits by the middle of the twenty-first century. Professor Jorgen Randers, in an update to *The Limits of Growth*, has argued that we have already overshot many of these limits (with the most pressing being greenhouse gases), and that governments are not doing enough to adapt to these new limits.[2]

One optimistic view of resources is that natural resource stocks are often greater than we fear, as technology can "unlock" stocks that are difficult to reach and allow us to use them wisely, creating a world of "abundance." But just because resources are in the ground does not mean that we can use them cost-free. Extracting these resources comes with a big price tag: destruction, displacement of people, and the various impacts of conversion, use, and disposal. Fracking is a good example; those who herald it as a way to yield cheap energy do not include the methane released,[3] the increased risk of seismic activity,[4] or chemical pollution[5] in the price tag.

Growth, when it happens, is financed through debt: we are borrowing tomorrow's resources in order to pay for today's growth. Eventually, this strategy will lead to a crash, and many of the signs are already visible to those whose heads are not buried in the sand.

Arguing that growth must eventually reach some sort of steady state is not the same as saying that the economy will shrink. Economist Herman Daly developed the idea of the "steady-state economy," in which there are "constant stocks of people and artefacts, maintained at some desired, sufficient levels by low rates of maintenance 'throughput.'"[6] This would create a "circular economy," often considered the holy grail of sustainable development, whereby the outputs of the economy are recycled back into its inputs, thus reducing, if not removing entirely, the need to consume "new" resources.

To counter the views of those who argued that he was calling for a shrinking economy, Daly responded by noting that "the verb 'to grow' has become so overladen with positive value connotations that we have forgotten its first literal dictionary denotation, namely, 'to spring up and develop to maturity.' Thus the very notion of growth includes some concept of maturity or sufficiency, beyond which point physical accumulation gives way to physical maintenance; that is, growth gives way to a steady state. It is important to remember that 'growth' is not synonymous with 'betterment.'"[7]

I do not go quite as far as Daly to think we have reached a stage in the economy where we have fully reached "sufficiency." The level of poverty still present throughout the developing world is proof of that; whatever steady state we reach cannot have billions of people living without access to basic needs. Ensuring that these billions gain that access will require "growth," in the sense that we will need to consume more resources to make that happen. For example, ensuring that every Indian has a home will "grow" the Indian economy—buying the materials, paying labor for construction, building the home itself, and the like. And this is without counting any of the positive spillovers that will come from providing every Indian a home.

But this growth would be in service of a social purpose: providing one of the basic rights of life to the vast majority of Indians. It's not immediately clear how growth pursued through free-market mechanisms would be able to deliver this (given that there are an estimated 600–700 million Indians who do not have permanent homes) or have the same direct social impact. This gets at the central claim of "trickle-down economics": that the benefits of economic growth, even growth without any defined social purpose, ends up benefiting the poor by virtue of growing the economy.

Daly himself dealt with this question of how growth connects to poverty alleviation. In 1993, he asked

> How far can we alleviate poverty by development without growth?
> I suspect that the answer will be a significant amount, but less than half. One reason for this belief is that if the five- to tenfold expansion is really going to be for the sake of the poor, then it will have to consist of things needed by the poor—food, clothing, shelter—not information services. Basic goods have an irreducible physical dimension and their expansion will require growth rather than development. . . . Angelized GNP [a version of the economy that has reduced resource inputs] will not feed the poor.[8]

But in a world of constrained resources, growth of any kind has an environmental and resource impact. Societies will need to think more carefully about what type of growth their resources are spent on, and then how to best handle that impact. The sustainable state will need to determine which impacts to the economy must be borne, and how they must be accounted for. It must also determine what kinds of growth are not worth the cost.

When we are faced with finite resources, growth is possible only through productivity growth: doing more with the scarce resources we have. Massive productivity gains in the nineteenth and twentieth centuries, combined with a smaller population, allowed for consistently high growth. Yet no such productivity gains appear to be forthcoming today, despite the hype around digital- and internet-enabled technology.

We often understand *productivity* solely as how cheaply and quickly we can make something. However, this narrow definition misses the effects on the poor majority in the developing world. If we included external costs in our understanding of productivity, many of the world's major industries would no longer seem as productive.

For example, let us compare industrial farming and organic farming. The former relies on economies of scale, leading to higher yields at reduced costs. The soil is worked hard: crops are farmed intensively, with injudicious application of chemical fertilizer to add nutrition back to the soil. The overuse of fertilizers leads to soil and water pollution, and the spread of chemical pesticides and herbicides can negatively impact the health of both laborers and consumers.

Then there are the effects of driving food prices as low as they possibly can go. Industrial farms have undercut smaller farms on price, enabling them to dominate the market. Low food prices—especially for certain foods—have transformed eating habits the world over, leading to the global rise in obesity and exploding amounts of food waste (which, if the waste were its own country, would be the third largest emitter of carbon emissions).[9]

Organic farming, by contrast, is labor-intensive and relies on natural inputs in their production. This often leads to smaller yields at higher costs, so is portrayed as "less productive" than its industrial counterpart. However, organic farming generates much lower external costs. By relying on natural inputs and focusing on soil health, organic farms do not pollute with chemical runoff. By avoiding chemical pesticides and herbicides, organic farms protect both their workers and consumers. By employing more labor, their operations benefit the wider community.

This is true of the entire economy. Most major industries seem productive if one compares the amount they produce with their private business costs. However, include costs on the environment, and suddenly their productivity is erased. Imagine how far "productivity" would fall if we included costs on society as well?

Automation is another example. On the one hand, robots are hugely productive: companies can now produce goods without paying even low wages. On the other hand, when we consider costs to the wider community, robots suddenly seem much less helpful. Growing unemployment, caused by increased automation, has a social cost. One wonders how productive robots would seem if these costs were included.

We need to think about growth more carefully. We should not pursue economic growth for its own sake, nor should we foster mindless consumption in the hope that it leads to economic growth. Instead, we need a version of growth that accounts for living standards: *developmental growth* or *sustainable growth*.

• • •

In 1962, the free-market economist Milton Friedman famously wrote: "There is one and only one social responsibility of business—to use its resources and engage in activities designed to increase its profits so long as it stays within the rules of the game, which is to say, engages in open and free competition without deception or fraud."[10]

For many years, business leaders treated this as gospel. But times have changed. Few business leaders worth their salt would utter these words today. Yet it is a sign of the magnitude of the challenge we face that rejection of Friedman's statement still does not get us far enough in solving our civilization dilemma. This quote gives us one definition of what corporate responsibility really is—and gets at the heart of why markets and businesses are ill-suited to tackle the sustainability challenge.

Any improvements in resource efficiency will not change the simple truth at the heart of a corporate business model: companies are in the business of "doing more, cheaply," to maximize revenue and profits by selling products to the greatest possible extent, not "doing less, responsibly."

If companies were truly concerned about sustainability, they would need to decide to limit production and sell fewer products *even if* that sacrificed revenue and profit. Some companies may have the long-term vision to willingly limit production to sustainably manage resources. However, this can be difficult for the world's largest companies, which tend to be public and thus beholden to outside investors and shareholders who want maximized returns on their investments, even if at the same time they pay lip service to sustainability and facile environmental, social, and governance (ESG) regulatory demands.

If this is the case, why then do companies get involved in "sustainability"?

One possible reason is that corporations, as the biggest economic entities in the world, feel compelled to project leadership on these issues, even as they seek to preserve the free ride inherent in their business models. Their involvement in sustainability allows them to define the terms of the sustainability debate. Companies can ensure that regulations are not too invasive and remove any threat to their business operations. If they instead rejected any push for new rules on climate change and sustainability, they would risk harsher and stricter rules if new policies were ever formulated. An open rejection of sustainability efforts might even get some pushback from consumers. By embracing it, albeit superficially, they can appease the public.

This is why companies like ExxonMobil and Royal Dutch Shell express support for a global solution for sustainability and climate change, even though ExxonMobil, for example, is currently accused of suppressing internal research into climate change for decades. As some of the major culprits behind global carbon emissions—and as some of the likely targets of carbon regulation—these companies have an interest in light, non-invasive regulation. By supporting a lighter hand now, these companies may avoid a heavier hand in the future. This is no different than what the tech companies are doing now to push back against regulation, even enlisting the support of a poorly informed public.

Some companies have sincerely tried to offer an alternate way of doing business, but have struggled as they come into contact with economic realities. Some American jurisdictions, for example, allow companies to declare themselves as "benefit corporations," or B-Corps. B-Corps are declarations by companies that they have goals beyond just maximizing revenue, such as offering workers better conditions or ensuring that their practices are sustainable.

Some B-Corps, such as Patagonia, are in private hands, which mean that they can operate according to the whims of their owners. But the few examples of B-Corps going public, such as the e-commerce website Etsy, show that they suddenly find it very difficult to reconcile their other goals with the primary objective of maximizing shareholder value. After Etsy went public in 2015, its share value dropped by 63 percent over the next two years. Shareholders demanded that Etsy cut costs, and its socially aware CEO was fired by the board. Most analysts now expect Etsy to let its certification as a B-Corp lapse, turning the company into an ordinary shareholder-value-maximizing corporation.[11]

The idea of maximizing value to shareholders has put companies in a bind when it comes to serving other ideas or masters. CEOs introduce measures friendly to consumers, suppliers, workers, or the environment, only to be criticized or even fired by angry investors who believe that the company is "overly concerned." When the American Airlines CEO offered to pay its staff the industry average, one angry analyst from Citibank complained that "shareholders get leftovers."[12] Shareholders can even resist the minor superficial changes of corporate social responsibility. Unilever's current CEO, Paul Polman, has started to talk about growing a culture of responsibility within the major company (and, to his credit, banned the term *CSR*). Yet Polman has had to fight off both internal dissent from activist investors demanding that the company cut costs, and an external threat from Kraft Heinz, owned by a private equity firm with a pure growth-at-all-costs focus.[13]

This is not to criticize companies for what they do. There is nothing wrong with their goal of maximizing revenue within what is legally allowed. Nor am I saying that business has no role in the implementation of sustainable development. A business, operating with the right incentives and parameters, can be a valued partner for the state as it implements public policy.

But to hope that business solutions are a viable replacement for strong government action would be foolhardy. On their own, they will not be enough to solve the global sustainability challenge, especially if the state is unwilling or unable to act. It is only the state that can decide in the public interest whether the goods of a company are detrimental to society, be they guns, cigarettes, or junk foods, and what license may be provided. Companies alone are not capable of this.

• • •

Both the previous chapter and this one have criticized the hope that markets alone—whether expressed through trickle-down economics, a faith in technological development, or a belief in corporate social responsibility—can achieve sustainable development. The hoped-for market dynamics will at best fail to solve, and at worst exacerbate, resource constraints and unsustainable economic practices.

Instead of looking to the invisible hand of the market, we should instead look to the "visible hand of the state"[14] to guide the economy toward a more sustainable outcome. Chapter 4 will argue that the state is the best vehicle to exert governance over the economy. Although both global governance and local governance have their place in a twenty-first-century sustainability agenda, they both currently lack the capacity, legitimacy, and accountability to consistently intervene in economic decision-making. Only the state currently has the authority and legitimacy to make the difficult choices that face developing economies and to define a new meaning of prosperity in the developing world.

CHAPTER 4

WORKING WITH THE STATE
Building the Social Security Net

E arly in 2017, in the midst of the despair of the US environmental movement in the aftermath of President Trump's election, a strident call for optimism was released by Michael Bloomberg (former mayor of New York City) and Carl Pope (former executive director of the Sierra Club). Their book was titled *Climate of Hope: How Cities, Businesses, and Citizens Can Save the Planet.*

Bloomberg and Pope were sanguine, writing in their book's preface that "through our work with cities, businesses and communities, we believe that we are now in a better position to stop climate change than ever before." The book falls into many of the pitfalls of the free-market approach described in chapter 2, almost to the extent of parody. But Bloomberg and Pope call for an additional shift in thinking that sounds perfectly reasonable in theory (especially if we separate it from market-based nonsense). The authors argue that "instead of putting all hope in the federal government, let's empower cities, regions, businesses, and citizens to accelerate the progress they are already making on their own. We believe that by changing the way we think and talk about climate, we can lower the temperature of the debate—and accomplish a whole lot more."[1]

The argument is that local communities are more able, more capable, and more willing to tackle the issues of climate change (and, by extension, sustainability) than a lumbering national government. As engines of the national and global economy, city governments could, through concerted action, transform enough of the economy to make a serious difference.

This is the hope, at least, of those who support a "bottom-up sustainability," whereby local, community, and grassroots initiatives take the lead in transforming the world economy. The argument is that states, especially in the developing world, are ineffective and corrupt. Even well-meaning government officials are hampered by a lack of resources and weak institutions, which limit their ability to execute government policy. Finally, there is the question of justice: the idea that communities (rather than states or markets) should benefit from local resources, both in terms of profits and of minimized costs.

Chapter 2 discussed why neither markets nor technological development are appropriate alternatives to a state-led policy of sustainability. It highlighted the need for some social institution to exert governance: to make choices about what economic actions are appropriate in a resource-constrained world.

This chapter will explain why governance must be exerted by the state, rather than by international institutions and agreements (i.e., global governance) or by villages, cities, or provinces (i.e., local governance). The state is the social body with the best combination of authority, accountability, and legitimacy to consistently manage the economy to support sustainability and to preserve resources for future generations. Neither the global nor the local communities have the capacity and institutions to directly exert governance themselves, especially when it comes to the complex and systemic issues of operationalizing sustainable development.

•••

Chapter 5 will go into more detail as to what a strong state would look like, but it is important to bring up some definitions at this point so that we know what limits both global and local governance.

Authority is the ability to make decisions and implement them without resorting to violent coercion or naked bribery. When a totalitarian dictatorship forces its people to follow its orders or when a state buys loyalty through dividends from natural resources, then the state does not have true authority and is, almost by definition, not a strong state.

Legitimacy means that the government is seen by the population as a true representative of the "popular will." This is connected to authority: the reason why people listen to a government, even if they personally disagree with its decisions or are even negatively affected by them, is that they see the government as the legitimate representative of the population.

In the mainstream discussion of politics, there is one way a government is seen to be legitimate: democratic elections. Even if nondemocratic states have performed better, directly elected governments are seen to be more legitimate. However, although Westerners see elections as the sole sufficient condition for legitimacy, elections are only one way to confer legitimacy, and may not be enough without a well-functioning government. A democratic system that encourages gridlock and political paralysis, or trades on existing divisions between classes, groups, or people, may have a fragile legitimacy, despite holding elections.

This is not to argue that all states should jettison democracy and become single-party authoritarian states likes China or Vietnam. But it remains true that these nondemocratic states have gone further in improving the lives of their citizens than democratic developing countries like India and the Philippines. And, to be frank, the Chinese Communist Party, despite not being elected, likely commands more popular support among the Chinese people than the Indian National Congress Party or the Bharatiya Janata Party have among the Indian people.

Finally, there is *accountability*: that a government is responsible for how its decisions affect the population, and that it has a system for changing policy if its policies end up hurting more than they help. If a state continually hurts the majority, yet does not change policy despite clear evidence, then it is unaccountable. Democracies can struggle with this just as much as nondemocratic governments. The US, for example, continually fails to pass even limited gun control legislation, even though a majority of Americans (67 percent, according to Gallup),[2] and even a majority of gun owners (83 percent of whom support mandatory background checks on gun purchases),[3] support "reasonable" controls. This is my definition of a weak state that does not represent the will and needs of the people to protect the public good.

• • •

One can understand why people look to global governance as the path to a more sustainable society. The externalities of our global economy are themselves global. When a consumer buys a smartphone in New York City, the repercussions ripple as far afield as South Korea, the Congo, and Ireland. Pollution from Chinese factories affects air quality in South Korea, Japan, and even California. Global consumption of plastic has led to massive islands of waste floating in the Pacific Ocean.

Then you have climate change, a problem so large and so systemic that it seems that only a concerted global effort will tackle the problems that underlie it. If any one of the world's major emitters, be it the US, Europe, China, India, or any of the other rising economies, fails to meet its commitments, then the whole solution risks falling apart. The externalities of carbon are global: increased carbon emissions in the developing world lengthen droughts in Africa and the Middle East, erode shorelines in North America, melt permafrost in Russia and Northern Europe, and expand deserts in Western China. If externalities require government to resolve them, then the implication is that global externalities require global government. This is why a great deal of time and effort has been spent in successive climate change negotiations in the hope of creating a functional climate change agreement.

There have been some successes when it comes to global governance on environmental issues. The Vienna Convention for the Protection of the Ozone Layer, one of the earliest global environmental agreements, was passed in 1985. There are international agreements to manage wetlands, to clean up and provide compensation for oil pollution, to control the trade in endangered wildlife, and to address other environmental and conservation issues. Even if the results of these international agreements are mixed, they still represent an international consensus.

However, we must remember that states are ultimately responsible for enacting and enforcing international agreements. The institutions of global governance have few enforcement mechanisms, and a state unwilling to implement global directives—inevitably because it is weak—can stall the entire process. For example, the US has refused to join compacts such as the Convention on the Rights of the Child, the International Criminal Court, the Convention on the Law of the Sea, and now, most recently, the Paris Climate Accord—and in doing so has weakened each of these institutions. Washington has sometimes rejected these agreements in spite of the wishes of the US president and the foreign policy establishment, leading to strange situations in which Washington calls for countries to follow global rules while refusing to follow them itself.

What is more common, however, is the inability of states to implement the directives of global governance. Many international agreements are signed with a lot of fanfare but little discussion of how to actually achieve them and to distribute resources between signatories to ensure that action can be taken. This means that developing countries are asked to take on international obligations yet are offered no assistance to help fulfill them. The global agreement thus ends up being ineffectual, despite the best intentions of everyone involved.

Global governance can still play an important role, namely in presenting a global consensus on an issue. The Paris Climate Accord shows what global governance can and cannot do. The accord was the first global agreement on climate change in which each state both declared its responsibility for its own emissions and promised to develop a plan to slow, halt, or even reverse the growth in carbon emissions.

However, the accord provided no enforcement or punishment mechanism. It did set up a Green Climate Fund to help developing countries fund their carbon reduction plans, but doing so was a tense part of the negotiations (and ultimately one of the reasons cited for the US withdrawal).[4] Its strictures are purely voluntary and depend on leadership at the state level. The global consensus on climate change has seemed to survive US recalcitrance for now, but there is still the risk that countries—advanced or developing—will slack off on their promises. And although leaders can sign up, their ability to act at home depends on how strong the state is. A weak, disjointed state will have no chance of pulling off the massive economic reshaping needed to meet the targets of the accord.

Perhaps the thorniest issue comes from attempts to regulate the global commons. As discussed in chapter 2, fisheries have been particularly difficult to manage, due to the ease of illegal fishing, the difficulty of monitoring large areas, and the benefits that come from "cheating." Governments have tried to develop international institutions to monitor fisheries and report on illegal fishing. These Regional Fisheries Management Organizations (RFMOs) often include several countries as members and do their best to promote conservation. But it's a big ocean out there, and the RFMOs are often underfunded and underequipped. They often need to cooperate with the fishing industry, which is, perhaps unsurprisingly, unwilling to provide much help.

• • •

When it comes to the authority of global governance, the exception that proves the rule is the European Union, which is perhaps the only supranational institution with real power to intervene in the affairs of its member states. The EU has a parliament, an executive, border controls, and a central bank. It can regulate goods and services across the common market, overriding state regulations if they come in conflict. It redistributes funds across the continent, collecting money from its members and delivering it to different projects. Although the EU does not have as much power as both its supporters and detractors often claim, it does have enough to actively manage and regulate a continent-wide economy. The EU's directives are listened to by its member states, even if it is somewhat begrudgingly.

The United Kingdom's decision to leave the EU both vindicates and shows the limits of the EU's authority. The United Kingdom chose to leave the EU out of a wish to "take back control"—over immigration, economic regulation, and the funds it would send to Brussels. This argument implies that Brussels really did have authority over Britain, enough to make it want to leave the EU. But Brexit also shows that, even in Europe, states play a central role. Despite all the authority the EU had over Britain, the country was still allowed to exit. If Scotland had made the same unilateral decision vis-à-vis the United Kingdom, it would have been ignored. The state's authority, even in systems of global or supranational governance, remains central.

Global governance also has serious issues with accountability and legitimacy: international institutions are neither seen as representations of any global opinion nor are they held responsible for the effects of their decisions. The most successful international institutions were, for the most part, constructed by the West at a time when the rest of the world was weak, and thus these institutions privilege Western countries, economies, ideas, and experts. They are now increasingly being challenged by "the rest," leading to fears in the West about the rewriting of the world order. Some of these fears explain the rise of populism in the West.

Many of the most prominent institutions follow a Western paradigm, which can be inappropriately applied to the developing world. This is not to doubt the sincerity of the experts and analysts who work at USAID, the World Bank, the United Nations Development Program, or the Asian Development Bank. But, for the most part, the people working in these institutions have gone to Western schools, live in Western cities, and apply a Western historical experience to the rest of the world. They work within the fickleness of short-term aid cycles, are unable to commit to the long period of time necessary for development, and are institutionally handcuffed to the ideology of the main Western powers. Development experts in these global institutions devise countless projects that never succeed, and many white elephants are abandoned, with little long-term benefit for communities.

At worst, these institutions of global governance reinforce and maintain the superiority of Western ideas and of its military and economic power, which can blind those in the developing world to alternate solutions. This is also true today with regard to the shaping of the sustainability agenda.

The developing world will ultimately have to create its own institutions based on its own experiences and principles, much as what China has attempted to do with the Asian Infrastructure Investment Bank (AIIB). But the AIIB's experience shows that the West may take a dim view to the creation of these alternatives. Despite Western and American commentators arguing that China needed to act as a "responsible stakeholder," the launch of the AIIB was received coolly by Washington, which pushed its allies (e.g., Japan) not to join and publicly disapproved of those that did (e.g., the United Kingdom). The implication for the rest of the world was that a globally governed financial system was all well and good so long as the United States had the largest influence and can dictate terms.

But even if the developing world creates these institutions and signs more international agreements, they may mean little if developing countries are not strong enough to implement them. China, India, Indonesia, and other major economies may sign whatever agreements they want, but those agreements will mean little if no one ends up implementing them.

• • •

The day after President Trump withdrew from the Paris Climate Accord, a leader from the other side of the continent hopped on a plane to China. California governor Jerry Brown was greeted with a red carpet, and even Chinese president Xi Jinping took time out of his busy schedule to meet him.[5] Governor Brown has highlighted California as a place where America could continue to pursue climate change action, yet he is merely the most prominent member of a growing contingent of local leaders who have stated their wish to continue the fight against climate change after the US withdrawal from Paris.[6]

One can understand why the environmental movement has latched on to these statements. California is the world's seventh-largest economy. New York City (whose current mayor, Bill de Blasio, also expressed his support for climate action) is one of the world's most important cities. Even if the federal government was unwilling to enact changes, cities and federal states may make up enough of the national (and perhaps global) economy to make a difference.

This argument has mostly come to the fore in the US, whose federal government seems to be stuck on almost every political issue (not just climate change), encouraging Americans to look elsewhere for necessary policy change. But, given how easily commentators expand American experiences to the rest of the world, it is only a matter of time before something similar is proposed globally.

The argument is that, in today's modern economy, cities can act faster than larger and slower national governments. Cities could use their economic power to encourage people to make sustainable economic decisions even if national governments are unwilling to implement regulation. Cities attract talent, expertise, and business, and therefore have the resources to tackle sustainability in a way that poorer regions may find more difficult. Finally (if proponents were being honest), cities consume vast quantities of energy and raw materials, often at the expense of the hinterland, and thus have an obligation to improve themselves first before calling on others to do the same.

However, a focus on cities ignores how closely cities are integrated with their surroundings, drawing on resource extraction and agriculture in the countryside. Mass consumption of resources in the city encourages unsustainable industrial practices out in the hinterland, with large externalities placed on those who live there. These rural populations have no way to pressure the city government to change its economic practices; the city government is thus *unaccountable* to these groups.

Then add the global dimension: that major global cities engage in activities with repercussions across not just the country but the entire globe. For example, take one central element of city life (at least in the cosmopolitan centers of the world): the daily cup of coffee. World coffee consumption now stands at 152.1 million bags and will likely continue to grow.[7] Yet coffee prices have remained low despite this increase in demand, which implies that costs are being kept low due to overproduction and underpricing. Coffee farmers are not benefiting from the coffee boom, because of both low prices and being forced to specialize in cash crops over foodstuffs.

Some cities may be altruistic enough to force local changes on behalf of those that live farther away, but they will likely be few in number and unlikely to go far enough. The urban economist Richard Florida noted that "blue-state knowledge economies run on red-state energy"[8]; in other words, the American states that are focused on services, technology, and "the cutting edge" are powered by cheap fuel and food from poorer states—Louisiana, North Dakota, Oklahoma, and others. Florida was writing within an American context, but his point could be extended globally: rich urban economies are fueled by poor rural economies. Rich cities can make themselves as environmentally friendly and sustainable as they like, but they will still extract excessive resources and "export" huge externalities around the world.

I will make one additional warning. The massive drive to urbanize has come at the expense of the countryside, whose economies and communities have stagnated, if not declined. This has encouraged a great deal of political resentment against the city for taking resources and talent from the countryside without giving anything in return or, worse, distorting the rural economy.

New Delhi and its constant struggles with water scarcity show the connection between the city and the countryside. India has built massive reservoirs that, during the dry season, release water saved during the rainy season. These dams are also used to provide electricity for India's growing urban population.

These projects are controversial, as they often divert water that would normally go to sustain rural villages. The construction of more dams, irrigation systems, and canals deprives locations further downstream from being replenished, reducing the water resources available that sustains numerous smaller rural communities. But it also leaves New Delhi in a rather unstable position: the canal bringing water to the city is often a target for protestors who sabotage it in an effort to exert political pressure. One such protest in early 2016 disrupted water supplies to the whole city, reducing water flow by over two thirds. Schools and businesses in Delhi were forced to close, and water needed to be rationed.[9] It should be noted this is not just any city in India. This is Delhi, the capital of the largest democracy in the world.

If a major city then tries to use its economic leverage to force rural communities to restrict economic opportunities in order to support sustainability in its immediate area, a backlash could emerge. A rural resident—already paying so much for a city's massive growth—will be upset at being asked to sacrifice even more.

Finally, it is not clear that cities have much real independence, especially in the developing world. The tradition of municipal self-government is rare in the developing world (and in the West as well). Given that the problem stems from rapidly growing megacities in the developing world, it is not clear that city-driven sustainability will be applicable anywhere outside of a few rich Western countries.

Even if cities were to drive the sustainability agenda, the state would ultimately need to build the institutions that would allow cities to govern themselves. Thus, a precondition to municipal autonomy, especially in the developing world, is a strong state willing to set the preconditions for institutional development.

I want to make clear that these criticisms are not meant to impugn the principles behind city-driven sustainability. Cities should do everything they can to create a more sustainable urban economy. If their efforts move the needle in their countries, then all credit to them. But city-driven sustainability efforts are still a rich-state solution. Only rich cities have both the economic resources and the local autonomy to pursue sustainability initiatives on their own. More important, it is a solution that only makes sense as a stopgap solution if the state government has abdicated its responsibility (i.e., has become a weak state).

• • •

One final alternative is to focus on the local village and community as the body that exerts governance toward sustainability. Local communities are often closest to the environmental repercussions of resource extraction and depletion. They would have the best information as to what would work in terms of resource management. But most important, perhaps, is that a focus on villages would restore power and dignity, eroded by centuries of modernization, to local communities. Globalization, centralization, and marketization have overturned many of the communal structures that govern local communities and encouraged the growth-at-all-costs mentality that has ravaged the hinterland. Urbanization has drained these areas of the young and skilled.

Pushing sustainable development at the local level could reverse these trends. It could build a local authority that restores power to the village, brings back economic opportunities, and encourages people to stay (or even move back). It would invest power and meaning in small communities that have lost much in recent decades.

From my own experience, I know that villages will happily pursue sustainable development when given the opportunity and resources to do so. My work has brought me to numerous rural communities across Asia. In every one of these locales, work was being done to develop structures that would give villages access to the best agricultural techniques, expertise, inputs, and equipment that would allow them to farm cleanly, efficiently, and productively. The solutions often involved enterprises, including cooperatives, that could bring sure control and self-determination to the producers. These enterprises were designed to bring farmers and communities together to decide the future of the company and to strengthen their bargaining position with other entities along the supply chain. We tried to create a model that was easily replicable, so that other villages or regions could implement these ideas for themselves.

But I also know from experience how difficult driving local sustainability efforts can be. Many of these villages had lost real authority years ago. Community leaders found it difficult to overcome years of mistrust and neglect and to get their communities working together again. Some groups had been co-opted by large business, and corruption was a pervasive concern. Supply chains had been designed to disadvantage producers and rural people working the land, to allow urban consumers—the "engine" of economic growth—to consume more underpriced commodities. But more fundamentally, any initiative would have required time and effort on the part of villages and community leaders: resources they might not have been able to spare over an extended period. Some communities had even lost knowledge of farming techniques that had been developed over generations.

Much of the work with which I have been involved regarding rural development and sustainability was trying to build structures that could overcome these barriers. But this capacity building was limited by both our and their resources. This leads to a new question: How best to build governing capacity on the local level? Villages and NGOs can try to do it themselves, but their lack of resources will limit the speed and scale of their actions. Over time I concluded that the institution with the resources and authority to build local authority on a national level is the strong state.

• • •

In a perfect world, governance for sustainability would be carried out by a combination of strong states, empowered local communities, and trusted global institutions and agreements. Such a world could tackle both the local effects of environmental degradation and resolve the large-scale global externalities in our globalized economy.

We are not yet in that world. Too much work needs to be done to build governing capacity at both the global and local levels for either of those to take the lead on sustainability.

Focusing first on state strength can lead to village- and community-driven sustainability later. A strong state can build local and community governance, delegating and embedding its "strength" in strong local institutions with the power, authority, and capacity to sustainably manage their surroundings. The same can be said about global governance. If one starts with strong states, then international agreements and institutions will be backed by governments that can actually do what they promise to do.

Of course, few states in the developing world are perfect. All the criticisms observers have made about these governments, though perhaps exaggerated, do reflect real concerns. They have problems with corruption. They can be easily captured by vested interests. Many have problems with accountability, with politics being dominated by a few elite families. Their reach is limited, and they have few resources with which to implement their decisions. Finally, there is the issue of competence: Can states actually carry out their objectives?

But those interested in creating a future based on the principles of sustainability should not use imperfection as a reason to ignore the state as an ally. The globe, the city, or the village, despite what people around the world may argue, cannot be a replacement for an imperfect state. Instead of looking elsewhere, people should instead strive to build strong states.

Chapter 5 will put forward a vision of what such a strong state would be.

THE STATE'S OBLIGATIONS

Imagine a large, economically powerful country. It's large in land area and population, with a booming manufacturing sector exporting to the world. Yet despite its huge strides, poverty is still a real issue. Smallholder farmers are seeing their livelihoods fail, their farms affected by desertification, soil degradation, and unstable global prices. Factory workers are working in unsafe conditions for little pay. Cities are expanding, but are also seeing expanding slums, with more urban migrants living in insecure and unsafe housing.

Despite these challenges, the government has adopted a bold vision of how to manage the economy. It institutes price controls, both to sustain important industries and to ensure that necessary goods are not too expensive for ordinary consumers. Generous support is offered to farmers, the young, the unemployed, and the elderly. The government puts constraints on the banking system to prevent it from destabilizing the economy. It intervenes in the labor markets, putting government weight behind workers' attempts to ask for better wages and working conditions. It tries to bring together important industries to prevent cutthroat competition leading to overproduction and waste. It drives mass support for private home ownership, bringing needed wealth to people who had never owned a home. It increases taxes on the wealthy to redistribute the nation's income toward its poor.

More important, the government embarks on an ambitious program of rural investment. Labor in rural communities is put to work expanding government infrastructure, building roads, trains, dams, airports, hospitals, and schools across the country.

As similar as this sounds, this is not China in the twenty-first century. It is the US in the 1930s during President Franklin D. Roosevelt's New Deal recovery from the Great Depression. The program featured many elements that would be unthinkable in today's America:

- Controls on the financial sector to prevent instability, such as deposit insurance implemented to protect ordinary people from bank failures. Regulation also separated retail banking from investment banking, preventing banks from gambling with their clients' deposits.
- The National Labor Relations Board, which helped mediate labor disputes, and the Fair Labor Standards Act, which instituted minimum wages and maximum hours.
- The Social Security Act, which provided retirement income for elderly Americans.
- The National Recovery Administration, which managed private industries to increase industrial output.
- The Agricultural Adjustment Act, which provided farmers with economic relief and financial support to ensure that small farmers could remain a going concern.
- The Works Progress Administration, which employed millions of people around the US to work on important projects. Workers built city halls, bridges, tunnels, dams, schools, hospitals, and other public buildings. There was even money allotted for artists, writers, historians, and playwrights.

With his New Deal, President Roosevelt has been credited with not just saving the US from economic catastrophe but also building a durable political coalition that sustained these programs for decades afterward. This was a broad-based platform of activist government, engaging in protecting the economic rights of both urban and rural areas. And the population largely supported his actions, with Roosevelt winning landslide electoral victories and record-high approval ratings (though some of this was inflated by the outbreak of World War II).

Despite the success of the New Deal, its lessons were lost in the 1970s. Faced with economic stagnation and the energy crisis, conservative politicians promised that economic growth and regeneration could only occur when the free market was unleashed and government was shrunk, beginning the period of so-called Reaganomics. Slowly the government institutions that had helped support, manage, and regulate the economy were rolled back, weakened, or removed entirely.[1]

Much of this move was driven by ideology. Conservative movements in the West, such as Margaret Thatcher's Conservative Party and Ronald Reagan's Republican Party, embraced the free-market ideas of "neoliberalism," which simplified all of society down to market principles. Questions of value—rights, morality, obligations, and so on—"must be submitted to a purely economic analysis," as Stephen Metcalf explains. He continues that "economics ceases to be a technique . . . for achieving desirable social ends, such as growth or stable money. The only social end is the maintenance of the market itself."[2]

As neoliberalism took over, first in academia and then in politics, the West began to push other societies to more closely follow in its footsteps: cutting social spending, cutting regulations, and placing wealth creation at the top of the agenda. International institutions such as the International Monetary Fund (IMF) and the World Bank pushed these policies on numerous developing countries, often when those countries were in dire straits; the IMF consistently attached these neoliberal policies to its debt relief packages for countries in crisis.

But the success of a more state-driven economic agenda in the middle of the twentieth century reminds us that there is nothing inherently Asian, African, or anti-Western about the strong state. State strength in the US, in China, and elsewhere around the world has led to broad-based economic development. In some cases, such as Vietnam, Rwanda, and Cambodia, a strong state has been able to improve economic outcomes in the aftermath of devastating conflict.

Rwanda in particular is a compelling example. Commentators have marveled at how well the country has recovered from the genocide of one million people. President Kagame has accepted donor and international aid, but rather than following external strictures, he has pursued his own agenda on how best to "have a country that really works, everybody speaks English, the Internet is super fast, the airport is free of corruption, [and] lure to Rwanda all the companies and economic interests that are working in this entire region."[3] The country now has the longest life expectancy in the region, improving from 48.3 years in 2000 to

66.1 in 2015, and its economic growth, at 8 percent, is among the best in Africa. The *Financial Times*—not normally a publication that celebrates more activist governments—described the country as "Africa's most orderly and disciplined society" where "flowerbeds are immaculate, villagers wear shoes (by decree) and local officials strain to make targets, whether raising cassava yields or reducing maternal deaths."[4]

It is time to use the lessons of the New Deal and other instances of state-driven economic development after World War II in the developing world to tackle the next challenge: building an economy that will survive a hot, crowded, and constrained twenty-first century. One where the state is judged by the establishment of peace, rising education standards, law and order for the needs of the time, security, and health.

Chapters 1 through 4 discussed why arguments for non-state-led governance to address sustainable development need to be challenged, as only the state has the ability to intervene and coordinate throughout an entire economy.

This chapter will present the book's alternate model for meeting our sustainability challenges: the sustainable state. This is a government which ensures that all people receive the basic "rights of life" through equal and fair access to resources. It needs to be competent, committed to the task of nation building through self-sufficiency (not dependent on aid), and strong but trusted by the people by virtue of results—not by ways that appease posturing political leaders from the West or the international media. The government has obligations toward its whole population; its legitimacy and accountability derive from its ability to universally provide these basic rights without overextending its use of resources in an unsustainable manner. In a resource-constrained era, this means directly working to provide these rights among the poor and middle classes, while constraining the consumption of the upper classes to ensure that resources are not overexploited, or mismanaged by elites.

The sustainable state must have the ability and the will to consistently intervene in and ultimately manage the economy. This means that the state must be strong—that is, it must be able to both define and carry out social, political, and economic objectives. A weak state—one that is unable or unwilling to act or that delegates its responsibility to third parties—will be of little use in implementing sustainable development. Figures 5.1 and 5.2 compare the traditional understanding of the state with this book's understanding.

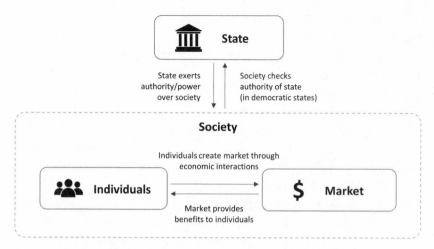

Figure 5.1 The traditional understanding of the state.

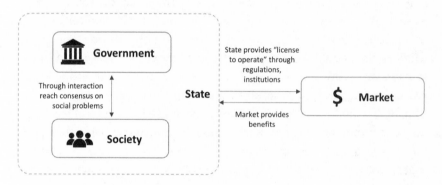

Figure 5.2 This book's understanding of the state.

What are the basic rights of life? They are the necessary elements of a basic standard of living; by virtue of being human, each person deserves to have these rights fulfilled.

People deserve the very basic necessities to survive: an adequate amount of nutritious food for oneself and one's family; clean water; and a shelter that is sturdy, secure, and safe from the elements. They deserve safety from violence, whether from natural disasters or from human conflict.

People deserve the ability to live long and healthy lives, which in practice means living with adequate sanitation, access to disease prevention materials, and high-quality and affordable treatment. They also deserve access to a good level of education for their children, not to build software or to become wealthy entrepreneurs but instead to provide valuable assets and skills to local economies.

Finally, there is the ability to work. Everyone deserves the opportunity to work so that one can provide for oneself and one's family, thereby making a societal contribution and escaping the indignity of being a burden. This does not have to be a formal career: working the land on a smallholder farm can be more compelling, even though it may "pay" far less, than working in harsh conditions in a factory. But whatever calling one follows, it needs to be able to provide enough for a person to live on and support dependents.

These rights define "sustainable development" for the world's majority. This is why artificial intelligence, robotics, and automation are so threatening to sustainable development in the developing world and must be challenged. These technologies deny ordinary people access to careers and occupations that can provide for a proper household. Workers lucky enough to keep their jobs will be forced to work harder and for less pay to compete with automated factories. Further, small businesses and farms will no longer be able to compete with mechanized and automated factories and farms, pushing more and more market power (and thus political power) to big, and often foreign, companies. All these repercussions have been seen in Western countries, such as the US, which at least had the benefit of a few decades of nonroboticized manufacturing that grew the middle class; developing countries have not had the same luxury. So, apart from taxing robots (as suggested by Bill Gates), governments should not rule out banning robots in certain parts of the economy.

The basic rights, the concept of "rights" in general, and how they connect to "prosperity" will be explored in greater detail in chapter 8. But I want to highlight that creating the conditions through which these basic rights are met for the majority requires fair and equal access to resources. When this access is restricted, we see income and wealth disparity, entrenched poverty, and social unrest.

• • •

The book's introduction brought up "the India question," or the idea that it is impossible to achieve both sustainability and development at the same time through the free market. The way out of this dilemma can only come from governing the economy through active state management to deliver on its obligations to what will soon be the largest population on the planet. Such a state will need to treat resource management as the center of economic planning, rather than treating it as an afterthought to growth, consumption, and production.

This is what differentiates the sustainable state from the developmental state discussed in chapter 1: whereas the developmental state uses state resource management to drive high economic growth, the sustainable state will use it to create a more sustainable, universal economy—which may come at the expense of meeting perpetual high growth rates, but guarantees stability and human rights as defined via the lens of sustainable development, and vastly reduces our currently disastrous impacts on the environment.

The current sustainability crisis means that the state needs to take a more active role in managing resources. As common resource stocks become more strained, the government must step in to assure that populations have equal access to these stocks.

The sustainable state has three main objectives:

1. It must protect public and common goods to ensure that all people have equal and fair access to them. This would help ensure that all people have access to and receive what I have called the basic rights of life.
2. It must define a path toward a moderate prosperity (as opposed to the no-holds-barred understanding of prosperity we have today) that is better suited to the resource constraints of the twenty-first century and the national need for built-in self-sufficiency.
3. It must structure the economy to internalize market externalities, allowing for a more honest understanding of productivity, economic benefit, and economic cost. It must also invest in "infrastructure": the supporting capital and services that act as the foundation on which resources are equitably shared and smaller, cleaner, and more sustainable businesses and economies can be built.

Some of the implications of these terms will be described in chapter 8, but in short: *moderate prosperity* refers to a standard of living that goes beyond just fulfilling basic needs, enabling people to live lives of relative comfort and ease. It is not built on the dream that everyone can get rich. It is an understanding of prosperity that looks at how the collective is living rather at individual levels of wealth and comfort. That is what a

Table 5.1   Examples of state obligations and some associated trade-offs arising from tough policy action.

State Obligations (Examples)	Tough Policy Action and Resulting Trade-Offs (Examples)
Affordable housing for all	**Implement controls on the housing market** Would give up using state land for private profit maximization (with resulting tax revenues) Thereby ensuring affordable housing for whole population
Rural economic development to reduce urban drift	**Direct investment to infrastructure in rural areas** Would create a shortage of cheap labor from rural areas to benefit urban areas Thereby building more vibrant and stable rural economies
Resource management	**Take a long-term view of resource management** Would give up short-term economic growth that could be gained from resource overexploitation Thereby avoiding the spread of irreversible damage and starting to resolve reversible changes, thus supporting intergenerational equity
Protection of forests, wilderness, and nature parks	**Create "no-go" areas that cannot be used for economic development** Would give up short-term economic growth benefits from such developments Thereby rejecting vested interests in the timber industry, industrial agriculture, and tourism
Prevention of obesity among young people	**Ban fast food in schools and institute compulsory physical education** Would restrict economic activity by private enterprise in schools Thereby contributing to better student health

true democracy would aim to do: work to support the whole population in its collective growth, rather than merely opening the path for some to succeed at the expense of everyone else. One of the jobs of the sustainable state will be to define what standard of living is sustainable. But one thing should be clear: "relative comfort" is not the same thing as the "middle-class lifestyle" as understood by the West.

What follows is a brief discussion of how the sustainable state might achieve these three objectives, using the tools of state management of the economy. Table 5.1 presents some key obligations a sustainable state might try to achieve as well as the trade-offs that would arise from such tough policy actions.

Objective 1: Protecting Common and Public Goods

The first objective of the sustainable state is to protect public and common goods to ensure that all members of its population receive the basic rights of life. This depends on an equal and fair access to resources. A country's population has equal claim on these public resources; it is the sustainable state's responsibility to sustainably manage these commons so that each person gets his or her fair share either directly or indirectly.

The state can actively manage these resource stocks by starting with a vision of the economy built on resource management, not on the archaic belief that full resource exploitation delivers growth. It should invest in strong institutions, trusted and reliable monitoring, and independent enforcement agencies. These bodies can monitor how resources are used, granting licenses to private operators to exploit natural resources, using the revenue for the public good. The state can invest in monitoring technology, changing policies if resource overexploitation begins to occur.

More important, these agencies need to have the power to punish companies that "cheat," and the politicians and community leaders who enable it. Whether they are dealing with poaching, illegal deforestation, wildcat mining, or fishing over quotas, government agencies need to step in quickly to sanction these companies, seize illegally exploited resources, and recover costs to the wider environment.

The need for strong regulators may sound obvious, but even countries with supposedly strong institutions struggle with this. Republican administrations in the US have neglected important agencies when they are in power, starving them of funds, resources, and talent. Government agencies that are vital to the lives of many Americans, from the Environmental Protection Agency to the Department of Housing and Urban Development, are left to wither by Republican governments.[5] It has also been suggested that attempts to cut the budgets and staff of individual members of Congress meant that they no longer had the independent resources to create policy—opening up a space for lobbyists and vested interests.[6]

Even Hong Kong—the city where I am based and a government prized for its civil service—has seen its institutions captured by vested interests. The government's close links with property developers has stopped it from intervening forcefully in the property market, even as Hong Kong's housing prices reach astonishing heights.[7]

Enforcement power is necessary and critical to the success of the sustainable state. An easily evaded management system will fall apart. No one will have an incentive to follow the rules, and the tragedy of the commons will occur.

One problem is that government punishment tends to be reactive to an offense or crime already committed, rather than aimed at preventing illegal resource exploitation before it occurs. This leaves governments with a quandary. These poachers have a stock of (potentially valuable) resources and thus the financial clout to work the system; this breeds corruption, as the government is encouraged, forced, or even "bought out" to look the other way. Punishments, when they occur, are light, often smaller than the windfall profits the poacher or offender will make.

However, we can think of a harsher system that would place much stronger punishments on those who cheat. Any illegally exploited resources would be seized by the state, or all revenues would become government property—no questions asked. More important, any illegally exploited resources would count toward the overall total resource exploitation. Companies would not be allowed to exploit as many resources next time. Some may criticize this as unfair, as it punishes companies who followed the rules, but it would add some punch behind obviously self-serving industry attempts to self-regulate and self-monitor, which currently do not work.

State management of these common resources can take a variety of forms and be exercised to various degrees. For countries with mature industries and resources where a lighter touch may be all that's needed, the government can simply add its support to industry attempts to self-regulate. For example, industry-led monitoring organizations often suffer from a lack of resources (as big businesses are often and almost deliberately uninterested in funding their watchdogs). The government can provide resources (via some form of taxation or mandated funding) and can ensure that the make-up of these organizations is truly independent. It can also ensure that agreements within an industry have the force of government regulation, adding state enforcement behind industry regulation.

Finally, the state can provide a space where industries can arbitrate and decide disputes over common resources. A "natural resources court" that judges how to equally distribute common and constrained resources and that arbitrates disputes between companies and communities will be one way to add state capacity to industry self-regulation.

However, there will be some resources for which there is no free-market way to provide fair access, so state institutions, or heavily regulated companies, must determine how to apportion access. The success of these measures depends usually on the maturity, competence, and stability of the institutions. In some cases, nationalization may be the only option, ensuring that only the state has the authority to (sustainably) manage these resources. Nationalization also ensures that the revenues from resources are in state hands, which means they can be reinvested for future generations. There is already a model for this: oil-exporting states have long used state oil companies as a way to invest in public services. The usual argument against this approach is that nationalization leads to the "resource curse," where countries abundant in natural resources have seen lower economic development than resource-poor countries. But this happens only because the state is weak: a weak state sees resources as a source of easy revenue rather than as "seed capital" (to borrow a business term) for future growth. When the state is strong, it can transform resource revenues into a foundation for future development. Of course, some states have done this better than others. Some state oil companies are public in name only: Petrobras, the Brazilian state-owned oil company, acts more like a private company (and often bribes the government). Other oil-producing states, such as the US state of Alaska, directly share oil revenues to their populations in the form of dividends, which can have little long-term benefit. Finally, other states, such as Bahrain, Abu Dhabi, and the Nordic democracies, have invested oil revenues into long-term public and social services, improving quality of life even as oil reserves begin to deplete.

There are clearly several mechanisms through which to manage common resources. But letting them be exploited by an unregulated free market prevents these finite resources from contributing to long-term economic development and the equal well-being of people.

Objective 2: Defining a Path toward Moderate Prosperity

In developing countries, the state is obliged to help bring the majority at the bottom up to a basic standard of living, while also constraining inappropriate and rent-seeking resource appropriation and consumption at the top to prevent resource overuse and overexploitation. When a large segment of the population sits at the bottom of the income distribution, the country is more difficult to manage. It is in the state's interest (and arguably in the interest of the ruling elite as well) to lift the living standards of this part of the population, as a moral, political, and economic imperative. Take away the drudgery, and populations will thrive in almost all spheres of human endeavor.

The simplest way to do this is to directly provide cash or resources to poor families. One of the most successful antipoverty initiatives is *Bolsa Familia,* the initiative by President Luiz Inácio Lula da Silva to reduce poverty in Brazil. Bolsa Familia combines short-term poverty alleviation with long-term investment in public health and education. The Brazilian government offers direct cash transfers to poor Brazilian families in exchange for keeping their children in schools and ensuring they were up-to-date on vaccinations. At its height, Bolsa Familia covered over twelve million Brazilian families, making it one of the largest such programs in the world.

Governments can also take greater control of certain sectors of the economy to ensure that economic opportunities exist throughout the country, rather than just in a few central locations.

For example, China relied on "town-and-village enterprises" (TVEs) in the early stages of its economic reforms. These were community-owned enterprises that provided much of the initial growth that eventually fueled China's economic boom a decade later. Unlike purely private corporations, which were still largely distrusted in Communist China, the TVEs combined public and collective ownership to ease their operation. Nominal public control meant that these enterprises could be brought together to fuel economic development.

A smaller-scale example is Malaysia's Federal Land Development Authority, or FELDA. This was a program launched in 1965 to resettle poor Malaysian farmers (mainly indigenous Malays who had been left behind by British colonial rule) into newly developed areas, and organize them into smallholder cash-crop farms. Priority was given to those rural residents who did not own farmland themselves. Originally designed around cooperatives, FELDA soon instituted a policy whereby plots of land would eventually be granted to the resettled residents farming them.

FELDA has since been hailed as one of the most successful land redevelopment and resettlement policies in the developing world. Settlers gained access to both land—a source of wealth—and a steady source of income, guided by state support and advice. In return, the state grew a stronger agricultural sector, which provided useful initial capital to Malaysia's early development.

It should be noted that FELDA focused on cash crops such as palm oil over more socially beneficial products like fruits, vegetables, or staples. FELDA has also since created large private sector entities, such as FELDA Global Venture Holdings, that engage in large-scale industrial plantation farming of palm oil, straying from rural (re)development. However, FELDA, at least initially, showed how wise government management, intervention, and resource allocation can lead to an objectively better outcome both for the economy as a whole and for individuals.

Objective 3: Allow Societies to Prosper within Hard Resource Constraints

In addition to helping the bottom, governments must also focus on constraining the top. Much of elite consumption places excessive costs on the rest of the society, which are not covered in the market price. The government needs to work to "internalize" these costs and ensure that they are included when a person decides to consume something.

Take golf courses, for example. The huge amount of space required for a full-size golf course could be put to several other purposes with much greater social value, from housing to farming. Yet these tracts of land are put aside for an elite sporting activity enjoyed by a select few. And that just concerns the land: maintaining the course also consumes a great deal of resources. One golf course in dry California, for example, uses as much water in one day as a family of four does in five years (and specifically a *US* family, who likely consumes more water than the average household in the developing world).[8]

Tackling consumption inequality is different from tackling income or wealth inequality. Although these are likely to be correlated, one can easily think of a middle-class household consuming far beyond its (or society's) means, even if the family's income is not particularly high in the grand scheme of things. Perhaps they splurge on a second car, or engage in energy-inefficient lifestyles. The same can be said of corporations and private businesses. Like individual consumption, corporate consumption is probably correlated with corporate size—but not necessarily in all cases. Some sectors have external costs much greater than their overall size. Chapter 1 pointed to ranching—a sector dominated by smaller suppliers rather than massive corporations, yet the cause of huge external effects from deforestation, agricultural pollution, and underpriced meat.

Income and wealth inequality and its corporate counterpart, monop-
olization, are important issues that need to be tackled by governments.
And they are very likely related to consumption inequality. But they are
not the same thing, so the policy responses need to be different.

One straightforward way to internalize the external costs of overconsumption is taxation. This would increase the market price of a good or
service so that it better reflects what it would cost if external costs were
included. Many industries have an environmental impact far in excess of
their revenue; in other words, their external costs are far greater than the
private benefit of companies. Taxation would help close that gap.

Imagine that a government knew exactly how much a good "should"
cost (by accounting for externalities), then used taxes to ensure that the
good sold at that price. Revenue would be directed toward policies meant
to reduce the externality and ameliorate any harms. It would provide a
direct incentive for companies to find a more sustainable way of producing things: if the "true cost" of a company's product has truly been made
smaller, then that company can undercut the price of its less sustainable
competitors. Some goods may never be able to be priced both sustainably and competitively. They may drop out of the market—which will be
precisely what is needed in a resource-constrained economy.

The benefit of taxation is that it provides revenue for state governments, which can fund efforts to help the bottom. But there are other
mechanisms to restrict overconsumption. Quotas and licenses are one way
to limit consumption of certain goods and services: both Singapore and
Hong Kong, for example, institute high vehicle license fees to discourage
vehicle ownership. Licenses can strictly delineate the total sustainable
amount of a product that can be allowed in an economy. Cap-and-trade
systems largely work on this principle: a government decides how much
carbon is allowed to be released each year, then sells portions of that to
businesses, who can then sell these portions among themselves. Cap-and-
trade systems have stumbled as an attempt to control carbon emissions,
but if anything, their failure has been due to the "and-trade" part of the
equation: attempts to build a functioning market in carbon permits have,
for various reasons, been difficult to sustain. But a more forceful cap system, less attached to a marketplace, may do well: the government would
decide the capped level of emissions and decide the best avenue to distribute the "stock" of emissions among different sectors of the economy.

Of course, there may be some goods and services that exert enough
harm on the majority that there is no way to recoup their cost. In this case,

the government can use the "nuclear option": outright bans on some kinds of consumption.

In most countries, the archetypical example is weaponry—guns, specifically. It is difficult to think of *any* positive social upside of mass gun ownership, whereas the social harms are easy to quantify. This is why most countries—with the significant exception of the US—have expansive, if not total, bans on privately owned arms.

In between help for the bottom and constraint at the top lies the middle: moderate prosperity. This is a standard of living that goes beyond the basic, and thus the government is not obliged to directly provide it. At the same time, this level of prosperity does not go as far as the exuberant overconsumptive standards of living seen at the top, and so does not warrant government action to control it. It lies in between: an achievable and, more important, sustainable aspiration for populations in the developing world.

The economic activities that encourage moderate prosperity may require state assistance and investment to get started. The state needs to invest in alternative revenue models and economic activities that can succeed within hard resource constraints.

Certain small-scale sustainable activities may be economically feasible only when built on already existing infrastructure. By "infrastructure" here I mean the array of businesses and services that support agricultural, manufacturing, and service businesses (especially small-scale businesses operated on a sustainable basis). This infrastructure reduces the costs of doing business, making small and medium-size enterprises viable; large corporations avoid these barriers through economies of scale and direct funding.

These businesses include, but are not limited to, cold chains, payment processors, banks, vocational schools, and arbitrators. Each of these reduces the costs of doing business. For example, a network of cold chains across the country, especially in rural areas, will reduce wastage in fresh produce and helps the rural economy by increasing productivity. Payment processors allow money to be transferred in a trusted way across large distances, reducing transaction costs. Arbitrators can help resolve disputes between enterprises, increasing trust between different businesses. All of these "smooth" the creation of new small businesses. One key effect of this is the slowing of the unhealthy (yet deemed almost inevitable) trend of urbanization in the developing world, leading to megacities that are increasingly becoming unlivable.

In the developing world, however, we have a "chicken-and-egg" problem. An economy built on small and medium-size enterprises will not arise naturally without these foundational services. But these services may need a critical mass of private economic activity to survive. After all, a payment processor cannot make money if there are no payments to process.

If the private sector cannot create this infrastructure and the foundational services, the strong state must create them. Banking, for example, has long been understood as one of these foundational economic activities that can unlock greater development in other sectors of the economy; this is what spurred the focus on microfinance and the current development focus on "financial inclusion." Yet, despite the centrality of banking to our current conception of no-holds-barred free-market financial capitalism, governments have long used state banks to create a managed financial system that apportions capital for a country's future development. Germany created a system of government banks throughout the country as it industrialized, allowing for broad-based economic growth; China's state-owned banks lent money to state enterprises at preferential rates, jump-starting industrial growth.

States need to invest in these industries and this infrastructure because it must provide alternatives to those currently working in unsustainable industries. These people are often themselves poor, not benefiting from the goods they (unsustainably) produce. Thus, if governments are to ensure that basic needs are met for the whole of their population, they must ensure that these workers are given sustainable opportunities to earn an income and engage in fulfilling work.

• • •

Despite its removal from most mainstream discussions of economic development, strong state governance in central roles has been a feature of the history of some of the world's most developed economies.

As mentioned earlier in the chapter, the New Deal in the US was a form of extended government activism in the economy. However, despite the proof that strong state governance had helped the American economy, the United States turned toward the underregulated, trickle-down economics it follows today.

Later, as the US was turning away from activist state government, many of its experts went to the postwar economies of Japan and Germany. Berlin, Tokyo, and Seoul (as South Korea also tried to recover from both

World War II and the Korean War) worked with major corporations to give them (managed) market power in exchange for their assistance in meeting each country's economic objectives.

A smaller, but no less important, example is Singapore in the 1970s and 1980s. Since its independence in 1965, Singapore has grown from a small Third World country to a First World city-state with a quality of life equal to, if not exceeding, living standards in the West. Despite the city's reputation as a free-market utopia, Singapore invests heavily in public services. The Singaporean government uses its power to manage socially and critically important sectors of the economy: the city has created a publicly managed system of cheap and widespread housing finance to encourage home ownership, and directly negotiates with drug providers and medical practitioners to control medical costs (leading to cheap health care).

Finally (and first mentioned in chapter 1), we have the developmental states. These countries used protectionism, state support, state investment, and, in the case of China, direct state ownership of companies to build globally competitive manufacturing sectors. Whereas other developing countries focused on import substitution—building local industries that would replace imports—these countries focused on the export market, developing industries that would sell to the developed world. They attracted foreign investment due to their lower input costs, yet rather than relying on it perpetually, instead used it as a first step to gain necessary expertise and experience with foreign business practices and techniques.

These countries were largely successful in building strong, developed economies, but they unfortunately focused on high-growth, high-consumption models of development that are unsustainable in the long term. They also wedded development to a narrative of overconsumption (i.e., the American Dream, and potentially the China Dream), which makes it difficult to shift toward a more moderate lifestyle. Although these countries do recognize the costs of consumption, they are still largely focused on alleviating pollution and environmental damage, and not on the resource management and controls needed in a true sustainability agenda.

The lesson we should draw from past examples of state strength is that consistent state intervention and management in the economy can achieve social and economic objectives. These countries actually achieved the goals they set out to achieve (even if these goals were ultimately unsustainable). By contrast, countries that hoped the free market would achieve these goals have largely seen disappointing results.

Rather than use the tools of state management to foster a high-growth, high-consumption economy, the sustainable state in the developing world will turn those tools toward the management and sustaining of resource stocks for more equitable development, wealth creation, and the welfare of future generations.

6

AUTHORITY, NOT AUTHORITARIANISM

I n 1984, the band I played for in Swaziland was invited to play in Soweto, Johannesburg. On my very first day, I saw a South African black man shot in the leg for stealing a pair of socks. The white shopkeeper that shot him stood as if he'd done nothing wrong—in fact, under apartheid, he hadn't broken any laws. As a nonwhite *kaffir* (or foreigner), protesting would have led to my arrest as well.

During that same trip, I attended an anti-apartheid demonstration at the University of the Witwatersrand, which was dispersed with tear gas and dogs set on the mainly black students. We all ran for our lives.

A few months later, I found myself in Maputo, Mozambique, for another concert. The newly liberated country had a charismatic leader in the form of Samora Machel, a former revolutionary. The state had the support of the majority to make changes, be tough, bring back law and order, stop the rich from distorting the economy, and continue the fight against elements of the previous colonial government.

This got me thinking about "situational authority", and how countries—especially those ravaged by colonial rule and civil war—needed to secure themselves quickly with a strong and capable state.

So how should we think about state strength and authority? Should we consider apartheid-era South Africa to be a "strong state" because it was willing to use force against its own people? But the apartheid regime eventually fell. Should we think of Mozambique as weak or strong, even though the government was weak initially (due to the war) yet had the trust and support of most of its people?

There is a tendency when we talk about state strength to equate a strong state with an oppressive one. The concern is that a larger government presence in the economy will eventually correspond to a larger government presence in political and civil society, making state intervention in the economy the first step down the road to repression, corruption, and a totalitarian dictatorship. This has made it difficult in mainstream Western liberal circles and platforms to propose and support a more activist government that can, and does, intervene in the economy to directly solve social problems.

This concern is present throughout the West, but is perhaps strongest in the US, whose history and culture have fostered a deep skepticism, if not outright hostility, toward a powerful domestic government (though its people often support a powerful and overbearing America abroad, with often disastrous consequences).

It is not clear how deep the American wish for a weaker government is. In the aftermath of the World Trade Center attacks in 2001, many US politicians supported an expansion of America's domestic intelligence services in order to tackle domestic terrorism. One can disagree with the problem the government highlighted, or the extent of the policies that were created. Many Americans, especially those on the left, disagreed with both. But America's expansion of its state, and the acceptance of this by both political parties, shows that when faced with a social problem, real or perceived, individuals and communities look not to themselves or NGOs but to the state for solutions.

Concerns about state strength have been exported and even imposed on others. These concerns led commentators to see democracies, even poorly functioning democracies that are barely holding together, as better than an alternative, less democratic system that is providing better outcomes. Worse, the less democratic nature of some successful states is used as an excuse to dismiss important lessons that can be learned from their experience.

This chapter will explain why we must consider the question of "state strength" separately from the question of whether a state is or is not democratic. When I talk about the strong state, I am not talking about a totalitarian dictatorship. Nor is it a state rife with corruption, where the government twists the arms of economic actors to ensure that profits flow upward to the elites at the top.

Instead, I understand a strong state as one that is willing to set bold objectives to solve the most pressing needs of the populace, and then actually takes steps to fulfill them. Such a state is accountable to the majority in that it must do what it promises. This trust allows it to work toward the collective interests of the majority, even if it must work against some individual interests in order to do so. That state's responsibility is granted by mandate—though whether that is granted by elections, good performance, or some other mechanism can depend on the situation and the country's political history.

This is not a criticism of democracy, nor an apologia for authoritarianism. Both democracies and nondemocracies have shown the ability to set bold objectives and achieve them, without resorting to the repression, coercion, or corruption seen in weaker states. State weakness also crosses the democratic/nondemocratic divide: some formerly strong democracies have seen their strength erode over time, meaning that their current democratic structures now reinforce, rather than counteract, their weakness.

But if sustainable development is to be a reality, the state must have authority. Resource constraints require the state to make tough decisions about how to allocate resources, and not wholly delegate it to the free market. This will be true regardless of the actual political structure of the country.

$$\bullet \bullet \bullet$$

There are two answers to the concern that state strength will lead to political oppression. The first that there is nothing about state strength that violates democratic principles, especially if that strength is aimed at protecting public good and putting collective welfare ahead of individual rights. In fact, if democracies are to be effective, they *must* be strong. Otherwise, they would be unable to implement any of the promises made to their citizens and voters. This neglect of state strength in both Western and developing world democracies has led to stagnation, political gridlock, new threats, and—perhaps most dangerously for a democracy—disillusionment.

The second point is that state strength does not inevitably lead to oppression or repression even in states that are not democracies (though that is always a risk). By definition, a truly strong state—whether democratic or nondemocratic—does not need to resort to the tactics that weak states use to stay in power, whether that is widescale repression or bribery. The strongest states have an authority that is listened to and respected, even as the source of their legitimacy can differ between different states. It can be

Table 6.1   This two-by-two matrix shows how states can vary in terms of both state strength and whether they are a democracy. Strong states are those that can achieve a consensus on social issues. Weak states, by contrast, are unable to make forward progress on social issues.

	Weak State	Strong State
Nondemocracy	"Failed states," totalitarian dictatorships	China, Vietnam, UAE
Democracy	Modern-day US, India, South Africa	Germany, Japan, South Korea

argued—and perhaps best understood by citizens of states that have clawed their way out of war or colonial repression, such as Korea, Malaysia, and Cambodia in Asia, or Rwanda and Uganda in Africa—that there needs to be a period of tough discipline to get over the hump (See Table 6.1).

Perhaps the source of the problem lies in how we traditionally understand the state. Or, more accurately, how a Western understanding of it was exported around the world. The state is often seen purely as the government that sits over a population, with the power to encourage (or force) its population to take certain actions. The state is thus defined in opposition to ordinary people and the general population; even if the state is benign, it is still a separate body. In democracies, this has led to a belief that the people provide a check and balance on the operations of the government, changing leaders if necessary.

However, the developing world requires a different approach, as the risks are much higher. Mature and wealthier developed states can probably withstand a few mistakes or a few bad leaders, as they have the resources to alleviate the damage. Developing states, by contrast, do not have as much margin for error: a mistake in those states will be hugely devastating to their poor majority, and developing governments do not have resources to cover for their mistakes. A mistake, whether through domestic economic mismanagement or imposed through misguided foreign pressure, can set countries back years.

Climate change mitigation is an example of the large differences in risk between the developed and developing worlds. The consequences of climate change fall disproportionately on the developing world. But even if we assume that consequences were borne equally, developed countries have the resources to pay people to move out of threatened areas, provide compensation, and invest in technology and infrastructure to mitigate the damage. Developing countries must be more judicious and efficient in how they help their people.

• • •

Rather than seeing the state as a body that sits on top of a population, I see it as something that grows out of the relationship between the people and the body that governs them. A strong state is one where the people and government work together to successfully achieve a social outcome. The people feel that they are included in governance and that their views are reflected in the social objectives followed by the government. The people buy into the struggle of development as defined by the state and appreciate the trade-off between a free-for-all approach to development and the need to develop within constraints as managed by the state. And in the developing world, the prime political and economic challenge of this century will be attaining a measure of sustainable development.

Violent suppression and oppression is thus not evidence of a state's strength, but rather its weakness. Overt coercion is a weapon of last resort, what a state turns to when other options no longer work, due to poor governance, lack of competence, weak institutions, and an erosion of trust. Truly strong states, democratic or not, do not need to resort to force.

It is important for the government to actually achieve its objectives, thereby demonstrating its sincerity and its competence and building accountability in the eyes of the people. If people trust that the government can actually follow through when it promises to improve living conditions, then they will trust it in other areas. Thus, when the government decides that potential sacrifices down the road are necessary to achieve some objective, people will largely accept them, trusting that the government is making these decisions for some social purpose. Chapter 12 will discuss some possible objectives that a strong state could follow in order to deepen the social contract between the government and the people.

Performance legitimacy requires cooperation between groups, rather than an endless fight over "ideologically perfect" solutions. Political gridlock leads to inertia, a lack of progress, and division. A good comparison is between Singapore and Hong Kong, as shown in Table 6.2: both city-states have service-based economies that face many of the same challenges (e.g., housing affordability and aging populations). Singapore's government, through its aggressive action to resolve these issues, has gained a great deal of trust from the people, which is why they regularly reelect

Table 6.2   A comparison between Singapore and Hong Kong and how they perform on different indicators.

Indicator	Singapore	Hong Kong
Political Process	Multiparty democracy, but the ruling party consistently wins elections due to long and successful track record when in power.	Quasi-democracy, with elected legislature and unelected executive. The government and opposition are severely polarized, which limits the state's ability to act decisively on social issues.
Legitimacy and Accountability	A long track record of success by the People's Action Party has led to trust in government. It is generally trusted to make correct decisions.	The government lacks both popular legitimacy and performance legitimacy. The population sees government as separate from its interests, and the government does not decisively solve social issues.
State of Media	Major newspaper and television station are state financed (though not necessarily state controlled). There are controls on certain kinds of speech.	The media landscape is competitive in both Chinese and English in several mediums (print, radio, television). Hong Kong is a hub for international media.
Public Housing	There is near-universal adoption of public housing due to government construction of housing and forced savings into home ownership funds. Land use is not subject to free-market principles and is not a major contributor to government coffers.	Although public housing initiatives were initially successful to a limited extent due to aggressive construction of housing during the colonial era, land was seen as a market asset to be traded to fill the coffers of the colonial government. Since the handover and democratization of the legislature, there has been paralysis due to strong vested interests, leading to a housing affordability crisis.
Health Care	A dominant public sector role in health care controls costs, keeping services affordable for patients. The government also forces Singaporeans to save money for medical care, and automatically enrolls citizens in coverage for catastrophic care.	The public health care sector in Hong Kong is even more dominant than in Singapore. Heavy subsidies of the public health care system ensure that even the poorest people in Hong Kong have access to affordable health care. There is no system of public health insurance.
Traffic and Vehicle Congestion	Singapore is the first city in the world to implement electronic road toll pricing to alleviate congestion. This program works in conjunction with high vehicle and gasoline duties that limit vehicle ownership.	The government debated implementing road pricing, but never followed through after resistance from lobbying groups. It has also resisted other ways of limiting vehicle ownership (e.g., by increasing gasoline tax).

the People's Action Party to power. By contrast, Hong Kong has routinely missed chances to resolve its problems, so the population has little trust in the political process. This has motivated people to give up on Hong Kong as a project or, worse, call for radical and unrealistic changes (e.g., the independence movement).

Trust between the government and the people is what leads to a strong state. The people trust that the government is working in the public interest, and the government is accountable in that it actually tries to work for the common good. The strong state also hinges on competency and leadership, which, in Singapore, the system nurtures. Hong Kong has a competent civil service, but its political system has thwarted the development of strong leaders. The strong state can intervene, even significantly, in the economy and civil society precisely because people will accept the government's argument that these moves are truly for the common good, as past evidence shows the sincerity of the government's arguments.

This good governance arises when a state has legitimacy and accountability, which I defined earlier: legitimacy means that the state is trusted as a legitimate representative of the public interest; accountability means that the government actually works in the public interest.

Unfortunately, the Western understanding of these terms has become mainstream, often implying that Western democratic understandings of legitimacy and accountability are the best, if not the only, workable definitions of these terms that exist in today's era. These definitions bound our search for solutions to the sustainability crisis by limiting us to technological and market-based solutions. These terms are often applied unthinkingly and simplistically outside of the West without considering the non-Western historical and cultural context, the country's lack of institutional development, and the nature of the challenges faced today.

We can look to Thailand as an example of how Western democratic norms were applied unthinkingly, simplistically, and too quickly. Thailand long prided itself as being the most democratic country in Southeast Asia, using this status as a way to attain Western investment in the 1980s.

Now, with the country trapped in a cycle of military coups, followed by protests and elections that are in turn followed by coups, no one would consider Thailand a well-functioning government, let alone a role model for democracy. Many middle-class Thai people have turned away from elections and democracy, believing that it leads to "instability" or, more accurately, to policies not in their own interests. In his book *Democracy in Retreat: The Revolt of the Middle Class and the Worldwide Decline of*

Representative Government, Joshua Kurlantzick, a senior fellow for the Council of Foreign Relations, notes:

> The never-ending cycle of street protest, by both the middle class and the poor, paralyzes policy making, hinders economic growth, and deters investment at a time when authoritarian competitors like China and Vietnam are vacuuming up foreign capital. Few Thais now trust the integrity of the judiciary, the civil service, or other national institutions. . . . The Thai military now wields enormous influence behind the scenes, a dramatic reversal from the 1990s, when most Thais believed the military had returned to the barracks for good. . . . Once-groundbreaking Bangkok newspapers now read like Asian versions of the old Pravda, lavishing praise on the red shirts or yellow shirts [referring to adherents of two protest movements] depending on the paper's point of view.[1]

The example of Thailand shows that democratic mechanisms in themselves are not enough to ensure legitimacy and accountability. The democratic government in Thailand was not seen as legitimate by the whole Thai population: the urban middle classes were perfectly happy to support a coup against a democratically elected government that did not suit their interests. Meanwhile, however, rural concerns were ignored, weakening the government's accountability among nonurban populations. Thailand's democratic process did not elect "good" leaders. In the case of Thailand, no side comes out looking particularly good.

The problem with Thailand was that elections were seen as all that was needed for a well-functioning democracy. The country did not invest in the institutions that would support democracy and that would have enabled the government to work in the interests of the entire Thai population, rather than the interests of a select few.

However, if institutions are able to ensure that democracies can work toward the public good and remain stable over the long term, one wonders whether they can help nondemocracies fulfill the same goals. Table 6.3 shows what the different elements of statehood could look like in a strong, sustainable state.

We need to understand state strength, and the legitimacy and accountability that underpins it, as separate from whether or not a state is democratic. Several democracies do have good governance, and thus strong states. One could even plausibly argue that democracies are more

Table 6.3 How different elements of statehood might look in different kinds of states: the dictatorship, the Western-style democracy, and a hypothetical sustainable state.

Element of Statehood	Dictatorship	Western-Style Democracy	Sustainable State
Accountability	May respond to economic and social problems among base of support; relies on communication from elites to government.	Post-facto accountability through regular contested elections.	Agreement between government and population on social problem to be tackled within resource constraints; the state judges solutions against agreed-on criteria based on a new definition of prosperity.
Legitimacy	May appeal to national, cultural, or religious identity as a way to justify its position.	Legitimized through regular elections.	Granted through the successful resolution of long-standing issues of social and economic development.
Resource Allocation and Management	Allocates resources according to internal political purposes, routing resources toward elite groups or toward base of support.	Generally relies on free-market dynamics to allocate resources; may have light interventions in the economy to support popular industries or sectors.	Allots resources according to social consensus on socioeconomic goals (i.e., meeting basic needs and "rights to life") for whole population.
Judicial Oversight	Weak, if not nonexistent. Judges act in support of government objectives as opposed to objective judgment of the law.	Independent judiciary adjudicates rule of law (as legislated by democratic processes), but can be hamstrung by vested interests.	Independent judiciary adjudicates according to rule of law, and helps ensure the fair distribution of resources, as state is not usurped by vested interests.
Creating Legislation and Regulation	Government sets certain legislation and regulation according to government/elite priorities.	Government sets legislation according to democratic processes. Can be affected by party politics and vested interests. Extent and speed of legislation and regulation can be limited by short-term focus and government unpopularity.	Government sets legislation and regulations according to socioeconomic priorities agreed to by both the government and the population. Can take longer-term view. Trust in government may allow more expansive and speedy actions.

(continued)

Table 6.3   (continued)

Element of Statehood	Dictatorship	Western-Style Democracy	Sustainable State
Efficient Civil Service	Politicized civil service; tenure is linked to relationships with those in power.	Independent civil service with clear social goals. However, shifts in power between different governments can affect resources available to civil service, and thus its ability to monitor and manage parts of society.	Independent civil service with clear economic and social goals. Ability to take longer-term view and social consensus on social objectives allow stable resources and jurisdiction for government departments.
Provision of Basic Needs and Social Services	Uneven distribution of basic needs and social services according to political importance. May provide some groups with unsustainable support to shore up its political standing.	Democratic processes can (slowly) expand provision of basic needs and social services. However, can be subject to party dynamics (e.g., when there is a switch from prowelfare to antiwelfare parties) and vested interests (e.g., private providers of social services).	Universal provision of basic needs and social services as a central goal of the state. Major element of accountability is the speedy and successful provision of basic needs.

likely to be strong states. But several democracies are not, and their weakness is sometimes reinforced by how their democracy is structured. The same point can be made for nondemocratic states, some of which, despite Western criticism, do exert good governance.

One can argue that democracies are more likely to be good governments, and thus have strong states. But being a good government is not the same thing as being a democratic one. Kishore Mahbubani, former dean of the Lee Kwan Yew School of Public Policy, noted in his book *Can Asians Think?* that

> . . . authoritarian governments can be antithetical to development.
> However, it is equally true that some authoritarian governments
> have been good for development, as shown by the dramatic eco-

nomic growth of South Korea and Taiwan in the early years. The point here is simple: The crucial variable in determining whether a Third World society will progress is not whether its government is democratic but whether, to put it simply, it has "good governance."[2]

We need to think about how nondemocracies can also be strong states, and how a poorly-structured or poorly-implemented democracy can lead to state weakness.

A few examples of nondemocracies and democracies around the world show how state strength and democracy are not the same thing. For example, despite the common portrayal of China as a totalitarian dictatorship with little interest in the people's long-term welfare, the majority in China likely believes that the Communist Party legitimately represents their interests. It's clear that people in China have a reasonable understanding of what is happening in their country, good and bad. Finally, despite not having electoral politics, policy responds to popular concerns, as shown by Beijing's current focus on environmental protection and corruption, which were implemented alongside growing public consciousness of these issues.

In contrast, India has not been able to universally achieve the basic rights of life across its population. Hundreds of millions still live in dire poverty, with poor access to food, clean water, sanitation, secure housing, or electricity. Many in rural communities have no access to proper toilets, which has been blamed for the country's stubbornly high rates of child malnutrition (higher than poorer sub-Saharan Africa), as children's bodies spend more time fighting infection than growing.

India's major political parties have rarely commanded countrywide legitimacy. Regional parties, such as Tamil Nadu's All India Anna Dravida Munnetra Kazhagam, Maharastra's Shiv Sena, or Kerala's Communist Party often command more legitimacy amongst ordinary Indians than the national parties do. The BJP built its national base by appealing to Hindu nationalism, whereas the Indian National Congress, despite running India for much of its post-independence history, has few recent economic achievements to show for it, perhaps contributing to its electoral collapse in 2014.

India did have to build a democracy from scratch in the aftermath of colonialism, so its struggles can be understood. What is more illuminating (or distressing, depending on your point of view) are those formerly well-functioning democracies that have seen their strength erode.

In the middle of the twentieth century, the United States' government intervened forcefully in the economy to protect its citizens and manage the economy to provide widespread prosperity. One should not ignore the serious inequalities within the country at the time (namely surrounding race and gender), but the government positioned itself as an ally of working- and middle-class groups by promoting access to basic needs.

However, the country's more recent pursuit of unfettered rights, deregulation, and "small government" has eroded its state strength. Its agencies are hamstrung by slashed funding, interference, and confused political priorities. Finally, the consensus among politicians on where the country was going has since devolved into political polarization.

This means that Washington is unable to solve any long-term problem. Despite a majority of Americans supporting action against climate change, limited gun control, expanded welfare systems, financial regulation, and reducing money in politics, the American government is unable to move forward on any of these issues.

• • •

We need strong states—democratic and nondemocratic—if we are to confront the challenges of the twenty-first century. We need to mainstream the idea that strong states can be created to protect and serve their citizens, especially in the developing world.

But I do understand the concern that the tools of a large government can be turned against its citizens. And, as recent experience in some democracies shows, there are increasing concerns that democracies can adopt authoritarian tendencies just as easily as nondemocratic states.

The next chapter will dive deeper into the institutions and processes that will underpin a strong state and ensure that such a state works in the interest of the majority rather than becoming twisted to serve the interests of an elite, an eventuality that is possible even in democratic states such as the US.

CHAPTER 7

CHECKS AND BALANCES

I n northern Myanmar, in the state of Kachin, a controversial Chinese-funded dam project has been stalled for nearly seven years. According to the plans, the Myitsone Dam was projected to be one of the largest hydroelectric facilities in the world. Under the original deal signed by Myanmar's military government, around 90 percent of the generated electricity would have crossed the border into Yunnan Province in southern China, while the remaining 10 percent would have gone to Myanmar's people. Even with the project on hold, villagers have already been moved away from land that would have been flooded if the dam were ever completed.

With Myanmar's transition to a democratic government, one could easily explain why the Myitsone Dam got stuck: it's unpopular. Its nature as a Chinese-funded project raises immediate questions as to why China isn't constructing it in its own territory. It also crosses the Irrawaddy River, central to Myanmar's self-image. And those who have been forced to leave their homes are a ready-made constituency radically opposed to its construction.

Except the project was stalled before Myanmar had its general elections in 2015. Thein Sein, then-president of Myanmar and former member of the military junta, announced in 2011 that dam construction would be suspended until at least the end of his term. The move was shocking at the time: although President Sein had technically resigned his military commission, few expected him to act any differently than the army-led government. But Sein's statement highlighted the importance of public

opinion, stating that "being the government elected by the people, it up-
holds the aspiration and wishes of the people. It is also responsible to solve
the problems that worry the public."[1]

• • •

In the immediate decades after the fall of the Berlin Wall and the end of
the Cold War, the first step for states in the new world order was to hold
elections. As the US started to selectively turn away from supporting dictatorships (from Marcos in the Philippines to Noriega in Panama) purely
to push back against Communism, many dictatorships fell to public protest. For these new democracies, having clean elections, free of interference,
corruption, and intimidation, was seen to be the most important part of
being a democratic state. The prescription on offer was to get elections right,
and the rest—prosperity, cosmopolitanism, and stabilizing institutions—
would follow.

Yet even as Western observers were still celebrating the spread of
democratic systems around the world, observers in Asia (both local and
Western) were raising concerns about the inherent weakness in many
Southeast Asia states.

The struggles of democracies in Southeast Asia (and elsewhere) show
that more than just elections are needed to overcome decades and centuries of domination by foreign powers and feudal social structures. Michael
Vatikiotis, former managing editor of the *Far Eastern Economic Review,*
takes a pessimistic view of the region, writing that "little has been done
to address the fundamental problem plaguing Southeast Asian societies.
Profound inequalities of wealth and welfare have fuelled unending unrest and conflict within the ten countries [of Southeast Asia] . . . even more
troubling, these inequalities provide tinder for the flames of religious extremism and conflict."[2] He continues that Southeast Asia is in "a state of
demi-democracy" that "has yet to deliver effective change." One reason
for this is the trauma of colonization and the scars and wounds left by the
struggle for independence.

One problem with many developing democracies (and with many
other states in the developing world) is that they are "underinstitutional-
ized." Another term for institutions could be *checks and balances*: mechanisms which ensure that societies and states are working toward everyone's
best interests.

The American view of checks and balances, as shown in Figure 7.1,
is that their only purpose is to prevent the concentration of too much

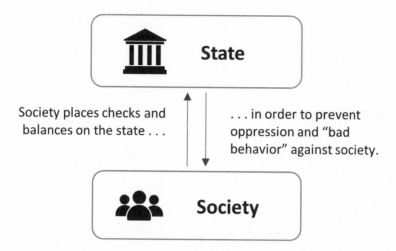

Figure 7.1 The traditional view of checks and balances, whereby the state is constrained in order to prevent it from wielding too much power against the wider society.

power in the government, or in one part of the government. This is why the US government is split into three coequal bodies, why the US Congress has several rules and systems to ensure bipartisanship, and why the US Constitution is exceedingly difficult to amend.

The American view is important, but it gets at only half the equation. One can be concerned about concentrating too much power in the state, but one also does not want a state that is too weak to act as a check and balance on other social actors, such as vested interests, large corporations, and the free market. One can argue that this is the situation in the US today. An incompetent or ineffectual state cannot be a check on anything, especially if it is usurped by private money. Such a weak state would be co-opted for the elite's benefit, increasing income and wealth inequalities and weakening the legitimacy and accountability of the state (despite all the checks and balances in place). This can be argued to be the case in many developed economies and even explains the rise of populism.

The other purpose of checks and balances is to ensure that what power the state does have is channeled toward socially beneficial purposes. Checks and balances in the US may ensure that a state does not slide into a totalitarian dictatorship, but do not provide any guarantee that the state that remains would act to promote the public interest. This has been the case in the US: a Pew survey in 2016 found that only 27 percent of Americans believed that elected officials acted in the best interests of the

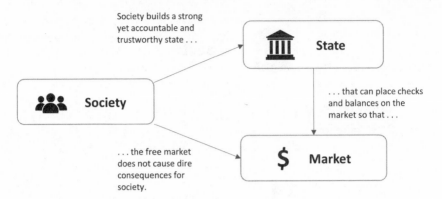

Society builds a strong
yet accountable and
trustworthy state . . .

State

Society

. . . that can place checks
and balances on the
market so that . . .

. . . the free market
does not cause dire
consequences for
society.

$ Market

Figure 7.2 My view of checks and balances, whereby a strong state empowered by the society places checks and balances on the market, ensuring that social aims are pursued and that the free market does not harm the wider society.

public.[3] This has been the experience in many budding democracies around the world: their systems may ensure that no politician declares himself or herself dictator for life, but they don't stop politicians from enriching themselves from their position in the government. My view of checks and balances, in which a state also acts as a balance against a rampant free market, is expressed in Figure 7.2.

There are several mechanisms that could support "good governance" within a strong and effective state. These include channels that communicate public opinion to the government and establish space for robust debate on issues. They include sources of expertise and planning that can combine long-term priorities with responsiveness to short-term challenges. And they must include a consensus on a long-term project for the government, beyond just keeping itself in power. These mechanisms and institutions can function in either democratic or nondemocratic states.

In the context of sustainable development, these checks and balances are needed to ensure that the state's authority is not captured by vested interests. Merely expanding the power of the state will do little if that power is put into the service of extractive, damaging purposes. The developmental states expanded state presence in the economy, but toward ultimately unsustainable ends. Several states with government-driven economies, in practice, rely on resource extraction and polluting manufacturing in service of vested interests.

This chapter will start by running through some brief examples of countries and governments to explore the full range of possibilities. Some countries, despite mainstream opinion to the contrary, have shown that they are capable of working in the public interest. Other countries, despite being held up in the past as models for others to follow, have seen their progress stall.

The chapter will then discuss some mechanisms that an ideal strong state could possess that would ensure that its strength is used appropriately. Each of these mechanisms will be described in both democratic and nondemocratic forms.

• • •

The strongest check and balance in a democratic system is the election. Even if elections and democratic structures may not always choose the best possible leader, they should certainly be able to get rid of clearly bad ones. If a leader has proven, during his or her time in office, to be a poor choice to lead the country, then democratic structures should eventually get rid of him or her. That is the entire purpose of popular democratic legitimacy. The advocates of this apparent inherent strength often ignore the damage that can be done by someone in a four- or five-year cycle, or the fact that the promise of "change" does not always deliver a better government, even if it does deliver change.

The fact is, several developing democratic states have been unable to get rid of leaders who either no longer have popular support or are failing their societies. I am not referring to, for example, Recep Tayyip Erdogan of Turkey, Rodrigo Duterte of the Philippines, or Viktor Orban of Hungary, who are criticized abroad yet command significant support at home. Rather, I am referring to those whom even the local populations judge to be poor leaders, yet their multiparty parliamentary democratic systems have allowed them to keep their jobs.

Malaysia is one example. Former Prime Minister Najib Razak was alleged to have funneled monies from Malaysia's national development fund to his own personal accounts. Despite coming in promising to reform some of the harsh security legislation that has been used against press outlets that criticize the government, he brought them back into effect once the corruption scandal broke.

Despite these scandals, he was not deposed as prime minister. Even before the scandal, Malaysia's political system allowed Barisan Nasional to keep a majority of seats despite not winning a majority. The coalition was not willing to remove Najib as leader of the party, because many in office owed personal loyalty to Najib, rather than to Malaysia or even their own party.

It took an election to remove him from office, showing that, in the end, elections remain a powerful mechanism for accountability. But it was also the last available option after a great deal of damage had been inflicted on the country. At no previous point did Malaysia's institutions step in to ensure accountability despite the supposed democratic checks and balances.

Surprisingly, this is not a problem faced by Pakistan, often portrayed as a "near-failed" state by the media (and especially by India). Pakistan's prime minister, Nawaz Sharif, was recently pushed from office by the courts after accusations of corruption. Even Pervez Musharraf, a former military dictator, was ousted by Pakistan's court system in response to accusations that he had orchestrated the assassination of political opponents. For all of its problems, Pakistan can exercise that most basic of checks and balances: getting rid of a bad leader, even if the choices for replacement are limited and not necessarily favorable.

One can compare Pakistan with another struggling democracy, Thailand. When after losing an election Pakistani politician Imran Khan declared that he would march on Islamabad to demand the seat of prime minister and overturn the election results, there were concerns that this would spell the end of Pakistan's young democracy. But, in the end, Pakistan's middle class rejected Khan, deciding to preserve democracy.

By contrast, when the Thai army moved to overthrow the Thaksin government, there was widespread approval among Thailand's urban middle classes. Thailand's middle class recently voted to approve a constitution that gives a great deal of authority and power to the Thai military, who preserve the right to interfere in Thailand's politics as it sees fit.

The difference likely comes through in institutions, which have built different relationships between the government and the people. Pakistanis know that their government is supremely flawed and that many of their politicians are corrupt. However, they also know that egregious behavior can be, and has in the past been, checked by the courts. Thus the system "works"—perhaps not well, but well enough.

By contrast, Thailand's political system devolved into a split between wealthy urban elites and poorer rural residents. The elite no longer believed that democracy worked for them, and so were happy to dismantle it if it meant their benefits could be preserved.

Vietnam is another single-party government whose state has been turned toward long-term economic growth and development. Unlike what the mainstream media would suggest, the country is not ruled with an iron fist by a cabal of ruthless military men out to secure their own position and power. If that were the case, the Vietnamese state would not have been able to turn a country devastated by decades of conflict into an economic power in just thirty years. After all, it had to take a dedicated and highly disciplined group of people to fight two colonial powers (France and the US) and then set about building a fairer society than the country had previously known.

One does not need to have an altruistic view of the Vietnamese Communist Party to understand why the government decided to improve economic development and the lives of its people. State officials understood that the population's trust in the government depended on their ability to deliver better living standards for Vietnam's people, so the best way to secure the continued existence and power of the Vietnamese Communist Party was to ultimately improve people's lives.

And it has largely worked. Vietnam is now one of Southeast Asia's major players and is poised to be one of the region's biggest drivers of growth and development.

Each of these cases illustrates how checks and balances can differ among countries. Some nondemocratic countries, despite not having elections, still have systems that channel authority toward socially beneficial ends. Some democracies, by contrast, have not been able to implement even quite basic checks and balances or to instate a culture of democracy in their populations.

• • •

What follows are several mechanisms that an effective strong state would need in order to ensure that its strength is channeled toward social justice and the interests of the majority. Strong versions of these institutions would build the accountability and legitimacy needed to create truly strong states.

Element 1: Channels That Communicate Public Opinion to the Government

If a government is to be trusted by the people, it needs to be able to respond to the concerns of the majority with regard to what I have defined as the basic rights of life. It needs to be guided by insights into the effects of its decisions (or lack of them) on the majority's quality of life. In the democratic mainstream, this is accomplished through competing political parties, the free press, an active civil society, and regular elections. Representatives are meant to be the vehicles for public opinion, ensuring that it is reflected in the writing of legislation and policy; if public opinion changes and the views of representatives do not change with them, then an election would lead to a government more in line with public preferences.

In a democratic system, the channel between the government and the people is meant to be the free press. The media help ensure that politicians know what their constituents think, feel, and believe, as well as inform them of the consequences of their decisions. On the other end, the press ensures that the public knows the preferences of the politician, and the actions he or she is actually taking (so that they can connect a policy change with a change in conditions).

There are limits on its effectiveness, as the "marketplace of ideas" can be less open and free than people think. Media consolidation driven by business interests ends up allowing a few voices to dominate the airwaves and can make it difficult for alternate views and opinions to exist on a financially viable and sustainable basis. Vested interests can also flood the airwaves with messages that support their point of view, drowning out criticism and other opinions. Politicians can become the cronies of certain media empires, as has happened in the US and the UK.

One nonelectoral mechanism to communicate public opinion to the state is to have an extensive network of local government officials accountable to their communities. This ensures that government institutions actually know what conditions are like on the ground. They know what people think and believe, and how they are affected by government policy. They may also be able to respond to problems faster than more centralized government departments.

This is a mechanism for communicating public opinion that is not contingent on whether or not a state is democratic. Both democratic and nondemocratic states can have a large and integrated yet distributed body of government officials who are aware of how local communities are faring.

Element 2: Spaces for Robust Debate on Policies

To ensure that states evaluate all the available solutions, governments should create and support spaces for open and robust debate. Such spaces help build consensus as to what the problem is, what its causes are, and what solutions will be most effective. So long as debate occurs, whether it does so in the public sphere or within governing and legislating bodies does not really matter.

Democracies generally focus on external debate, which they consider a badge of honor. Solutions are debated in the media, which influences voters and the representatives they elect. Open legislatures also feature debates between multiple parties, which inform the public of the preferences of various legislators. The hope is not that external debate is an objective process or that those engaging in it are acting free of self-interest but rather that enough people are involved so that these distortions come out in the wash.

However, these external debates can be colored by political partisanship. Good ideas can be dismissed, and problems may even be denied entirely, if doing so avoids granting the "other side" a win. It can turn objective facts into cultural arguments, which are harder to resolve.

Debates can also take place within governing institutions. Governments can have discussions on policies and policy outcomes on an objective basis. This has the benefit of avoiding political partisanship: people are allowed to propose and criticize ideas and policies without fear of letting one's political opponents win (though factionalism can exist in single-party systems as often as in multiparty systems).

The risk with relying on entirely internal debate is that it can close off the government to ideas from outside the paradigm. Governments, like any large organization, can suffer from groupthink and bureaucratic infighting where certain points and opinions are dismissed or, worse, never even considered. Governments—democratic and nondemocratic—have long been surprised that their assumptions about the world had no basis in reality whatsoever. Governments would need to make sure that they actively seek outside expertise, highlighting other points of view.

Element 3: Multiple Sources of Expertise and Planning

States need to have multiple sources of expertise as they develop policies. This is especially important for strong states in the era of sustainable development, as they will need to first understand the science, economics, and web of interconnections. More forceful intervention throughout the economy requires a level of economic planning, regulation, and control that is missing in most states today.

Thus there need to be many different agencies—each well funded, well staffed with qualified professionals, and empowered with significant authority—to monitor, plan, and regulate different sections of society and the economy. These bodies must be isolated from the day-to-day politics of the government, in order to ensure that they can work without interference from political interests.

One problem in many democracies is that they focus on putting out fires in the short term; this is understandable, as it is the short-term crises that tend to topple sitting politicians. Longer-term problems tend to call for more complex, comprehensive solutions that require some groups to sacrifice before they benefit, which is unpopular in the short term. Solutions, if developed at all, are meant to put off the day of reckoning—until it is too late. Long-term problems are left to fester until they become crises, leading to suboptimal solutions developed under tight circumstances.

Governments that are insulated from short-term swings in popular opinion can focus on the long-term planning that is necessary to solve long-term problems.

That being said, governments shouldn't be so insulated from conditions on the ground that they don't consider short-term consequences at all. People, rightly or wrongly, do judge the performance of their governments according to short-term concerns. Ignoring them will weaken the accountability of the government, in that people will not believe that the government cares about their concerns.

Element 4: A Long-Term Goal beyond Just Keeping the Government in Power

Governments need to have a long-term goal aimed at the betterment of society, beyond just keeping themselves in power. A "national project" tends to orient the expression of state authority toward some useful end, rather than have it exist for its own sake.

Democratic systems have an added wrinkle, in that there are multiple parties competing against each other for power. If political parties are focused on keeping themselves in power, they will not cooperate with the other side, even if such cooperation might benefit the country in the long term.

The lack of a long-term project in nondemocratic states leads to a pure focus on patronage, bribery, and coercion, as the state drifts away from helping the people and toward helping those in power. In democratic states, the lack of a long-term project leads to gridlock and stagnation. Neither are good for the optimal running of the strong state.

Another reason to have a long-term, national guiding project is that, without one, it is difficult to ask a population to make sacrifices for the future. Governments often claim that short-term sacrifices and struggles are needed in order to achieve some long-term goal, but they often leave this goal undefined and unclear. Worse, governments that lack a guiding vision may just end up not doing very much of anything, with leaders resorting to lofty and meaningless slogans.

Finally, a long-term national project around the critical challenge of sustainability helps bind the population together, which can be especially important for ethnically and religiously diverse populations who risk exploding over resource access issues. By presenting an image of the country in the future, a long-term and universal national project can overcome these divisions.

You can see the benefit of a long-term national project by comparing Singapore and Hong Kong. Both are largely free-market cities, with advanced economies, a general avoidance of regulation, and high quality of living. However, since independence, Singapore's governance has preserved a long-term agenda of improving the economic development of the city to First World levels (if not beyond). This has driven long-term strategies to improve the delivery of health care and housing, including quite aggressive government intervention and management of certain sectors of the economy.

By contrast, Hong Kong's government has lacked a long-term project for what the city might look like in the decades after its handover to China. There are various reasons for this—one of which being that the government's unsteady legitimacy has left it unwilling to make bold promises or choices. But this ultimately means that Hong Kong's government is usually concerned about the next crisis, and lacks a long-term agenda to guide its policies, thus fueling discontent among its population, mainly the young. It ends up not doing much of anything, letting crises fester rather than tackling them.

Element 5: Competent Institutions and the Rule of Law

Institutions help stabilize government practices and make them less prone to being overruled at a later date. These need to be bodies in which trust, legitimacy, and accountability can be invested by society. These institutions must be separate from the actual individuals who run the government. Things are done to support the institution (which has its own objectives) rather than to support the people in charge. They are run by competent people, some of the best in the country, who are looking to serve.

Even the Chinese Communist Party itself can be seen as an "institutional check" on the ambitions of Chinese leaders. The most uncharitable view one can have of China is that leaders are acting in the best interest not of themselves but of the Communist Party. But the party is still a body that exists, with goals and interests, outside of individual politicians. Pure dictatorships, by contrast, merely act in the interests of the dictator.

Democratic institutions are probably less effective overall. Even good, mature democracies tend not to be very good with long-term radical change, as it would lead to mass public disruption—and thus massive public unpopularity. But, assuming elections and institutions are respected, a democracy may be less likely to "go wrong," at least in the short term. A government that is really terrible will, in theory, be booted out of office. Thus the accountability and legitimacy relationship is less reliant on any government's performance in any one instance. Nondemocratic states, by contrast, rely entirely on the state's performance.

• • •

Competence is core to the idea of the strong state. The ability to govern, devise sound economic and social policies, and implement policies effectively and without recurrent mistakes is a central part of the social contract between the government and the people, and thus core to the strong state. This strength is instilled by a high level of institutional competence. It does not necessarily have to be the Singaporean or German model, but a basic level of competence is foundational. Without it, states resort to coercion, fear, and bribery to enact its objectives, or simply do not act at all.

Competence explains why single-party nondemocratic states like China and Vietnam are stable (even though they are not perfect by any means) compared to what we normally consider to be dictatorships. Dictatorships are, in general, incompetent: they do not deliver better living standards for their people, so they have no social contract with their populations. Dictators thus have to resort to force. By contrast, China and Vietnam have built competent administrations and institutions, and actually achieve better conditions through calculated and tough decisions in the interest of the majority. Thus populations are comfortable with these governments, even without direct popular representation.

Competence also goes beyond just the government to be a feature of society. Japan's government seems quite weak, with a quick succession of prime ministers over the past decade. Yet the country has fostered a culture of competence that pervades its institutions, which helps to keep the country running effectively. Perfection is sought in all aspects of life (and creates some other tensions), but things work. It's a culture where the train company actually publicly apologizes when a train leaves the station *early.* The commitment to seek perfection creates a collective culture of competence, which is the glue that holds Japanese society together.

But competence is not just grown in advanced, comfortable societies. Vietnam has built social competence in the face of adversity, in the aftermath of three major wars. Vietnam had to build competent institutions because it had little choice: without them, the state would surely have collapsed.

Competence is built through education and systematic nurturing of talent, which creates a population of highly skilled, publicly motivated people who can be drawn on to run the country. Institutions need to be highly respected and thus attractive as places to work and serve the public, to ensure that the best people are chosen.

There are perhaps two forms of competence. The first is *leadership competence*: the ability of a political leader (or body of leaders) to set priorities and effectively administer the government. The second is *institutional competence*: the ability of government bodies to anticipate, analyze, plan, and implement policies.

Each influences the other. Singapore is a good example. Lee Kuan Yew was clearly an extremely competent leader, building a small city-state unceremoniously ejected from Malaysia into an effectively First World country with world-class services. But all his work would have been for naught if he didn't demand and foster the growth of institutional competence (in this case, based on meritocracy); a new, less competent leader could have lost Singapore's advantages. But Singapore's good institutions allowed the city's success and competence to persist beyond the end of Lee's time as prime minister.

But institutional competence is not invincible. Strong institutions can survive mediocre leaders, but truly disastrous leaders will eat away at them. We have started to see this with Malaysia's prime minister Najib Razak, whose political survival in the face of blatant corruption has threatened to make a mockery of Malaysia's whole government and its until now fairly competent institutions.

Institutional competence comprises four components:

1. Administrative expertise
2. Public policymaking
3. Leadership
4. Meritocracy

Administrative expertise is the ability to set up state structures that are led by individuals who are qualified and experienced. They are teams who are able to minister and manage a department and execute on decisions. It's a tax collection department that can design appropriate tax systems and find and collect revenue, or a pollution regulator that conducts regular inspections to enforce the law without fear or favor. Without this expertise, institutions are "paper tigers," unable to fulfill their obligations.

Public policymaking is the process through which institutions identify issues needing new policies and have experts able to design options to address legislative needs. Institutions thus require setting priorities and deciding on the best way to achieve them, and competent ones will have systematic ways to monitor conditions on the ground and figure out the best solutions to problems.

Leadership refers to the need for the head of the institution to embody its values and ideals. An agency head who is not respected either within the institution or by the wider society will be hamstrung in his or her efforts to manage and monitor society. Talented civil servants will become disillusioned and leave for the private sector, while the institution's public reputation collapses. However, a strong and respected leader at the top can enhance the effectiveness of the agency.

Finally, *meritocracy* means that the institution has a process for finding and hiring people on the basis of talent and capability, rather than political connections or meaningless status symbols.

One can easily think of how institutions in the developing world may lack one, if not all, of these components, thus rendering them incompetent: a stinging charge, but a true one that must be faced.

• • •

The ultimate limits on what the sustainable state can do are political will and competence. The former is the ability to agree on a long-term vision for society and a willingness to make the tough decisions and suffer the trade-offs needed to implement that vision. The latter is the ability to actually follow through on those decisions, including pushing back against vested interests.

Some states have the will, but not the competence to follow through. India is an example: both the Indian National Congress and the Bharatiya Janata Party agree on the need to tackle sanitation, river pollution, corruption, and further economic development. Despite this bipartisan agreement, however, India has been unable to implement further changes. India has large reserves of very competent people, including in the government, but not enough to overcome the systematic institutional failings that are typical challenges in such a large country. China, by contrast, has over the last ten to fifteen years striven to move the government institutions to the next stage of competency by installing young, energetic, and competent administrators and technocrats across the country.

Other states have managed to build high levels of competence, yet currently lack the will to do anything with it. The US is an example of this phenomenon. American institutions are extremely competent, attracting bright people who want to work for the betterment of society. The country could tackle some of its most serious social problems in a short period of time. However, its political institutions are trapped in a vicious cycle of animosity toward the other side (often aided by vested interests) and have been unable to agree on a long-term vision for the country, meaning that the government is stuck.

An example of the importance of institutional competence—and the length of time needed to build it—comes from the misguided US policy of "de-Ba'athification" after its invasion of Iraq. Once Saddam Hussein had been toppled, the Americans enacted a policy whereby all public sector employees with ties to Hussein's Ba'ath Party would be removed from office, then barred from any future public sector employment. Several observers at the time argued that such a policy would be hugely disruptive. Even the State Department and the CIA, at the time, argued for a less extreme policy of "de-Saddamification," rather than removing Ba'ath Party members en masse.

The dire predictions were borne out almost immediately. The mass removal of public sector expertise meant that the Iraqi state quickly lost the ability to provide even basic public services, which contributed to the break-down of Iraqi society into the mess we see today. Iraq has *still* not been able to recover the institutional competence it lost due to the US invasion.

Where competence is low or absent (or not given priority), the state fails, even in the absence of extreme events such as war or famine. It can struggle to provide even basic government services, which drastically lowers people's faith and trust in the government. Pakistan is an example: low institutional competence has significantly weakened the social con-tract, even though the country has (fortunately) not suffered any extreme conflicts, natural disasters, or climate events.

• • •

These arguments do not simply apply to nondemocratic or developing world states. These observations are just as relevant to emerging and es-tablished democracies as well, which can be prone to capture by vested interests.

In an increasingly globalized world, democracies would seem to be having a tough time strengthening themselves, let alone becoming sus-tainable states. The short electoral cycle makes it difficult for politicians to take a long-term view or make unpopular decisions, for fear of losing office. Yet the electoral system provides popular legitimacy and account-ability, and there are the moral and philosophical reasons and arguments for why a society would want to keep a democratic government.

I am not an expert in democratic political theory, but here I offer a few suggestions on how a democracy could become a strong, sustainable state while preserving the democratic values it holds dear.

First, democracies need to have clear lines of accountability, which can be muddled by unruly coalitions and protections for the minority party. In these systems, political parties, whether they are minor coali-tion partners or opposition parties, have an incentive to be disruptive and obstinate. Democracies around the world can be rendered ineffective. But partisan gridlock can also benefit the party in power: if the party's poli-cies never come to pass, its leaders will never actually be held account-able for the changes they want to make. Stronger majorities, whether achieved by removing procedural barriers such as the filibuster or by us-ing runoff voting, enable democratic governments to get things done while also ensuring that, if things go wrong, people know exactly who is to be blamed.

Decision-making bodies should still be designed to embrace and allow for bipartisanship, so as to reduce damaging petty politics and also because having multiple stakeholders invested in a solution will ensure continuity after power changes hands. But when this does not work, mechanisms should allow the elected government to act decisively if an obstinate minority party is blocking reasonable, or even routine, decisions.

Accountability must also be deepened among the people. Many democracies have shockingly low voting rates, especially among the poor and the young: the former because it is too difficult to vote, the latter because they have yet to turn voting into a habit. If democracy is so cherished on the basis that it creates checks and balances, then a strong democratic state should make voting as easy as possible: more polling stations, lower barriers to voting, and more ways to vote, even electronically if need be. But this should be backed by mandatory voting, so that every person engages with the political process. This would strengthen the state and give true legitimacy to democratic elections and the elected leader.

Second, democracies should consider longer terms for their politicians: perhaps somewhere between six to eight years. Short terms mean continuous election campaigns and wasteful politicking, leaving only a short time to get anything done. Long terms can enable leaders to make an impact and voters to really understand their objectives. These longer terms can be balanced by strict limits—for example, only one or two terms, which would also force politicians to develop their ideas and policies in future leaders, growing a new crop of political talent.

Third, the independence of the civil service and the institutions of the state needs to be further insulated from political pressures or interference. Legislative meddling in the civil service, from appointing leaders wholly opposed to the ministry's mission to slashing their budgets, can leave government officials hobbled and demotivated. If they leave for the private sector, the government is deprived of much-needed competence. In addition, the increasing trend of revolving doors in democracies needs to be halted, even with legislation, to help strengthen the state so that it is not usurped by private interests over time.

Many democracies have informal norms that discourage meddling in the civil service, but these norms are not as strong as firm rules. Democracies should consider institutionalizing and legislating many of the behaviors that protect the civil service.

Fourth, democracies need to tackle the issue of money in politics. In short, it is too expensive to run, and sometimes even hold, office. Politicians are either beholden to wealthy donors and corporations or must be independently wealthy themselves. Thus politics reflects the elite of society, rather than the full range of individuals and social groups found within democratic society. Many democratic leaders are unable to make decisions on long-term sustainability issues that affect lobbyists and corporate donors.

Campaign finance laws, public financing, and even benefits for politicians (such as government-provided housing) can both limit the ability of the wealthy to influence politics and make it easier for people from all walks of life to run for and hold office without the help of private interests.

Fifth, democracies need to be wary of media consolidation, which can get to the point where media outlets are large enough to become kingmakers. News Corporation, Fox News, and its associated entities are the archetypal example, with its newspapers and news networks fueling right-wing politics in the UK, the US, and Australia.

The media landscape needs to have enough competing voices to ensure that no single outlet gets too big, and that a viable, objective competitor exists at a price affordable to all (if not free). Democracies should set firm rules to ensure that no one media outlet dominates the airwaves. When they get to a certain size, they can be taxed at a different rate, with the revenues used to support public media: not-for-profit media outlets, supported by government funding yet completely independent, with strict rules about objectivity, fairness, and breadth, and with a clear mission of informing the public. These outlets provide an easily accessible way for everyone to stay informed, especially as the whole industry is disrupted by the rise of the internet and social media. And with social media that have run amok, democracies will need to properly regulate these companies if they are not to be further manipulated and weakened.

Sixth, democracies need to revisit their constitutions (if they have them). These constitutions were written decades, if not centuries, ago, in a much different context than we are living in today. Democracies need to be willing to reconsider how their governments and societies should work, and develop a new narrative for how democratic structures should operate in a more constrained future.

Should legislation concerning sustainability be protected from changes for a set period of time longer than a party's term in office, to ensure that long-term goals are completed? Should an independent body to evaluate a leader's performance be created, with the ability to take action if need be? How should authority be split among the city, the countryside, and the national government in order to best manage resources? These and other questions will need to be answered by democracies as we move further into the twenty-first century.

• • •

The previous sections have described a few of the mechanisms that will serve to ensure that the strength of the state is oriented toward the benefit of the majority. The strong state in an era of constrained resources will end up intruding into the lives of populations to a much greater extent than in the past, and therefore must have strong institutions, and all the necessary checks and balances to make a viable state to ensure that the government remains legitimate and accountable.

Strong states will need these institutions as they start their most important task: redefining prosperity and rights in an age of constrained resources. This task will require managing the expectations of a population who may have come to expect a consumption-driven lifestyle with high resource consumption as the end result of development. It will require asking people to sacrifice in the short term to ensure a sustainable level of resources for future generations. States will need every tool in their arsenal as they work to alter how their societies and economies operate.

Chapter 8 will discuss these redefinitions in more detail.

CHAPTER | 8

REDEFINING FREEDOM, RIGHTS, AND PROSPERITY

M y view of moderate prosperity in the context of twenty-first-century resource constraints arises from my own experiences: growing up in a poor developing country, working in Africa as a young engineer, and visiting many countries over the last twenty years to work on projects at the crossroads of poverty alleviation and sustainable development.

When I was working in the small Kingdom of Swaziland in southern Africa, I lived in a very small housing estate. Many of the other residents were, for the first time in their lives, living in a "modern" house. Before, they had lived in traditional homesteads built from mud, stone, and thatch.

I was struck by how satisfied they were with something so basic, but that still had all the trappings of being "modern": a tile roof, brick walls, running water, a toilet, and electricity. This brought them immense joy, and there was no mad rush to make themselves even richer. They did not have air conditioners, washing machines, or even kettles, but they did not mind. I remember having similar experiences as a child, as my family moved from the basics to something a notch up. There was a drive to be educated and a worthy member of society, but there was no burning desire among the people I knew to get rich quick and to be surrounded by material wealth.

What was also interesting was how my Swazi neighbors returned each month to their rural homes. There, they had a more basic level of prosperity, but it also provided them with a greater human connection to the land, their past, their relatives, and their animals—a sense of belonging and a reassurance of identity.

But as the pressures of urban life started to set in, one could see shifts begin to emerge. A more modest, caring, and simple model of community life gave way to one driven by desires, rather than needs, and to a lifestyle completely out of sync with local conditions, traditions, and values. A moderate way of life, one that provided basic needs while existing in harmony with both nature and traditional culture, disappeared, in exchange for a lifestyle modeled after high-end global lifestyles. Inequalities grew and began to widen. This pattern has been repeated throughout the developing world, and lamented both within and outside of it.

• • •

This chapter will present new definitions of the fundamental concepts underlying my idea of a viable economic model and the strong state: *freedom, rights,* and *prosperity.*

If our societies—especially those in large overcrowded nations—are to survive a resource-constrained twenty-first century, states will need to define these concepts differently, because they guide popular expectations and aspirations. Expansive understandings of freedom and prosperity encourage people to expect a standard of living and a level of consumption that will be impossible within a few decades, and prevent them from fully understanding the constraints we live with and the implications of ignoring them.

A common refrain by those that understand resource constraints but are still unwilling to embrace controls on consumption is to argue that it is impossible to suppress these aspirations. But we need to start with the understanding that overconsumption will wreak havoc on society, and thus we have no choice but to manage unrealistic expectations.

One can understand why people argue that constraints will unfairly cap their rights or potential. For all the problems with the free-market narrative and the American Dream, they are, at least, an internally consistent and appealing idea: work hard to earn money, then spend it on all the comforts of life.

But this is a simple narrative, and we cannot think in simple terms. This book lays out a new economic and political model that does not rely on perpetual growth through mindless consumption. It does not accept "progress" as its ultimate goal, especially if that progress comes with a high social cost and vast inequalities. Instead it aims to create a positive vision of living within limits and moderate prosperity that does not just focus on what people will no longer be able to do, but also presents a compelling image of what such a life might look like and how it is the only possible guarantee of social stability and collective welfare in large developing nations. Creating such a positive vision will mean that free-market ideologies can no longer claim that they are the only realistic path to human welfare and deem other approaches as utopian or inherently flawed.

Several political and moral concepts in the Western economic model imply that "free market economics" is the right and only option for human prosperity. This encourages the unrestrained use of public goods, overconsumption, and the neglect of external costs. Environmental damage and resource overuse becomes the price to be paid for prosperity. And true sustainability—lowering resource use by reducing production and consumption—becomes, at best, a fringe element in policy discussions.

The Current View of Freedom and Rights

Freedom is a difficult concept to describe. Hardly anyone, especially politicians and business leaders in liberal democracies, wants to talk about the bounds of freedom, for fear of being accused of inviting oppression.

The free-market definition of freedom asserts that people should be left alone to do as they so choose, if they have the desire and aspiration as well as economic means to afford it. The ultimate freedom is to be able to improve their economic situation and thus wealth with no restraints, without being honest about how they have used these freedoms at the expense of others, either on the individual level (purchasing a pair of denim jeans made using underpaid labor and overused water) or at the corporate level (e.g., large-scale strip mining that infringes on the lives of indigenous people).

The concept of rights is closely connected to freedom. In the Western model, rights are defined "negatively" as areas of activity where the government is not allowed to interfere. Rights are thus connected to the free-market narrative's conception of freedom: if people are free to do largely whatever they want, then they have expansive rights that must be protected.

Consumers argue at the same time that they have the freedom to use what they own in whatever way they wish for the sole reason that they paid for it and own it. Even more expansively, they may argue that they can do whatever they wish because they *can* pay for it (i.e., a sentiment that means one cannot tell people what they should or should not do with their own money).

An expansive understanding of freedom means that governments have taken a very narrow view of economic regulation, as they believe that such regulation will impinge on the freedoms of owners, consumers, and businesses. Governments in the developing world have over the past fifty years internalized this prescription, after being bullied into this by Western-led rule-making organizations such as the IMF and the World Bank. Regulations are only accepted if there is visible and drastic evidence of harm, and even then vested interests, unsurprisingly, will work tirelessly to argue that no harm has been done. One need only look at the power and wealth of lobbying groups to see this in action.

The Current View of Prosperity

In the Western economic model, which has been exported to the rest of the world, prosperity is equivalent to consumption. The more one consumes and owns, the more prosperous one is. In most societies, one's status in the world goes up. This is true even if the consumption does not serve any real personal or social purpose or if people could achieve the same standard of living with less consumption or fewer resources.

In this model, prosperity is continuous, stretching out to infinity. This has led to a great deal of waste, of which consumption of clothing is a good example. In developed countries, the middle and upper classes own far more clothing than they feasibly could ever need. Having a large and varied wardrobe is seen as one of the symbols of prosperity. Singapore's National Environment Agency estimated that, in 2015, Singapore threw out 156,700 tons of clothing and leather waste.[4] A Greenpeace study of Hong Kong found that one-fifth of all clothes bought by residents were never worn, totaling almost US$512 million in wasted purchases.[5]

At the level of the individual, it doesn't hurt consumers to buy more clothes than they need. These products are so cheap that even the extremely limited benefit of owning more clothing would still be greater than the price. But clothing is cheap for a reason: the massive underpricing of the resources (e.g., cotton, which has huge externalities as a crop) and labor that go into making them. One would expect that if clothing were priced more accurately, people would decide to buy far less of it and to try to preserve the clothing they already own. (And only then could fashion designers and the garment industry lay claim to any green credentials and give even an iota of legitimacy to their T-shirts with slogans about saving the planet.)

It is also clear that our current view of prosperity does not handle how long a product will last. When faced with the choice of buying multiple cheap products that will fail in a short period of time or buying one expensive product that will last a long time, many people will choose cheaper disposable goods. The market does not mind this behavior; in fact, it desires, cultivates, and thrives on it.

For example, the consumer electronics sector thrives on planned obsolescence, with companies producing faster and more powerful devices each year in the hope of driving new sales. The lifespan of these devices often extends far longer than the product cycle, yet companies encourage people to junk their existing devices and buy the newest. This leads to an increasing amount of e-waste, which is now plaguing landfills around the world. Worse, companies may even design products with the foreknowledge that people will replace them within a year or two, discouraging those companies from making reliable and optimized products. So much for "innovation."

We often leave it to the consumer to define prosperity, because economic models often assume that people can rationally judge the costs and benefits of their decisions. If the consumer always knows best, then it would be wrong to interfere.

However, experience and evidence shows that people are quite bad at making "rational" decisions, especially when it comes to day-to-day experiences. Even on an anecdotal level, people likely know this is true: how often does someone buy something they did not truly need during a "Black Friday" or "Singles Day" sale?

Governments too strive for a version of prosperity focused on symbolism and status. Governments in the developing world have often thrown money at projects in the hope of building national symbols and national champions, even if these things do little to improve the lives of ordinary citizens. Asian and Latin American countries can be especially culpable: they both have a history of colonialism and now believe they have the resources to "beat the West at its own game." Thus these countries want the tallest buildings, the most glamorous cities, the flashiest movies, and the largest companies.

Countries like China, Malaysia, Saudi Arabia, and the United Arab Emirates have sunken millions of dollars into building super-tall sky-scrapers, major stadiums, and other vanity projects. These make for nice headlines and press releases upon completion, but do little to actually improve conditions on the ground in these cities. The PR benefit is fleet-ing: the tallest skyscraper is rarely the tallest for very long, yet remains a blot on the landscape.

Sporting events and exhibitions are also attempts for countries to "buy" national prosperity. The past several years have seen several major events meant to be the "coming out" party for various emerging coun-tries: the 2010 World Cup in South Africa; the 2012 Winter Olympics in Sochi; the 2016 Summer Olympics in Rio de Janeiro; the World Expo in Astana, Kazakhstan; and the coming World Cup in Qatar.

•••

If the strong state is to consistently intervene in the market to preserve resources for future generations, protect the livelihoods of the poor ma-jority, and manage the expectations and aspirations of its population, it needs to have a drastically different understanding of rights, freedom, and prosperity as it simultaneously pushes for an economy that is not driven purely by domestic consumption.

Rights in the Strong State

In my understanding of the strong state, rights are all the basic neces-sities of the right to life: nutritious and clean food, clean water, sturdy shelter, access to energy, satisfactory health care, safety and security, and so on. The government has a moral obligation to ensure that these basic rights of life are provided and protected for its whole population at an af-fordable level. A government that does not see this as its core principle is failing in its core obligation to its people.

This basic standard of living would prevent people from living in destitution and toiling in drudgery. It is not a comfortable standard of living, and certainly does not include many of the modern amenities that current definitions of the middle class often take for granted and that are promised in the false narrative of trickle-down economic theories. People will work hard and may have little left over after paying for living expenses. But these people will not be in danger of starvation, being homeless, getting sick from preventable diseases, being unable to educate their children, living in an unsafe environment, or living without dignity.

These rights are not a replacement for the civil and political rights cherished in Western discussions—the individual right to free speech, freedom of religion, and so on. Those rights focus on a different realm of human experience. Rights in the strong state focus on a standard of living that delivers the basic rights to a decent and dignified life. These two spheres of rights can happily coexist. In other words, countries that place high value on Western-style civil and political rights can also focus on the basic rights of life without worrying about one contradicting the other.

In fact, the two types of rights can be combined—for example, a society can argue that a basic standard of living requires the ability to speak freely on a given issue (though, in practice, there should be protections to ensure that this right is not abused by those with greater wealth and resources). Combining economic and civil-political rights is not a new idea; it's not even an anti-Western idea. President Roosevelt's "Four Freedoms" (freedom of speech, freedom of religion, freedom from want, and freedom from fear) are an example.

Xi Jinping's recently announced "Four Comprehensives" instead combine economic rights and a focus on the legitimacy and accountability of the Communist Party. The Comprehensives call on Party members to "build a moderately peaceful society," "deepen reform," "govern the nation according to law," and "strictly govern the party." These goals combine the need for China to continue to lift people out of poverty while also ensuring the Community Party retains its legitimacy through self-discipline.

Economic rights should not be neglected: India, for example, is a country that respects civil and political rights. However, as noted previously, its provision of economic rights is dismal. South Africa is another country that, for historical reasons, is (rightly) protective of political rights, yet still struggles with providing economic ones.

In any case, the strong state's view of rights is that they are obligations to its citizens that must be achieved and protected. Doing so requires a much more activist and interventionist state than what is seen in the Western model, where rights are meant to prevent state action, and markets are trusted to solve fundamental social provisions.

Freedom in the Strong State

Under the sustainable state, the core definition of freedom will remain the same. People will ultimately be free to do what they want to do so long as their actions do not impinge on the rights and freedoms of others. This has often been called the "harm principle" and is an old concept in political and ethical philosophy.

However, we need to update this principle given what we know about the nature of modern economies and resource extraction/exploitation, and how our economic actions affect other people. We also need to clarify how we understand harm given the very strict resource constraints of the twenty-first century. For example, the overuse of resources by a minority in the "free market" makes it difficult for the majority of society to achieve a basic standard of living for themselves and their families, thus impinging on their rights. This is most prominent and hard felt in the developing world. The challenge is therefore to minimize harm while allowing the majority to access their basic rights to life. We must place many more restrictions and regulations on economic activity and economic freedom.

In the past, we largely assumed that externalities were limited, and freedom could be understood quite expansively. Regulation and constraints on freedom were justified only when externalities were clear and significant.

However, we now understand that external costs and the resulting negative impacts pervade the entire global economy. This must be factored into our economic models. There is not a single economic action that comes without some social cost or a cost placed on some third party. Every action we conduct in the economy places harm on another person.

Contrary to this understanding, people often operate under the assumption that consumption is innocent until proven guilty. In other words, any form of consumption is automatically assumed to be acceptable and that people should be free to consume as they wish until significant harm is proven. Only then is consumption of a given good deemed too harmful to remain unregulated. But almost all consumption is "guilty" in that they place externalities on others. Consumers can wear blinders that protect them from awareness of the true nature of harm.

For example, e-commerce has normally been portrayed as an expansion of freedom by allowing people to buy whatever they want, whenever they want it. However, although e-commerce does expand the freedom of consumers, it limits the freedom of everyone else. By making goods cheaper and more convenient to purchase, it contributes to waste creation. It displaces traditional retailers (which usually employ more people), replacing them with overworked and underpaid delivery and fulfillment careers. Finally, and more subtly, the rise of e-commerce seems to have led to the creation of massive monopolies; for example, Amazon now has enough money to dominate the US retail market (which was itself mature and developed). One expects that China, with a much less mature retail sector, is facing a similar prospect with the rise of Alibaba. There may come a time when Beijing will need to intervene in how Alibaba operates if it is seen to be a negative. But when Beijing makes this decision, it will have the tools to do so, unlike the US government vis-à-vis Amazon.

It is still too early to see whether e-commerce will be immune from regulation or how populations might react if regulations were put in place (which would ultimately increase prices or slow delivery times). But I expect that people would be upset and push to take such regulations down. We have seen this with reactions to Uber: despite clear evidence that Uber's business model ignores safety, puts drivers in poor working conditions, and blatantly breaks the law, Uber's customers fervently criticize any attempt to control the company, and actively lobby city governments to let Uber continue to break the law.

I suggest that instead of deeming consumption innocent until proven guilty, the strong state take the opposite approach: that overconsumption is guilty until proven innocent, or that people should only be allowed to overconsume once a government is reasonably sure that external costs have been accounted for. We should assume that all of our economic decisions have some repercussions on third parties, much of which are negative. Consumption and especially excessive forms should only be allowed to continue when these external costs have been reconciled, either by directly working to reduce them or by increasing the price to ensure that the true cost is being reflected.

We can see how this would work with car ownership. We currently assume that cars are innocent until proven guilty. Governments accept that poorly trained drivers have clear negative effects—namely, that untrained drivers cause accidents—so have implemented licensing regulations. There are also regulations against drunk driving and excessive speeding. Otherwise, regulations are few and far between, especially in the developing world. But there are signs that things need to change.

In the strong state, car ownership and usage would reflect the full effect of their social cost, such as their contributions to traffic congestion, pollution, poor public health, and carbon emissions. They would have to have been quantified and accounted for. This would serve to make cars significantly more expensive, but the price would accurately reflect the level of harm uncontrolled car ownership does to the rest of society and the environment. The tax revenues from more expensive cars can be used to build public transportation systems. The government can also discourage private car usage employing a range of economic instruments (and thus reduce all the negatives) by investing in public transportation.

Prosperity in the Strong State

Prosperity for the majority in the developing world starts with having their basic needs met, but is more than just a basic standard of living. Instead, it is a reasonably comfortable and compelling lifestyle that can serve as a suitable aspiration for people in a resource-constrained twenty-first century. *Comfortable* refers to a lifestyle that does not have the basic drudgery of everyday life, and that provides people with adequate comfort and free time to pursue their own ideas and hobbies, while providing enough opportunities for their families. The backdrop to this book's argument is that the majority of people in the world are either not free from drudgery or living lives that are far from even a basic definition of comfortable. It is the obligation of the state (and the state only) to address this challenge in the large developing countries, which demands a rethinking of the definition of sustainability and the paths toward achieving it. *Compelling* is more spiritual: Does the lifestyle provide meaning to an individual? A lifestyle purely based on consumption, in that case, would not be compelling.

These terms are open to interpretation, and different societies may choose to invest different meanings into these definitions according to their situation. But they must be understood within the hard resource constraints of the twenty-first century.

As noted earlier, we currently understand prosperity as stretching out to infinity. The more we own and consume, the more prosperous we are. I instead see prosperity at a societal level in the decades ahead as a threshold:

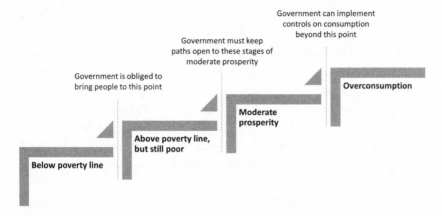

Figure 8.1 The stages of consumption. The lowest stage is similar to the poverty line; people consuming below this level do not have enough for basic survival. Governments need to bring people to this level as a matter of moral and political obligation. The highest stage is the standard of living that a government thinks is feasible given current resource constraints. The government can, if not should, implement controls on consumption beyond this point to preserve the resource base.

the point where someone is living a comfortable and compelling life. Governments can make it a matter of policy to help bring people to that level, or at least to preserve a path to that comfortable lifestyle. It can determine a set of policies that help people achieve that standard of living while consuming far fewer resources. Figure 8.1 illustrates the various "stages" of consumption and the government's role in each. The first is a basic standard of living, where people are no longer living in inhumane conditions (i.e., they have achieved what I've defined as the basic rights of life). The second is a comfortable standard of living, where people are able to live in relative comfort and are not working themselves to death (i.e., prosperity), while also not imposing a "cost" on collective welfare just because they can afford to do so.

Note that the government has no obligation to help those who are already past the moderate prosperity threshold. It can actively put regulations, costs, and quotas in place for any consumption beyond the prosperous level. People may still choose to consume more: to buy a second car, to own a larger house, have a swimming pool, to engage in polluting activities. But then, at the very least, they will be paying for the full cost of their activities and the associated luxuries.

Between the most basic level and moderate prosperity can be various other stages, where a person's access to basic needs is strengthened and deepened. For example, let us look at access to food. The basic stage would clearly mean that there's enough food to ward off starvation and malnutrition—not good food, or even healthy food, but just enough food. A middle stage could be access to enough food for a balanced diet, leading to better health. The moderate prosperity stage could be a refrigerator, allowing people to store food over time, improving their food security.

Another basic need we can analyze in this way is sanitation. The first stage would be some kind of structure to stop open defecation, and where the waste is not exposed to disease vectors and is concealed or carried away to a septic tank. This would not be "prosperous" by any stretch, but it would be better than the alternative. The next stage would be a private structure with some cleaning facilities, but still not what we would consider necessary for a cradle-to-grave sanitary treatment system. The final stage is what we would consider the "toilet": a hygienic facility with running water that isolates human waste from other systems and is treated at a central treatment plant before being discharged to bodies of water.

If we think about prosperity as a threshold, we also open up the possibility of thinking about a more energy- and resource-efficient way to achieve a prosperous standard of living. Can we get families hearty, nutritious meals in a way other than a meat-based diet? Can we build efficient homes that use natural cooling techniques, rather than rely on boxy structures cooled by wasteful air conditioning? Can we design our cities in ways that do not allow for density to be shaped by the dictates of market-based land prices, which in turn creates congestion and heating effects? Can we encourage certain kinds of leisure activities that do not consume huge amounts of energy and space, such as community sports and public libraries rather than golf courses, shopping malls, and air-conditioned movie theaters?

What would this version of moderate prosperity look like? It would be an expansion of the various elements of a basic standard of healthy living. Those living a prosperous life would have adequate nutrition for themselves and their families. They would be living in a home where each family member has enough living space to be comfortable (even if it may not reach the middle-class expectation of a single room for each child). People would have access to clean water and proper sanitation, the basis of any healthy living environment. They would not be energy-poor, but nor would they be entitled to being energy-rich via fossil fuels. They would have access to an adequate quality of health care for whatever condition they may experience. They would have access to good education for themselves and their children.

Another way to look at moderate prosperity is to look at some of the goods and services we believe to be hallmarks of prosperity and see what need or want they fulfill. Let us return to car ownership: why is owning a car seen as a symbol of prosperity? Cars, for all of their faults, do provide an appealing service to people by allowing them to travel from one point to another in an extremely convenient, private, safe, and speedy manner. Thus prosperity is not necessarily car ownership but rather the ability for an individual to get around in this way.

If mobility, rather than car ownership, is the actual element of prosperity, then we can think of ways to help provide mobility that avoid many of the external costs that come from private car ownership and excessive usage. A strong state can invest in a high-quality, inexpensive, and fast system of public transportation, which would allow citizens to travel from one point to another quickly, while freeing up space now taken up by roads and car parks.

A strong state can also tip the scale the other way: it can ban car usage in certain congested areas or where dense populations would be negatively affected by rampant car ownership. Reduced car ownership could even improve prosperity in other areas: land that would normally be used for expanded roads and parking garages could be repurposed for more socially beneficial purposes, such as housing, public facilities, or even just green/pedestrian space. A strong state can make the privilege of car usage in certain urban areas very expensive.

Hong Kong is one example. Although the city is not perfect (it has far too many cars on the road and has not implemented many of the controls and fees that would decrease car ownership), it has perhaps the world's best public transportation system. The Mass Transit Railway (MTR) is clean, cheap, and fast, and it is integrated with an extensive bus system. The entire public transportation network is connected by the Octopus contactless cash payment card, which makes it supremely simple and convenient to travel from one end of the city to another. There are many people in Hong Kong who would be considered prosperous who would never consider owning a car.

But, more generally, the strong state will try to develop paths toward a moderate prosperity: a lifestyle that achieves many of the needs and wants of a comfortable standard of living in a manner that consumes far fewer resources.

• • •

The redefinitions I've described in this chapter will act as the foundation of a new economic model that can better operate within the twenty-first century's hard resource constraints. Under this model, the objectives of an economy, and the government that manages it, are to ensure that every person has access to a basic standard of living, open a path to moderate prosperity, and prevent the overuse of resources and the externalization of costs.

The next three chapters will apply these concepts to some growing issues in East and Southeast Asia.

CHAPTER 9

THE TROPICAL HAZE CRISIS

On a clear afternoon in October 2015, I flew from Hong Kong to Kuala Lumpur—a flight I had made countless times before. But something was different this time around. As the plane approached the Kuala Lumpur International Airport, the scene outside my window seemed much less bright than usual, to the point where the glass appeared to be tinted. In my rush to get off the plane, I put the matter out of my mind.

I realized the cause when I left the climate-controlled and air-filtered airport terminal to wait for a taxi outside. What welcomed me to my home country of Malaysia was stale, acrid, choking air. Smog hung low in the sky, reducing visibility to only a few hundred meters at most. This was my first encounter with the legendary and crippling haze of Southeast Asia. NASA said it was the worst in twenty years.

I began to wonder what the cause of this pollution might be. With my training as an environmental consultant and my awareness of the region, I began to connect the dots. Burning forests on the island of Kalimantan. A worse-than-usual dry season due to La Niña. The expanding production of palm oil for packaged food, shampoo, and other consumer products. Industrial agricultural companies, many of which were based in Kuala Lumpur and nearby Singapore.

This was perhaps the greatest man-made environmental catastrophe in modern human history, yet no one seemed really capable of doing much about it.

• • •

The first third of this book laid out the problems with how we currently understand the economy and sustainability, and the solutions that are often put on the table. The second third portrayed what should replace it: a strong state with the necessary checks and balances—a state that provides universal basic needs, manages the expectations of its population toward a moderate prosperity, and intervenes in the economy to ensure that resources are shared more equally and also protected for future generations.

This final third of the book will look at several examples of sustainability crises in the world today: how the roots of the problems were nourished by weak state governance and the pursuit of unsustainable growth models and how a stronger state can take more aggressive action to resolve these crises.

The first of these is the haze that has for the last ten to fifteen years blanketed the countries of Indonesia, Singapore, Brunei, Thailand, and Malaysia (and sometimes as far away as the Philippines and Vietnam) for one to two months each year. This is a global environmental catastrophe caused by industrial agriculture, rural underdevelopment, and the rampant externalization of the costs of a global commodity product—palm oil—aided and abetted by the weak institutions of the state.

• • •

The region of Southeast Asia had for at least a decade viewed the haze as an acceptable "cost of living" and "price for prosperity" in the region. Transboundary haze had been reported as an issue as early as 1972, but the first major crisis occurred in 1997, which caused approximately US$9 billion in damages from health issues, disrupted air travel, and business. The haze has since become an annual phenomenon, with intense periods in 2005, 2006, 2009, and 2013. But even jaded Southeast Asians believed that 2015's haze season was especially bad. Haze blanketed the major cities of Jakarta, Singapore, and Kuala Lumpur, as people commuted under a hazy orange sky. Photos of politicians holding court in a hazy orange legislature, even indoors, were common on front pages.

The haze arose from forest fires on the island of Kalimantan (also known as Borneo). La Niña had created a drier-than-usual rainy season, so Borneo's forests and tropical peatlands were more susceptible to fire. That autumn, widespread fires released smoke and haze into the atmosphere.

Forty million Indonesians—a population equal to Spain's—were affected by the haze, which doesn't include the millions of others in neighboring countries. Approximately 140,000 people across the region visited hospitals for respiratory illnesses, and Malaysia closed its schools for several days to protect over two million students. One model from Harvard University suggested that more than 100,000 people died prematurely as a result of the haze crisis (though, admittedly, these results have been questioned).[1]

There were wider environmental repercussions beyond just air pollution. Borneo's rainforests are some of the world's oldest and most diverse. The island has 15,000 species of flowering plants, 420 species of birds, almost 400 species of fish, and 210 species of mammals—and perhaps more that have yet to be discovered. The fires destroyed much of this biodiversity and threatened its viability by reducing the available habitat for these creatures. Forests play a role in the water cycle, transferring water stored in the ground to the air. Deforestation leads to a drier region, which in turn sparks more forest fires.

Finally, there was the release of carbon emissions. Tropical peatlands store huge amounts of carbon, built up over millennia. And much as how melting permafrost in Siberia and Alaska is releasing millions of years' worth of trapped carbon, the burning peatlands risk being a "carbon timebomb." At the height of the 2015 fire season, Indonesia was releasing more carbon emissions per day than the much-larger US. Over a three-week period, Indonesia released more carbon emissions than Germany had in the entire year.

As mentioned, the drier-than-normal rainy season was the proximate cause for the 2015 fire season, but the problem had its roots in much earlier practices. After all, dry years had come and gone before, yet did not lead to massive fires and constant haze. These are some of the oldest and densest tropical forests in the world. They had survived centuries of climate variation.

The more fundamental cause was deforestation. Over half of Borneo's forest has been chopped down since the mid-1990s; forest cover will drop to merely a third of its original size by 2025 if current trends continue. The tropical peatland underneath, now exposed, becomes easy tinder for any fire that starts.

And fires are common on the island of Borneo, due to the widespread practice of slash-and-burn agriculture. Despite the fact that it sustains so much life, forest soil is not always best suited for the agriculture practiced by poor subsistence farmers and various other groups who live off the land. Thus farmers for millennia have converted forest to farmland by cutting down forest cover, letting the wood dry, and then burning it. The resulting ash and charcoal fertilizes the soil, making it more suitable for agriculture. The soil is then farmed until it is exhausted, at which point the farmers repeat the same process with a new portion of forest.

Slash-and-burn agriculture is sustainable on a small scale, and as noted, is a method that has been used by subsistence farmers for centuries. Abandoned fields regrow trees and shrubs, allowing the forest to recover over a period of decades. Farmers often then return to this regrown secondary forest and repeat the process (but often also enter virgin forest).

But when slash-and-burn is carried out on an industrial scale to serve the expansion needs of a highly productive cash crop such as palm oil, too much forest is cleared, and even secondary forest cover cannot be regenerated. As more farms and plantations expand, more of the forest is taken away. In addition, fields are no longer abandoned to be taken over by forest, but instead are adapted for other purposes by a burgeoning population, who in turn contribute to more slash-and-burn practices.

Borneo's agricultural sector is dominated by large plantation businesses, growing a monoculture of cash crops, such as palm oil or trees for wood pulp. Plantation farming is tough on the soil, as the monoculture leaches nutrients out of the soil without replenishing them. The soil is made unsuitable for agriculture, which gives plantations two options: artificially improve soil quality through chemical fertilizer or expand to a new field. Fertilizer is cheap, but cutting down more of the forest can be even cheaper, especially when forestry regulations are weak or poorly enforced. And there is a huge amount of money to be made from the lumber. Thus, when concessions are given, all parties enjoy a double benefit: immediate profit from the valuable timber and future profit from the palm oil grown on the land.

Not all slash-and-burn is carried out by plantation companies. When large plantations expand, they can push smallholder farmers off their land. These farmers must then find new fields for themselves, cutting down more forest and burning down the wood, only to be pushed off their land again later when plantations expand further.

• • •

The whole situation—the functioning of Kalimantan's agricultural sector, the island's deforestation, and the resulting catastrophic forest fires and haze—is ultimately the result of weak state governance.

In 1996, the Indonesian government, in an effort to alleviate crowding on the island of Java, resettled thousands of farmers to the island of Kalimantan. The government said it would convert over one million hectares of land for rice production, cutting down forests and building irrigation channels. Migrants were promised funds and their own land if they were willing to move from crowded Java and Bali to more sparsely populated Kalimantan. However, the migrant farmers had little experience farming on Borneo's soil, so much of the land was abandoned. The peatlands, left exposed, dried and thus became extremely susceptible to fire.

This virgin land was also a prime target for plantation owners, and weak governance in Kalimantan allowed these plantations to expand extremely quickly. An investigation by the Gecko Project and conservation news outlet *Mongabay* found that the Ministry of Forestry—technically the body with jurisdiction over the island's forests—granted only three licenses to plantations in the regency of Seruyan, a part of Central Kalimantan Province. The regency's leader, however, granted thirty-seven licenses, covering an area eighty times the size of Manhattan, or six times the size of Singapore. One license even overlapped with a protected natural park, but the ministry's moves to block the grant went ignored.[2] This was an expansion that was repeated throughout Kalimantan. Nor was it uncommon throughout other parts of Southeast Asia.

In 2002, the Association of Southeast Asian Nations (ASEAN) signed an agreement on controlling transboundary haze, but the organization has not done enough in practice, given the scale of the impacts, to control it. The agreement set up an ASEAN Center to facilitate "cooperation and coordination" to manage the impact of land and forest fires, but also asked member countries to monitor fire-prone areas, communicate this information to ASEAN, undertake prevention measures, and take the lead in combating the fires. Countries could ask for assistance, but other ASEAN members could refuse to provide it. The agreement provided no long-term channels through which to provide assistance.

The agreement does not reflect the fact that Indonesia is both the source of the fires and the country that will spend the most trying to combat it and change the root causes. Therefore, any international agreement which pretends that all countries face the problem equally (as the ASEAN agreement does) is unlikely to do much. One expects that Indonesia recognized this, which is likely why it only ratified the agreement in 2014.

But it is unfair to solely criticize Indonesia for its sluggishness. Indonesia is part of a regional and global economic structure that has encouraged deforestation and turned a blind eye to forest fires for decades, and has been forced to belatedly accept this situation at the behest of regional and global actors. Indonesia's vice president, Jusuf Kalla, when asked about the haze situation, noted that "for 11 months, they enjoyed nice air from Indonesia and they never thanked us. They have suffered because of the haze for one month and they get upset. . . . Somebody once told me that Indonesia must restore its tropical forests, and I told him, 'Excuse me? What did you say? Do you know who damaged our forests?' "[3]

Kalla was perhaps being overly defensive, but he had a point. Many of the plantation companies that engaged in slash-and-burn agriculture were based outside of Indonesia in the wealthier countries of Singapore and Malaysia, which were largely unwilling to crack down on their own companies (though this changed during the height of the 2015 crisis, at least in Singapore). Major plantation companies like Asia Pacific Resources International Holdings Limited (APRIL), Musim Mas Group, and Wilmar International are based in Singapore. Wealthier ASEAN countries and global consumers also benefited from the "cheap" products produced on Kalimantan plantations, such as wood pulp and palm oil. Palm oil is an ingredient in everything from chocolates and fast food to soaps, shampoos, and cosmetics. Singapore and Malaysia were happy to externalize the cost of their plantation companies so long as they saw no cost to themselves, and only woke up when the scale of the haze created a public backlash.

Products grown on Borneo, such as palm oil, are consumed globally, not just in the ASEAN region. Many of the world's largest commodity traders are involved, yet they took hardly any responsibility for the catastrophe apart from making pious statements at sustainability conferences. Major food companies, such as Nestlé, Hershey's, Mars, and Kraft Heinz, use palm oil in their products as a "healthier" food oil, but none of these companies have gone far enough in policing their use of palm oil. Nor has Europe or the US taken action against these companies despite the clear externalization of cost. Almost everyone has turned a blind eye.

At the height of the 2015 fires, both Singapore and Malaysia offered some assistance in the form of funds, aircraft, and expertise. But this was an ad hoc measure, considering the seriousness of the 2015 fire season. There was no institutionalized, long-term offer of assistance to help Indonesia tackle the fundamental source of the problem. And none was created in the aftermath of the 2015 fire season, after the firefighters and soldiers went home and things went "back to normal."

Indonesia did try to take action after the 2015 haze season. President Joko Widodo declared a moratorium on converting peatland within existing concessions and banned any new permits on palm oil plantations. He also extended the moratorium on converting primary forest and peatlands, which had been implemented by his predecessor, President Susilo Bambang Yudhoyono, in 2011.

It has yet to be seen whether these actions are enough to solve the problem. The year 2016 was largely haze-free; although six provinces in Indonesia declared a state of emergency due to pollution, Jakarta recorded 60 percent fewer hotspots in 2016 than in the previous year.[4] They were helped by a wetter-than-normal rainy season.

The other question is whether Indonesia can actually implement the proposed actions. There were fewer hotspots in fire-prone areas in 2017, which was credited to greater monitoring and quick action. However, fires also started in places not known for fires, such as the province of Aceh. Thus Indonesia is still struggling with implementing these policies across the country.[5] As one professor noted late in 2017, "Although 2015 was exceptional, every year now we're seeing fires. This is the new normal."[6]

The Indonesian government has also backed the creation of the Fire Free Alliance, a coalition of environmental groups and major plantation companies, such as APRIL and Wilmar, which tries to engage with communities to change agricultural practices. However, this alliance will likely run into the same problems as its palm oil–focused counterpart, the Roundtable on Sustainable Palm Oil, which includes environmental groups and major global companies yet has failed to solve the issue of unsustainable growth demands of the palm oil sector.

If the haze crisis is going be solved, then Indonesia is going to have to take the lead. Even if ASEAN countries provide some support, Indonesia is going to have to exert its authority as a sovereign state and, in the long-term interests of its people, protect its forests on the island of Kalimantan and create a more sustainable agriculture sector.

Indonesia's democratic system (which, we must remember, is still extremely young) will not quickly correct this issue through the electoral process. The ones most directly affected by the unsustainable business practices of industrial and plantation agriculture are poor smallholder farmers living in remote areas days from Jakarta. They are the ones being forced off their land by large agribusiness firms, slotted into a system that drives their prices down while not providing them with much in the way of security. They are also living at the very source of the haze.

The farmers have little political power. They are poor and poorly educated, and live far from the economic, political, and cultural centers on the island of Java. Their efforts do not go anywhere near as far as the efforts of the more moneyed plantation owners. This view is reflected in their level of political engagement; former journalist Michael Vatikiotis said that he "consistently found [Indonesians] to be profoundly disinterested in some of the basic elements of a functioning democracy, such as who represents them in the national parliament. . . . Not one of those I met during the 2004, 2009, and 2014 campaigns cared about their local member of the legislature, because it was assumed these politicians were all selected and then elected on the basis of money and patronage, and . . . their votes were bought and sold."[7]

The latter point is important. There is nothing inherent in Indonesian culture that makes it unsuited for democracy per se. As an Asia Foundation survey in 2014 noted, "While Indonesians are clearly keen on the idea of electoral democracy, they remain extremely critical of the main players: political parties and officials. This is due in part to the fact that most parties seem disinterested in making meaningful connections with their constituents. But of far greater significance is the rising number of corruption cases involving public officials and senior party representatives."[8]

The failure of Indonesia's electoral system to choose politicians who truly reflect the views of the people means that many ordinary Indonesians have given up on the process. Ironically, the perception of corruption and control by big business led to voter apathy, which in turn made it easier for big businesses and moneyed interests to control the process.

All the businesses and governments involved at different links of the value chain are benefiting from a business model that externalizes cost onto someone else or the commons. Southeast Asian plantations and the companies that buy their products are pushing costs onto ordinary Southeast Asians, poor farmers, and the global biosphere. Arguably, governments in the region want to externalize cost as well, in pursuing a solution to the haze crisis while getting someone else to pay for it.

However, this is not just a story of corporate greed, neglect, and consumer ignorance. It is also a story of rural underdevelopment and policy failure.

There are few obvious economic opportunities in the nonurban areas on the island of Borneo. The major industries focus on primary resource extraction: plantations, lumber, coals, metals, and oil. This has inflated the statistics in Northern and Eastern Kalimantan: as these are oil-producing provinces with small populations, they have high average incomes. By contrast, the provinces of South Kalimantan and Central Kalimantan are poorer than the national average. These regions have average incomes of US$3,102 and US$2,825 respectively, compared to US$3,574 for Indonesia as a whole.

Plantation farming—or working for the plantations—may be hugely damaging to the environment, but it is also one of the few economic options in the region. For poor laborers in Kalimantan and even those from some of the other islands, there are few options apart from working on plantations and cash crops. The cycle is self-reinforcing. By specializing in cash crops, plantations are able to drive costs down and sell at a cheaper price. They outcompete their small neighbors and expand further, increasing their external impacts.

Other forms of farming are not viable in this kind of environment. The presence of global mega-agribusiness forces smaller farmers to "go big" themselves (often putting themselves into unsustainable levels of debt and insecurity to do so), have their land bought out from under them, or be turned into suppliers for the big players.

Even corruption is a by-product of rural underdevelopment. It is well known that government officials are poorly paid, working in dead-end jobs. Their ministries are not given the resources they need to do their jobs. Local officials in this situation could easily turn to petty corruption just to survive. After all, their superiors in Jakarta are not willing to pay them a decent wage, and the government seems unable to ensure that officials on the ground actually do their jobs. Without much job satisfaction or a belief that their career means something, officials can find "looking the other way" to be a more financially rewarding option.

• • •

A strong Indonesia should first take a tough stand on all matters with regard to illegal encroachment of the forest, enforce the no-burning regulations that are in place, and start to internalize the external costs of plantation farming. This is of course easier said than done, but is a basic expectation of good governance of resource-rich nations. The core argument of this book is that large countries can no longer turn a blind eye and that there are no shortcuts or excuses: their very survival depends on getting this right. It must be noted that since the 2015 haze that drew great attention, the Indonesian government has begun to act on the first two issues.

Jakarta can tax the products of plantations before they leave the country. This would ensure that palm oil, wood pulp, and other environmentally damaging products are priced accurately before they are sold to suppliers. This would also act as a new source of government revenue for Jakarta, which can be cycled into improving monitoring and reforestation efforts on the island of Borneo. But the revenues need to be captured solely for this purpose—a Pigovian tax meant to resolve the externality. As the world's largest producer of palm oil, Indonesia does have enough leverage to be able to do this and even force the issue among other palm oil–producing nations.

Indonesia can also implement regulations that snap into place when Jakarta declares a national haze crisis. This could involve regulations that target slash-and-burn agriculture, deforestation, and plantation farming. When a crisis is declared, there could be greater enforcement of forest conservation measures, funded by levies that go into immediate effect on farms and plantations to help counteract the crisis.

Some of these measures would lead to greater resources for forestry and environmental protection ministries, which should be allocated effectively. One project that could be pursued by an empowered ministry is a well-resourced "inventory" of the full forest, to know the full extent of what needs to be protected and what has already been lost.

Finally, Indonesia can mandate that commodity traders disclose the details of their businesses and transactions, as well as detail where goods were procured. This can help determine the "inverse" of value creation along the supply chain: At what points are costs externalized to a third party? The Indonesian government can then stage economic interventions at these points to reconcile the difference between private and external cost.

Although Indonesia will have to do most of the work on its own, there are things ASEAN can do to help contribute to Jakarta's efforts.

ASEAN can set up a natural resource fund, to be provided by member states and administered by ASEAN. This fund can make the necessary investments in infrastructure and assist companies and smallholders in order to build a more sustainable agricultural and primary resource sector across the ASEAN region.

ASEAN can also set up a natural resources court to adjudicate disputes over common resources, including, but not limited to, the Borneo rainforest. The court could help adjudicate transnational disputes between different companies, or between governments and firms based in a foreign country. Singapore, given its reputation as a financial and trade center and for its rule of law, would be an excellent location for such an institution.

These regulations are only part of the solution, however. All of these place important sanctions and punishments on plantations and agriculture companies that are harming the environment of Borneo. The long-term goal of the Indonesian government should be to start to reduce the plantation industry in Kalimantan. But merely punishing plantation owners without ensuring that alternatives are available will guarantee that much of the punishment will fall onto poor farmers in Borneo, worsening the rural underdevelopment on the island.

An imbalanced solution risks creating blowback. Poor farmers may understand all the environmental repercussions of plantation farming, slash-and-burn agriculture, and the constant haze, but they will still pick those if the alternative is continued underdevelopment and deprivation. The government needs to invest heavily in a more sustainable agricultural sector that can provide farmers with livelihoods and a steady income to sustain themselves.

Perhaps it is best to start with what we would like the island of Borneo to look like, and work backward from there. In this vision for Borneo, the country has an economy based not on industrial agriculture but on smallholder farmers growing high-value food crops (to attain a decent livelihood and to be self-sufficient in the staples), which does not widen the threat to the remaining forest and even aids in the regeneration of degraded land. These small farmers are able to make a decent living from their work, grow enough food to provide food security to their communities, and have enough economic opportunity to encourage people to stay. There are limits on land expansion, with incentives for farmers to avoid the use of excessive chemical fertilizers and other inputs;

preserve, if not regenerate, the forest; and adopt practices that naturally restore soil quality. Finally, the island's resources are managed in a manner that preserves them for future generations.

What is currently preventing this vision from coming about? And what steps can be taken to make this more sustainable agricultural sector a reality?

The first step is land reform, which should ensure that poor farmers have their own plots of land, with firm protections against expropriation. Attempts to intimidate or coerce people off their land will be cracked down on, ensuring that farmers are able to live and work off their land in peace.

The next step must address one of the fundamental impediments to the achievement of our vision for Borneo: that the infrastructure that supports a more sustainable agricultural sector is just not present in rural Indonesia. We normally think of infrastructure as big construction and utilities projects: roads, plumbing, power lines, ports and airports, and (increasingly) internet access. However, we need to think more broadly about what we mean by infrastructure. Individual businesses are often themselves dependent on numerous foundational services provided by other businesses. A small family farm relies on other businesses to have access to inputs, to transport and store produce, to deliver produce to markets, to have access to finance, to arbitrate disputes, to handle payments, and to provide expertise, among countless other services.

In more developed economies, these are provided by the private sector, with (one hopes) enough competition to ensure that costs are low. But in less developed economies, the incentives are not in place to encourage the private creation of these services through the free market. It becomes a chicken-and-egg problem. Without enough local economic activity, other entrepreneurs will not invest in supporting services. But without these supporting services, local economic activity is not able to grow. The whole area remains underdeveloped.

This ends up helping large companies, which are often the only entities with the capital and resources to develop these services themselves. A large plantation has the resources to develop its own customized delivery and logistics systems (or to pay a premium for a third party to provide them). Smaller businesses, unsurprisingly, do not have these advantages. But if only large companies can create these supporting services, the resulting economic model is centered around large businesses.

It also leads to monopolies, enabling large companies to dominate smaller entrepreneurs.

This has been endemic in the agricultural sector, where large companies provide many of the supporting services for small farms. Large companies provide the inputs, handle the transportation, store the produce, and handle the marketing and retail side. The small farm is reliant on the large company for its business operations, and therefore has little actual power.

Neither outcome—rural underdevelopment, or an agricultural sector dominated by large business—is what we would want for Borneo. But if the private market is not going to invest in these services, then the government will need to provide them.

This entails state investment in cold chain networks, proper systems of logistics, transportation companies, agricultural banks, and other important supporting services, including education and health care. As the private market will not invest in these areas of its own accord, the government would need either to provide significant subsidies to encourage the creation of these businesses or to develop them itself as state-owned enterprises and government institutions. The mandate of these organizations is not to make a profit but to encourage the development of small family-run farms growing high-value food crops and, even more important, staples to build self-sufficiency.

We could imagine a public-backed corporation—the Kalimantan Agricultural Development Corporation or something to that effect—that provides these services on an affordable basis with a mandate of encouraging the growth of smallholder farming in Borneo. It can invest in cold chains, delivery systems, and harvesting equipment to ensure that farmers can rely on them. It could even act as a buyer and seller of last resort, providing price support to account for vagaries in world prices or poor harvests. Eventually (if the corporation becomes successful), it can be weaned off government support to become a quasi-public statutory body. Profits can be distributed to the population of Kalimantan, much as how other primary resource extractors distribute their incomes among a population. One can imagine a Chinese model where a strong state can encourage or even incentivize large private sector companies to invest in the region and develop it, much like China's western expansion, whereby Beijing promoted the development of poor western provinces.

The government could create other public institutions. A public agricultural university could act as a source of expertise and research for smallholder farmers. A state-backed contract arbitration center could ensure that disputes between farmers, suppliers, distributors, and other organizations are handled fairly and expeditiously. And a public statutory body could monitor the quality of Indonesian crops and help market them abroad.

The government might also need to intervene to stabilize this developing agricultural sector. Agriculture is a notoriously difficult market to predict as a smallholder farmer. Commodity and input prices change regularly, so farmers have little ability to predict revenue. Poor farming conditions can wipe out a crop, removing the farmer's only source of income for the year. But a bumper harvest can be just as damaging, as the oversupply causes prices to collapse.

The government could provide a combination of price support and insurance; it could step in during a bad harvest, paying out when a farmer's crop is devastated due to poor weather or pests. And it could provide price support at points when prices are low, helping farmers through difficult periods of low revenue.

Orthodox economists will complain that these measures would be propping up inefficient agricultural practices, keeping businesses and farms alive without letting them wither in the free market. And there is no question that governments should be wary of wasting money; it can be difficult to withdraw support from businesses and sectors once circumstances change (as shown by the US's continued support for corn, despite its distorting effects on the American agricultural sector and the American diet).

But this assumes that the government's only goal is to have the most "efficient" economy possible. Remember that these orthodox economists understand efficiency and productivity without considering the massive externalities many of these so-called efficient businesses place on third parties. The goal is to create not an efficient economy but a fulfilling and sustainable one that provides the basic rights of life and a path to moderate prosperity, while still conserving resources.

Regional institutions, such as the Asian Development Bank or the Asian Infrastructure Investment Bank, can also contribute to this support, by helping provide some of the capital and financing for these investments in infrastructure. In addition, some of the state-backed institutions would not need to be supported by Indonesia, but instead by ASEAN (which might lead this smallholder-driven agricultural sector also to be integrated with the other growing economies of Southeast Asia). The regional organization can also tailor its regulations and tax regimes to treat small farms and their produce more positively than the produce of large agribusinesses.

We should remember that the final goal of this investment is not to create an industrial agricultural sector like that in the US but rather to create an economy that can sustain a large rural population that has no choice but to live off the land. The state has to intervene to create more sustainable outcomes.

• • •

The haze crisis will only be solved in the long term if the government offers a quid pro quo. The state will provide universal access to basic needs and support toward alternate paths to prosperity, including subsidies and investments in supporting services. In exchange, the government will implement very strict controls on environmental protection, resource management, labor rights, land tenure, and sustainability. In other words: the government says, work within the rules and parameters we set down, in exchange for help toward a more moderate prosperity and a better economic model. Enforcement of the rule of law is critical to the success of this only viable approach, and for that a strong state is the only option.

The fundamental causes of the haze crisis are somewhat specific to Indonesia, but there are similar examples of rural underdevelopment, industrial-scale agriculture, and environmental degradation throughout the developing world. India has issues with tea plantations; the global drive to keep tea prices low in the West has led to some of the worst instances of what the Western media term modern-day slavery. Coffee and cocoa farmers in Africa are also forced to accept low prices for their cash-crop produce. Much of the deforestation in the Amazon rainforest is due to the expansion of soybean farming and cattle ranching (which also leads to slash-and-burn agriculture).

But a stronger state government that both enforces punishment and provides needed investment can shift these rural areas away from hugely damaging industries. By deploying economic regulations, subsidies, and state-backed institutions, governments can suppress environmentally damaging activities while laying down a path toward a rural economic model that is both sustainable and economically vibrant. Only a commitment to a free-market economic ideology prevents this greater investment in a sustainable rural economy.

But rural areas are only half the problem. If rural areas are underdeveloped, one can argue that urban areas are *overdeveloped*. Cities are becoming too big for their own good. Chapter 10 will explore this idea further by looking at some of the tropics' hot, overcrowded, and unsustainable megacities.

THE TROPICAL CITY
IS NO PARADISE

Jakarta, Indonesia's capital city, routinely wins the dubious honor of having the worst traffic in the world. Jakarta's policymakers keep trying to combat the city's daily, hours-long congestion, to little effect. In 1992, when Jakarta had only half its current population and one tenth the current number of vehicles,[1] the city introduced carpool lanes on some important thoroughfares. Commonly known as the "3-in-1 policy,"[2] it required cars to have at least three passengers.

Jakartans subsequently built an entire economy centered on circumventing the intent of the policy. For example, men, women, and even children would hire themselves out as professional hitchhikers, known as "jockeys," to serve as an extra body so that cars could travel in the carpool lanes. (Mothers with babies were in especially high demand, as drivers could thus get two extra passengers for the price of one.)

Some of these practices broke the law, but other issues made these business models unacceptable. Schoolchildren guided traffic instead of going to school. Female jockeys were sexually harassed. Newborns and babies were sedated so that drivers wouldn't have to deal with crying infants. To halt these sometimes hazardous practices, the Jakarta government finally ended the 3-in-1 policy in mid-2016. Traffic immediately rose on the former carpool lanes.

Only a few months after the repeal of the 3-in-1 policy, the new "odd-even license day policy" was introduced.[3] Again, this failed as a corrective to Jakarta's traffic problems. Jakartans acquired multiple fake license plates or just ignored the new law. Richer Jakartans simply bought a second car with a different license plate. (To be fair, Jakarta's government never declared that the odd-even policy would be the ultimate solution to traffic issues or that it was only a temporary instrument. True success is planned to come in 2019 with the implementation of an electronic road pricing system, which will implement a flexible road pricing program as a replacement for some traffic measures.)

Traffic is not the only negative side-effect of the massive increase in car ownership. Another is the explosion in parking spaces and garages in Jakarta, preventing the land from being used for more socially beneficial purposes, such as housing.

• • •

Indonesia's capital is not the only city with severe traffic problems. As of June 2017, Mexico City, Bangkok, and Jakarta led the TomTom Traffic Index, which measures congestion. All the most congested cites are in the tropics, whose residents spend roughly 400–500 hours per year in traffic.[4] And new cities are following in their wake. The *South China Morning Post* reported that Ho Chi Minh City's severe growth of traffic congestion and air pollution threatens to turn it into the next Manila or Jakarta.[5] And one estimate for the city of Bangalore stated that each year, over ten million people waste six hundred million man-hours due to traffic congestion.[6]

Furthermore, hundreds of thousands of people die each year on the roads of these tropical cities. According to the World Health Organization, many of these deaths are easily preventable. There is a lack of enforcement of simple government policies and requirements, such as mandatory seat belts and motorcycle helmets.[7] As Anucha Setthasathian, the secretary-general of Thailand's National Institute of Emergency Medicine, explained, more than one out of five emergency patients in Thailand die on their way to the hospital due to delays from traffic jams and uncooperative motorists.[8]

Finally, there are deaths caused by air pollution—not just from cars but also from surrounding industries and, in the case of cities such as Delhi, from a complex web of causes, including the burning of agricultural waste in the surrounding rural hinterland. In 2016, the World Health Organization estimated that air pollution causes almost 6.5 million premature deaths each year.[9] A 2017 study by the Lancet Commission on Pollution and Health found that India and China topped the list for premature deaths from pollution in 2015, at 2.5 million and 1.8 million respectively.[10] India's Supreme Court itself estimated that pollution in New Delhi kills three thousand people every year.[11]

• • •

Cities across East and Southeast Asia have grown tremendously as more people move from the countryside (where there are few economic opportunities as a result of economic policies of neglect) to the city (where there are meant to be many more economic opportunities but dire living conditions). These cities have been unable to expand to accommodate this huge inflow of migrants, yet policymakers allow them to stream in.

The growth of large cities has often been seen as the quickest means of spurring economic development. The theory goes that urbanization brings underutilized people out of the countryside to the city, where they can be put to more productive uses.

Proponents point to the developed world as evidence of this model's success: rich countries saw growth as people moved from the countryside to the city. But this urbanization occurred over a relatively longer time frame: decades, if not centuries. Rich countries also had the resources to manage the growth of these cities, even as they expanded to enormous sizes.

Poor countries do not have that luxury. The timescale for growth in the developing world is years, not decades. Rich countries would struggle to manage growth at that scale; poor countries have no chance. Nor do poor cities have the infrastructure to provide an adequate standard of living for their exploding populations or to deal efficiently with their externalities (e.g., solid waste, sewage, air pollution, traffic congestion, and so on).

Yet the idea that urbanization must be slowed down, let alone reversed, is not seen in the economic literature. Nevertheless, it is an option that must be seriously considered with the coming global crisis of sustainable development.

This chapter will illustrate the consequences of weak state governance in relation to rapidly growing cities. Policymakers continue to believe that urbanization is an inevitable benefit for their economies, in spite of all the evidence that the developing world's megacities have serious issues that require drastic measures. Why make something bigger when it is already so bad?

It will also explore possible solutions through greater state management of the economy. City and state governments of developing economies must act now; a hands-off approach will only make some groups better off at the expense of poorer groups and will result in irreversible trends and very expensive solutions. More active governance would enable every resident—in both growing urban economies and in the rural communities "left behind"—to have access to basic needs.

A radical concept for developing countries should be considered: deurbanization, or encouraging people to move out of cramped major urban centers. This would require government investment in the countryside and secondary cities to encourage a more sustainable population distribution across the entire country. I will argue that this would also help reshape the economies of these countries and be part of how we reshape capitalism in the twenty-first century.

• • •

In 2009, for the first time in human history, the number of people living in urban areas (3.42 billion) surpassed the number living in rural areas (3.41 billion), according to the UN Department of Economic and Social Affairs.[12] Many forecasters project that this trend will continue throughout the twenty-first century. As of 2016, twelve of the world's fifteen biggest urban areas were Asian.[13] In most cases, this news was greeted as inevitable and even as a sign of human prosperity or the path to it. But we need to be bold enough to challenge this unquestioned assumption.

Urban life has been made to appear to be what people want: excitement, bright lights, and modernity. What was justified on an economic basis has been transformed into some inherent part of human desire, combining arguments around growth, wealth, modernity, and innovation. As the narrative goes, cities are the center of modern life. They attract multinational corporations, as cities are big markets for their products. In turn, cities attract the young and talented. These stories are spread by the media, which share success stories of those who made it to the top.

Let us look at why and how urbanization appeals to two different groups: ordinary individuals and government.

Citizens. Modern literature often discusses how cities pull people to them (e.g., offering a reliable income, safety from the natural environment, luxuries, convenience, and even night life), and how people are pushed from rural areas (e.g., droughts, lack of jobs, economic decay, boredom, backbreaking work). Combined, these forces encourage migration from rural to urban areas.

In this narrative, many villagers are cited as saying they want to move to the city for a "higher quality of life." This is then accepted by many as the reason why urbanization is inevitable. What the narrative does not explore is why a higher quality of life is to be had in cities and not in the rural areas (leaving aside the more philosophical debate about what we mean by a higher quality of life). Most times, it boils down to one thing: lack of jobs. And why? Political neglect rooted in the false belief that urbanization is the mechanism for economic growth and development. An urban lifestyle is synonymous with a higher-paid, less physically demanding job (or often just any job at all) than what is available in rural communities. Urban communities can also sustain higher-quality public and social services, such as education and health care, as well as access to the comforts of modern life—again indicators of public policy neglect of rural areas. Communications networks in rural areas are also far less developed. The density of people in cites means that political and business leaders choose to invest in cities over more sparsely populated rural areas.

Cities are usually a country's economic hub, which in turn attracts a diverse domestic and international audience. This often makes cities the focal point of a country's cultural scene as well, as the place where most of a country's artists, musicians, and writers tend to live. Urban life is connected to success and the modern "meritocracy": as the famous song about New York City goes, "If I can make it there, I can make it anywhere."

Governments. For most countries, urban areas are engines of economic growth. They also host a country's political elites, naturally bringing greater attention to them.

Although estimates vary, cities cover between 1 and 3 percent of the Earth's surface.[14] However, they are now home to roughly 54 percent of all people and drive around 80 percent of the world's economy. They also contribute to our planet's pollution by the same share.[15] Empirical studies suggest that there is a significant correlation between the rate of urbanization and a country's per capita productivity.[16] However, this tells us nothing about the quality of life for urban residents, the long-term damaging effects on the environment, or the question of whether striving for the highest possible per capita output is the best goal for an economy in the first place. Claims that the best thing for economic productivity is to move people from less productive rural areas to more productive urban areas are not including these important external costs in their calculations.

Cities are of paramount importance to the economic and political elite. Local, regional, and central state governments generate substantial shares of their fiscal revenue from these urban areas, and thus rely heavily on their output. On the spending side, governments can take advantage of economies of scale when they provide public services, although these services are inevitably to address issues created by excessive urbanization, and rarely do so satisfactorily. Thus developing an urban area appears to be much easier than working through many small towns and villages.

• • •

Congestion, which I discussed in the opening of this chapter, and inadequate housing, which we will look at here, merely scratch the surface of how rampant urbanization could eventually lead to catastrophic and even irreversible consequences, from air pollution and common homelessness to untreated sewage, increasing urban temperature, and permanently submerged areas.

The rush to urbanize has pushed more and more people to live in very dense urban areas like Mumbai. India's largest metropolis, with a population of twenty-three million, is one of the world's most densely populated cities, behind only Dhaka in Bangladesh.

It can be difficult to grasp what the density really feels like. Demographia, the urban consulting firm, noted that "Dhaka's density is so great that the New York urban area, if as densely populated, would contain one-half billion (500,000,000) residents, more than the combined population of the United States, Canada, and Mexico. Paris would have 130,000,000 residents, approximately the same population as France and the United Kingdom combined."[17]

Overpopulation and overcrowding are two of the most prominent concerns for tropical cities. Landlords and property developers subdivide apartments into multiple tiny units, leading to new terms like "shoebox apartment," "coffin cubicle," and "cage home" to describe the ever-shrinking living space, even as rents keep increasing.

The city of Hong Kong, for example, has a long-standing and persistent problem with housing affordability. It has consistently been ranked one of the world's most expensive housing markets, with a "median multiple" of 18 between average home prices and average income. Hong Kong also does not have any minimum standards for living space, which puts downward pressure on home sizes. Property developers sell apartments little bigger than a parking space for millions of Hong Kong dollars, and landlords illegally split single apartments into multiple units. This problem is not unknown—every few months, dire images of "coffin homes" make the rounds on domestic and international media. Yet no action has been taken, as the state is riven with conflict and thus too weak to take action against vested interests.

Dense dwellings, air and noise pollution, contaminated water, poor infrastructure, untreated sewage, traffic congestion, slums, and homelessness are all immensely important problems to solve. But there are some other, less well known downsides of urbanization, especially in tropical regions.

Informal settlers are at much higher risk of harm from

- Land insecurity. The OECD defines informal settlements as "1. areas where groups of housing units have been constructed on land that the occupants have no legal claim to, or occupy illegally; 2. unplanned settlements and areas where housing is not in compliance with current planning and building regulations (unauthorized housing)"[18]

  Consequently, "squatters" are by their nature perpetually vulnerable to eviction. Governments must come up with solutions to satisfy the accommodation needs of informal settlers living day-to-day without knowing whether they will have a home the next day.

  For example, slum dwellers in Lagos—Africa's largest and fastest-growing city—have been pushed from the fringes by a government campaign to "clean up the slums," which just so happen to sit on prime waterfront territory. Slum dwellers have since been pushed to live in canoes along the Lagos waterfront, providing even less security from eviction.

- Damage from natural disasters. Informal settlements are usually at the mercy of natural forces, due to their geographical location. For example, the slums in Rio de Janeiro and Bogotá are constantly at risk from landslides and rainstorms, which can kill hundreds and displace tens of thousands.[19] Living by the water's edge, settlers in Manila, Jakarta, Yangon, and Lagos[20] are all threatened by rising sea levels, rainstorms, and floods. In some regions, earthquakes can level settlements to the ground. Unfortunately, governments largely abandon slums to their own devices.

- Man-made disasters. In densely populated slums, fires are fast spreading and disastrous, such as the blazes that Mumbai's Dharavi slum experienced regularly. Fire departments can find it difficult to reach the source of the blaze, due to the packed nature of urban slums. Other man-made disasters are related to pollution, such as waste contamination of water sources and spread of diseases.

Slums also serve as a cauldron for criminal activities, such as gang violence, drug consumption, and prostitution. Law enforcement in these areas is usually underfunded and thus insufficient. Inadequate public policing and poor city planning and governance all contribute to the poor circumstances for slum inhabitants.

Sadly, for many men, women, and children seeking prosperity in any fast-growing tropical city, their dreams often end upon arrival. Homelessness or a life in the slums may be inescapable. Soon, there will be more than one billion informal settlers, as the growth of urban poverty outstrips the rural rate.[21] The United Nations has estimated that if no action is taken to control the inflow of people, there might be as many as three billion people living in slums by 2050.[22]

Yet another downside of the city, especially in tropical areas, concerns the "heat island" effect. A heat island is an urban area that is substantially warmer (by 3°C–7°C during the day, and at night even reaching double-digit differences)[23] than its surrounding rural areas due to human activities and man-made changes to the environment. Originally, natural fauna or water surfaces would reflect incoming natural energy. But artificial materials, such as asphalt or concrete, trap that heat. Ambient temperatures are also driven up by the activity of millions of people.

As temperatures rise, so does the demand for air conditioning. These units in turn give off their own ambient heat, which calls for yet more air conditioning. This vicious cycle overstresses the power system, leading to frequent electrical blackouts.

Tropical cities with large populations are most likely to be the most severely affected by the heat island effect, as shown by a recent study of nearly seventeen hundred cities globally.[24] The urban heat island effect has severe ramifications for nature, wildlife, and people, altering water cycles and water availability, lowering the resilience of environmental systems, and causing health problems in both animals and people. It is thus little wonder that incidences of heat stroke are surging dramatically; India's National Crime Records Bureau found that there was a 61 percent increase in the number of deaths from heat stroke between 2004 and 2013 compared to the previous decade.[25]

This unbearable heat is accompanied by the high humidity of the tropics. Simultaneous high temperatures and humidity will slowly make several cities impossible for humans to live in.[26]

•••

Undoubtedly, cities are vital economic engines for any country. But, from Rio to Lagos, the need to optimize growth and lift millions out of poverty should be on the top of the agenda. Ignoring the downside is easier for officials in the city than seriously thinking about how the city and the hinterland are interconnected, and about the unpopular decisions that would need to be taken to undo the damage of past policies. Policymakers in the tropics must develop the ability to extract less from the hinterland and create a functioning system to correctly price the services of rural areas, such as food production and supplying drinking water, so that these areas can thrive and that cities do not become even larger while being parasitic. Bold leadership will be needed, as these actions will threaten the status quo and those that thrive on it. Only a strong state can withstand such interests and implement policies in the interest of the majority.

As mentioned before, in the West, people moved to cities due to their greater economic opportunities. Urbanization took place incrementally over the course of two hundred years, and on a much smaller scale due to lower populations. Governments and people had time to adjust: legal systems, law enforcement, infrastructure, and the administrative structure grew at rates adequate to the requirements. The growth also took place at a time when the West was the growth engine of the world and had access to resources worldwide due to colonization.

The situation in cities like Jakarta, Manila, Rio, and Lagos is more chaotic than the West had ever seen. Even by the second half of the twentieth century, these urban areas had reached a scale unmatched in Europe or North America (with the possible exception of New York City). Urbanization in the developing world seems to focus on a single city—Lagos, Manila, Jakarta, and so on. These areas experience intense urbanization within a matter of decades, and therefore do not possess the capacity to serve their growing populations, let alone the financial resources (due to inefficient tax systems and collection).

Where will the resources come from to host more than ten million people? City boundaries are pushed ever further to seize more surrounding underdeveloped land without adequate infrastructure or basic services. Cities cannot keep pace with their own growth, and so have a lower quality of life for the majority of their inhabitants.[27]

Megacities also have widespread effects on rural communities: "brain drain"; resource exploitation; soil erosion; power imbalances; economic instability; loss of culture, knowledge, and traditions; and social tensions. First of all, no city, tropical or not, is self-sustaining. From the raw material to build skyscrapers to the energy needed to keep engines running to the coffee served in thousands of cafés, all are found in rural areas in the hinterland.

Second, by focusing on major urban centers, governments leave rural areas behind. Thus young people in rural areas seeking an education will abandon their hometowns in search of a better life. Yet once awarded with a degree, few return to live where they were brought up. The elderly, young children, the unskilled, and those too poor for education are left behind. This hollows out rural areas and results in the myth-creating narrative of cities as the centers of prosperity and modernity. As the Asian Development Bank explained, "This loss of human capital in the fields of medicine, science, engineering, management, and education can be a major obstacle to economic and social development."[28] Urbanization has a similar effect, albeit domestically. The best and brightest abandon rural areas for the city, leaving little talent in the villages and countryside, thus perpetuating the cycle of poverty and underdevelopment.

• • •

There is little time to waste. These urgent problems won't disappear into thin air, nor will any new technology provide the basic needs that are still not met for over a billion people and billions more who are at the margins. The governments of today's rapidly growing cities and countries in tropical regions need to drastically rethink and reinvent the future of their cities before the damage is beyond repair. The success of the minority affluent population in cities, who live in much better circumstances, should not be the template for planning the future, as tempting and seductive as that might be. After all, it has become clear that this high-consumption lifestyle is not possible for the majority.

The only institution with enough power, capability, and authority to resolve the issues of urbanization is the state. The next sections describe some ways a strong government can change tack.

Basic Needs in Urban Areas

The most urgent task will be to provide access to basic needs (food and safe drinking water, appropriate accommodation, sanitation, education, and health care) for all people within a country and to lift them out of poverty.

One central need is affordable, high-quality, resilient accommodation. The most straightforward way to provide this is with public housing: government-constructed homes designed for low-income residents. Whether rented at subsidized rates to low-income people, made accessible at reduced prices with extremely generous public housing finance programs, or just provided to the very poor free of charge, public housing ensures that everyone living in a city has a safe and secure place to live.

There is another benefit of public housing: it allows cities to guide urban planning toward a more sustainable path. Rather than encourage suburban sprawl, governments can use public housing to drive high-density development that is integrated with public transportation, uses the latest sustainable building techniques, and is surrounded by adequate public and green space.

Contrast the performance of Singapore to the efforts of New York. Singapore has managed to fit almost six million people on a tiny sliver of land without leading to a massive housing affordability crisis. This is mostly due to Singapore's world-class provision of public housing: the city has some of the highest rates of public housing occupancy in the world, approaching 80 percent.

Singapore has achieved this by putting the entire housing sector under public control. The government builds the vast majority of homes in Singapore, but it has also created an entire system of public housing finance. Singaporeans can pay off their mortgages (offered by the government) by withdrawing money from their pension accounts (managed by the government). The government then uses these resources to build new homes, continuing the creation of more affordable housing for Singaporeans. This control over housing also allows the Singaporean government to use housing as a mechanism to achieve other policy objectives, such as encouraging children to move near their parents, thus saving money on elder care, or mandating the creation of ethnically diverse housing estates to encourage tolerance.

By contrast, New York City continues to struggle with housing affordability. The current mayor of New York, Bill de Blasio, came into office with a promise to build cheap homes throughout the city. However, rather than using the power of the city government to build or fund homes directly, Mayor de Blasio has chosen to encourage developers to allot some of their units to be sold at "affordable" prices. These units are then allotted to individuals on the affordable housing waitlist—a list that is now two million people long. This strategy has had limited success: de Blasio's office recently celebrated the construction of seventy-eight thousand affordable flats over the span of three years, and only six thousand in 2016. In comparison, Hong Kong, which faces its own (admittedly more severe) housing crisis, has pledged to build 460,000 flats over ten years—only half of what the government believes is needed to fully resolve the crisis, which itself is believed to underestimate what is truly needed.

It is somewhat unfair to compare these two cities. Singapore is a city-state, and therefore has much more authority to control its own affairs than New York City, which must comply with the laws and politics of both New York State and the wider US. Mayor de Blasio probably does not have the authority or political foundation to launch a massive public program to build affordable homes. Singapore also can control its inward migration, which New York City certainly cannot. But this reveals the necessary role of the state government in using its strength to help cities deliver basic needs and control rural-urban migration. We cannot expect cities such as Bangkok or Manila to have the resources or the authority to solve these problems alone; the state will have to work with them. But given the importance of these megacities, it is incumbent on the state to act and to do so even draconically if needed. After all, they will have the support of the majority.

Reducing External Costs: Traffic

Cities should strive to internalize all the costs of urban living, including those placed on rural residents as well as those placed on urban residents. One straightforward way to reduce social costs would be to implement controls on car ownership, which places numerous external costs on a city's population through congestion, pollution, and damage to public health. The best way to reduce these costs is not by investing in electric cars but rather to directly work to limit car ownership and expand high-quality public transportation.

There are numerous ways a city government could reduce the number of cars on the road. The government could increase taxes on both cars and petroleum, increasing the private costs of owning a car. It could also limit the number of licenses granted each year or add surcharges on parking garages and spaces. Or it could revise laws to discourage driving and drastically reduce the number of parking spaces.

Governments could also implement strict regulations not just on car ownership but on car usage. Although carpool lanes and alternate-use days based on license plates are both possible mechanisms to control car usage, such lighter mechanisms, as shown by Jakarta's experience (discussed previously in this chapter), are open to abuse. A stronger government mechanism would be to implement a system of road pricing to force drivers to pay for their external costs. More drastically, cities can designate areas as no-car zones (apart from public transportation and emergency vehicles).

City governments must do more than close off the overuse of cars, however; they must also ensure that urban residents still preserve some level of convenient and speedy mobility. In essence, this would be a clean, efficient, fast, and low-cost system of public transportation.

Much of the discussion about urban mobility tends to focus on the new, flashy, and expensive. Expensive subways are seen as a hallmark of urban modernity; thus many developing cities try to drill expensive tunnels. These systems are often designed with politics in mind, rather than actual need. Worse, some experts are talking about replacing private car ownership with fleets of cars for hire that can move people from one place to another. One expects these fleets will be privately owned, limiting government regulation and control over transportation.

But a good system of public transportation does not need to be expensive or flashy. Public buses, electric trams and streetcars, and ferries can cover a larger area more cheaply than subways, especially when they can operate efficiently once other measures are in place to reduce private car usage or ownership. Cheaper, less flashy, but just as effective alternatives can be found for the cars-for-hire system beloved by tech people: electric tuk-tuks and bicycle cabs are already cost-competitive with gasoline-powered versions. Governments can mandate that all tuk-tuks switch to electric versions and come under public control and management, in exchange for government assistance in bolstering their services.

Reducing External Costs: Heat

The problem of heat may be the most pressing and difficult issue to solve, especially in the tropical city. Governments will somehow need to curb the use of air conditioning with all of its ill effects and costs, while also finding ways to help people cope with the heat. Other critical steps would be to reduce the percentage of the city that is paved or covered in concrete, and to vastly expand green cover.

One initial step would be an aggressive move to replace old air conditioners with newer, more efficient, and less carbon-emitting versions. This can limit the environmental impact and external cost of air conditioners already in use. Governments can also mandate how air conditioners are used in major commercial and public buildings, such as office towers, shopping malls, and public facilities.

But this would only be the first step. Governments will need to start curbing, or even preventing, the installation of new air conditioners. The government could impose a tax on new air-conditioning units, using the revenue generated to encourage more energy-efficient methods of cooling. The government could encourage the use of less heat-generating cooling systems, such as the "swamp cooler," which uses water evaporation to cool rooms. It could mandate renewable energy facilities as the mainstay energy provider for air conditioners to combat carbon emissions, but this does not fully address the heating effect.

Cities should also embrace the building techniques of centuries past. Tropical communities had developed homes that could handle the heat long before the advent of air conditioning. But the ease of air conditioning has made architects lazy: its far easier to throw up inefficient, glass-covered, boxy homes and skyscrapers that are cooled by air conditioning than to take advantage of natural thermal dynamics.

Not every traditional technique can be modernized, to be sure. But few architects have tried, largely because they have relied on air conditioning. But a government mandate to limit, or even prevent, the use of air conditioning would force architects and engineers to come up with new cooling strategies.

Urban Design and Planning

Anyone who has been to one of the higher floors of Kuala Lumpur's magnificent Petronas towers will immediately see the topography of the surrounding Klang Valley. The view makes clear that the urban yet leafy sprawl of Kuala Lumpur is bounded by lush vegetation, forests, and ancient limestone hills—a hub of biodiversity. Elephants, tapirs, and tigers can be found a two-hour drive from the twin towers.

Ideally situated at the confluence of two muddy rivers (from which the city gets its name) and surrounded by tropical mountain ranges, Kuala Lumpur is ideally situated to become the world's first botanical city. Its population is expected to reach ten million by 2020 and needs a new model to overcome the unsustainable path of most megacities in the ASEAN region. This could open a whole new world of urban design and creativity, one not based on ideas from the West or other large modern cities unsuited to the tropics. It could encourage profound innovation and entrepreneurship to develop the talent, science, technology, and management capabilities required to make this transformation successful, thereby giving birth to a host of new business and job opportunities.

This vision would go well beyond preserving and restoring pockets of rainforests around the city, but would also bring the country's abundant and valuable nature into the city itself. This would include growing nature corridors that connect the urban center with suburbs and surrounding forests, embedding the rainforest into urban life. It would also require restoring Kuala Lumpur's polluted waterways. This will no doubt create a cooler microclimate to overcome the rising urban heat island effect.

Kuala Lumpur's potential to become the world's first botanical city is merely one example of how urban planning must try not just to lower the external costs of urban life but also to drive a new sustainable urban lifestyle better suited to a twenty-first century version of moderate prosperity. State governments should strive to answer the following question: What do we want our cities to look like in a resource-constrained twenty-first century? Do we want a sprawling metropolis like today's Bangkok or Jakarta? Or something novel?

Rural Development and De-urbanization

The most transformative action states need to take is to develop a framework for a more sustainable division of a population between major cities, secondary towns, and rural areas. Governments need to blunt the flow of migration from rural areas, and channel the migration that remains across a wider area. This means decentralization and de-urbanization:

encouraging people to live in rural communities and secondary towns, rather than in the major metropolitan area.

China has something that approaches this in the hukou: the internal permit that allows a person access to a given city's public and social services. Although the hukou probably does place some controls on urban migration, many rural Chinese have ignored it and still moved to the city. However, when migrants live in an area without the hukou, they are denied access to basic social services, thus worsening their quality of life.

Instead, governments should seek to build better economic opportunities in both rural areas and secondary towns. Chapter 9 presented some ideas of what governments can do in rural areas, especially when it comes to developing higher-value agricultural companies and providing for food security without relying on industrial agriculture. But there are other areas governments can focus on as well.

One motivating factor can be the spread of provision of basic needs (electric power, clean water, proper sanitation, safe housing, and so on) across large rural areas. Building this infrastructure and these services will help create important economic opportunities in the countryside, encouraging people—especially the young and the skilled—to stay put.

States also can go beyond providing only the infrastructure for addressing basic needs: they can invest in many of the amenities and facilities that serve urban areas, such as higher education, advanced health care, financial systems, and public cultural facilities. These things may never "make money," but that will not be the point: their purpose will be to provide in rural areas the moderately prosperous lifestyle people currently associate with cities.

Governments should also focus on secondary cities and towns, developing them into their own economic and business clusters. This will give migrants more options (and relieve pressure on the major cities) if they still decide to move to a city.

It may be too late and too difficult for mature countries like the US or European states to make these changes. But the developing world, as it expands its state institutions in managing the economy, can start to place important governing and regulatory institutions throughout the whole country, rather than centralizing them in one city.

Dealing with this issue on the level of the state allows for a national system of resource management and distribution, rather than leaving individual areas to work on their own. Governments could develop tax incentives to encourage people to stay, work, and set up businesses in rural areas and secondary towns. If this is done on a national level, state governments can ensure that any shortfall in revenue is made up through a national redistribution of income (as opposed to a federal system, where lost tax income stays lost).

• • •

The rampant scale of urbanization requires a strong and quick government response to alleviate external costs on both the vast number of new urban migrants and the many people in rural areas who are left behind. Only the strong state has the authority to control and regulate unsustainable practices in the city while still providing paths to basic needs and moderate prosperity in both urban and rural areas.

None of these efforts necessarily have to work against the city. In fact, city governments may agree with several of the prescriptions here, especially concerning traffic alleviation, public housing, and expanding utilities. They may even support programs that encourage people to move elsewhere, in order to lower the pressure on their utilities, infrastructure, and housing markets. But, due to a lack of authority and resources, cities are unable to do these things themselves.

Solving the problems of the city requires a national solution. And the strong state is the only entity capable of establishing one.

CHINA

The Strong State?

I t was a bitterly cold February 2011 in the Chinese province of Hubei. I was running a leadership program where an international group of executives was looking at how to organize Chinese agricultural coopera- tives into a network of social enterprises, where farmers could leverage their collective strength throughout the supply chain, both upstream and downstream.

It was here that I got my first glimpse of the highly competent and dedicated professionals working as rural officials, dispatched by the Chi- nese government. In the township, the cooperative had arranged a meet- ing with the mayor to brief us on his plans and vision for the township. I was expecting someone older, perhaps looking like the stereotype of the stuffy party cadre. Instead, I found a man in his mid-thirties. He knew his stuff: he spent about thirty minutes briefing us, without notes, and pro- vided detail after detail on everything from transportation infrastructure and energy to increasing agricultural output and improving livelihoods.

Some of the international group, who had perhaps expected a Mao- era figure, were completely taken aback. They began to appreciate that there was a big change taking place in China, much of which had to do with the strong presence of the state, even in these remote areas, in sending highly qualified young professionals to help build the China of tomorrow.

This phenomenon was repeated elsewhere. More recently, in Au- gust 2017, I was in the small historic town of Tongguan. Working on a project related to promoting large-scale circular farming among rural pop- ulations, we had the privilege of meeting the town's (female) mayor and deputy mayor. Here again the officials were highly qualified—the deputy mayor had two degrees—and appeared to be workaholics dedicated to a mission: an attitude one sadly does not normally associate with officials in remote areas of the developing world.

Perhaps these people would have found their way into public service on their own. But there is no guarantee that they would have ended up where they could have done the most good—especially in an out-of-the-way township in rural China. Somehow the Chinese government had helped give these young, confident people the chance to better their communities.

• • •

This chapter will investigate perhaps the best example of the strong state in the developing world today: China. At the time of this writing, China has, perhaps for the first time since the revolution began, garnered some respect from the outside world for the ability of its government to act decisively and effectively for the public good. Oddly enough, this had to do with taking a lead in the fight against climate change.

Over the past few decades, China has successfully used government intervention, support, and protection in pursuit of a single social goal: poverty alleviation and, by extension, wider social well-being. In the space of just a few decades, China has gone from a backward, underdeveloped, and mismanaged economy to a global economic powerhouse. Although we should be careful about overstating its success, China's different path to development has led to a record of poverty alleviation unmatched in human history thus far—half a billion lives over the past several decades.

It's important to remember what people predicted China would look like by now. When China first began to open up, Western observers predicted that its opening and entry into the World Trade Organization would lead it, if not necessitate it, to become a Western-style liberal democracy. Eventually, China would remove its controls over the economy, becoming a fully liberalized, capitalist society. The rise of the middle class would have increased calls for a Western-style democracy, building pressure to a point where widespread change became inevitable, eventually toppling the Communist Party.

When China's eventual transformation into a Western-style democracy looked less likely, the predictions changed. Liberalization in China may not have been inevitable, but it was still portrayed as the best policy choice for the country if it wanted to continue its economic development. If China did not undertake these economic and political reforms—in other words, Westernize—then it would either go through an economic collapse or be doomed to perpetual stagnation. These prediction were always premised on the assumptions that the Chinese government is repressive and that the Chinese Communist Party is only interested in its own power.

Even now, China is told that it needs to liberalize if it is to be "innovative" (however that is defined). One wonders what prescriptions will be made ten years from now. China has neither collapsed nor stagnated. Even during periods of slowdown, it has enjoyed healthy economic growth that would be the envy of developed countries. Politically, the country also seems more stable than its Western democratic counterparts. Most Chinese are satisfied with the performance of the government and are very aware of the trade-offs for a country as large as theirs. Some of this political stability is due to the government's authoritarian measures against dissent, but many Chinese do sincerely believe that the Chinese Communist Party is, and has been, good for China. No Western pundit would dare file a story that suggested this.

China is a clear example of how state strength can be oriented toward the social good, even for a large society with a recent history of turmoil. But its current path will not be enough to ensure survival in a resource-constrained twenty-first century. The Chinese population, on the whole, wants to live a Western-style life, and that level of resource consumption is unsustainable for a nation with over a billion people. Beijing often wants to reinforce its rise and power by building large-scale projects that win plaudits in the international competition for face, yet are hugely disruptive to the environment and to resource stocks.

Yet awareness in China is growing both at the highest levels of government and among many segments of its population. As early as 2012, Chinese leaders were starting to talk more about environmental protection; then-president Hu Jintao devoted an entire section of his address to the 18th Party Congress to "ecological civilization," citing "unbalanced, uncoordinated and unsustainable development" as one of the country's top challenges. His successor, President Xi Jinping, took things several steps further in the 19th Party Congress, changing some core parts of China's official economic orthodoxy to include concepts aligned with sustainable governance. China's current success also gives it the room to define a new model of political and economic governance that is more oriented toward sustainability.

More important, China's program of state-driven development gives Beijing the tools to create the more sustainable economy that will be necessitated as constraints continue to kick in. This will not be true of countries that continue to pursue a more free-market, small-government model. To become strong states, these countries will need to increase their governing capacity (if not create entirely new tools of economic management). This will entail tough political battles against vested interests, which must be won even before the state actually does anything.

China, by contrast, can flip the switch immediately when needed. For example, China announced in October 2017 that it was going to strengthen its environmental tax. Instead of charging polluters a fee locally (which could vary among regions), Beijing would instead charge a national tax on polluting companies. Analysts expected that it would increase the burden on large state-owned chemical and energy companies by anywhere between 40 and 300 percent. This tax was implemented quickly, going into effect on January 1, 2018.[1]

China has also announced the creation of a new program to create a carbon-trading market, where companies are forced to buy and trade permits to pollute or release carbon emissions.[2] The program is admittedly only a start: the market does not yet include an actual cap on emissions.[3] Nor has Beijing pursued more direct methods to control carbon, such as a carbon tax, instead choosing a more market-based cap-and-trade system. But this is still a big step for what is now the world's largest carbon emitter, and certainly more than what can be expected for any major economy outside the European Union.

A comparison can be made with India. The central government is clearly aware of pressing environmental and resource issues, such as the state of India's rivers or the continued inability to provide adequate sanitation for hundreds of millions. However, this awareness has not been translated into proper political action. The central government is not just too weak to implement its action plans itself; it is too weak to corral the governments of its federal states to do the work on its behalf. It has not been able to build the critical competencies through the various institutions of the state to execute its objectives. China, as everyone is aware, is able to.

Thus, when India comes around to developing its own model of sustainable governance, which one would argue is well overdue, it is going to be starting from a much more basic starting point than Beijing will. China's problem is one of orienting its tools for state management of the economy toward more sustainable ends, and less about the creating institutions that can organize and discipline society. India, by contrast, will need to develop these tools from scratch and find ways to strengthen its institutions, which are inept despite the enormous talent in the country.

• • •

As noted earlier, China has used government intervention, support, and protection in pursuit of a larger social goal: poverty alleviation. For example, China has preserved state-owned enterprises, which ensures some level of control over the country's largest corporations as they grow in size and scale. The government has also acted to regulate economic activity. It has preserved its influence over the financial sector, which ensures that other important sectors receive the capital they need to grow. Thus, even though China moved away from a command-based economy toward one where prices were set on a more market basis, the state presence in the economy ensures that it still works to bolster economic development by supporting export-oriented manufacturing and other important sectors. To do all this, it has found a way to attract highly competent people into the government and into a system that demands discipline, sacrifice, and results. In short, there is a high level of competence in the state.

As Arthur Kroeber, an economist based in Beijing, has noted, supporting state-owned enterprises is not the same as creating a government-owned monopoly.[4] Major reforms of the state sector in the 1990s created multiple competing, yet still state-owned, enterprises. This wedded some of the benefits of private market competition (e.g., lower prices, better corporate efficiency) without necessarily giving up state control.

Some of these policies had been implemented in the other major East Asian economies. Japan in particular used (less severe) forms of government-influenced finance and industrial strategy to ensure that the economy developed along lines considered socially and economically optimal.

China has also invested directly into basic needs and social services. It has improved the provision of rural education and health care, ensuring near universal provision of these services across its massive population. By 2016, almost all Chinese villages had access to electricity, and over 90 percent had both centralized water supply and garbage treatment. Almost all townships had libraries, primary schools, and health care institutions.

China is often criticized—sometimes, but not always, justifiably—that its nondemocratic nature means that it is deaf to the concerns of its citizens. However, the anticorruption drive of the last three to four years shows that Beijing is cognizant of what the population thinks of it. The idea that Communist Party officials are profiting off their position has often threatened to overturn the party's legitimacy; thus Beijing has consistently made strong efforts to crack down on corruption in order to preserve its legitimacy. Other elements of President Xi's reform program, such as encouraging less polluting industry and opening up more space for individual private enterprise, can be seen as reactions to what the general population wants.

Even the One Child Policy can be seen in this light. China really did have a problem with overpopulation. And even if fertility was declining, it was not declining fast enough for China to avoid massive resource issues as these new people were being born. The One Child Policy was a drastic measure, but it may have been a necessary one at the time. The Chinese Communist Party estimates that its population would be 300–400 million people larger if not for the policy; independent estimates place the number somewhere between 150–200 million people (or, in other words, the entirety of Brazil or Pakistan).[5]

A revisionist look at the One Child Policy argues that, through its aggressive intervention, China has slowed population growth and thus weakened its economy. But this, again, shows a limited view of how population growth does (or does not) contribute to the economy. Yes, a growing population does lead to an increase in working-age people who would, in theory, power the economy. But it also means more people to feed, house, educate, treat, and employ. This would strain natural resources—already under pressure from a massive population. In fact, from a resource consumption standpoint, a declining population can only be good for a large, overpopulated nation such as China or, for that matter, India.

To be sure, the One Child Policy has had ill effects, such as the growing gender imbalance. There were far too many cases of Chinese girls being abandoned as families pursued the chance to have a son. But there is also evidence that the One Child Policy forced families to invest in their only daughters, rather than neglecting them in favor of sons. Critics of the One Child Policy have pointed to the authoritarian way it was implemented, but this misses that China needed to get a handle on population growth—and quickly—or face possible catastrophe. Doing it entirely through market-based incentives (i.e., taxes and subsidies) would have reserved the chance to have more than one child to the rich, and China was too poor at the time to deploy economic instruments.

Again: one can disagree with China's nondemocratic nature, but it remains true that the country has had a much better track record in improving the lives of its ordinary people—and in a much shorter period—than many other developing countries. It is also not clear how China could have improved these standards of living so quickly without strong state action.

• • •

This chapter is not an apologia for China. The country has made several mistakes in how it has pursued development. Its current approach to the challenges of the twenty-first century will not serve the country well in a more resource-constrained future. Much of these problems are well known and well reported, but they are still worth repeating.

For all the differences between China's and the West's economic systems and political structures, they are similar in their objectives: a growth-at-all-costs attitude toward economic development, which ignores the external costs of economic activity.

The most visible issue is environmental pollution. Air pollution in the major cities, especially in Beijing and other northern cities, is legendarily terrible. Pollution levels are sometimes three or four times higher than what is considered healthy by the World Health Organization. WHO found that over half of China's cities had annual average pollution levels higher than the standard.[6] A team from the Chinese Center for Disease Control and Prevention estimated that following WHO standards for air pollution might prevent over three million premature deaths a year.[7]

China also has serious issues with water pollution. Heavy industry and industrial agriculture have contaminated both waterways and groundwater. A study in 2016 by the Chinese government found that 80 percent of shallow groundwater sources were contaminated. None were considered "pristine," and almost half were deemed unfit for human consumption of any kind.[8] Agriculture plays a role too: according to the Chinese Academy for Environmental Planning, 90 percent of organic pollutants come from agricultural waste. The issue of water pollution came to a head in 2013, when Shanghai residents woke up to almost three thousand pig corpses floating down the Huangpu River.[9]

China's energy system is also the world's most energy intensive. Beijing is correct when it argues that its energy usage per capita is much smaller than the rest of the developed world. Looking purely at oil, China's oil consumption per capita is slightly above the world average, and a third of what the US uses. However, China fares much worse when you look at how much energy is needed per dollar of GDP. The economist Arthur Kroeber calculated that China needs to burn 2,000 barrels of oil to produce a million dollars of output, compared to 1,000 barrels in the US and 600 in the European Union.[10]

There are wider concerns involving sustainable development and resources. Intensive farming, including the heavy use of agricultural chemicals, is degrading large swathes of China's vital agricultural land. One study by China's agricultural ministry in 2014 estimated that 40 percent of China's agricultural land was suffering from degradation.[11] China also draws on its rivers to provide water for farming, which has led to the drastic overuse of water. Since 1985, the Yellow River has dried up completely at least once a year.[12] China's Ministry of Water Resources has found that twenty-eight thousand rivers have disappeared over the past sixty years.[13]

China's development has, in practice, focused on urban areas over rural ones. Chinese cities have grown at alarming speeds, with secondary and even tertiary cities now large enough to rival, if not surpass, major cities in the developed world. Cities that hardly anyone outside of China has even heard of—Jinan, Shenyang, and Shantou, for example—have populations larger than major European capitals. This imbalance is expressed through income inequality within China. Average annual income in the city is approximately US$5,170. By contrast, rural households have an average income of only US$1,900 a year (though the ratio of urban to rural incomes has started to improve in recent years).

It should be noted that the Chinese government has recognized the problem, and has since launched several major initiatives to open up underdeveloped areas. This includes infrastructure investments in rural western China, provision of social services, and regulatory changes, such as the abolition of agricultural taxes in 2006. By 2013, almost all rural residents had some form of health insurance, up from 13 percent in 2000.[14] Beyond the western provinces, China's secondary cities now have international-standard airports, excellent road and rail connections, modern universities, major companies, and skyscrapers.

China has also seen a massive shift in population from the countryside to the cities, with all the negative repercussions discussed in chapter 10. These cities have become overly crowded. This has stressed urban economies, driving up the cost of social services. It has fed a property bubble as more and more people need places to live. For recent migrants who have come from the countryside with little in the way of income, finding a place to live can be extremely difficult. They are driven to living in illegal structures, often on the outskirts of the city. Some illegal homes for migrants are built in Beijing's underground tunnels, cramming four or five migrants to a damp, moldy room.

The factories that employ migrants also shunt them into poor working conditions. Hours are long, so that Chinese factories can produce the rush orders that sustain global consumerism. China became the "factory of the world" because the global consumer expects things to get cheaper all the time. Workers have few bargaining rights, both because the Chinese government disallows trade unions and because migrants are easily replaced by fresh faces from the countryside. There can be few options for a migrant stuck in this situation.

The explosion in China's consumption has also been well reported. The growth in consumption—and the growth in the effects of that consumption—have outpaced the growth in incomes. This had led to the rapid emergence of "rich-country" social issues, such as sedentary urban middle-class lifestyles and rising rates of youth obesity.

Finally, China's growth has not been matched by increased regulatory standards and oversight. As production in China increases, firms are incentivized to cut corners, using chemicals and industrial additives to increase productivity, lower prices, and thus capture more of the market. This has been endemic in the agricultural sector, which is characterized much more by small private and township enterprise than by massive state-owned agribusiness. This would not normally be a problem, but China exerts much of its regulation through its state control of large enterprises rather than through economic regulation per se.

We should also take care not to overstate the gains that China has made, impressive though they may be. The country has made historic achievements toward reducing poverty and providing access to basic needs. Yet many people are still poor. Even in China's own judgment, forty-five million people still live in rural poverty,[15] a population the size of Sudan. Further, this is a poor population that is by definition the hardest to help. Even those who are technically not living in poverty are still not prosperous, even under our more constrained idea of moderate prosperity proposed in chapter 8. The World Bank estimated in 2014 that almost 130 million people still lived on less than $3 a day—technically out of poverty, but still poor by any stretch of the imagination.[16] There are 430 million people who live on less than $5 a day.[17]

But the largest problem is that through its opening to globalization, China—or, more accurately, China's people—have been led to believe that they should and can have a Western standard of living. That means a consumption-driven economy with living standards that approach, if not exceed, what is found in the West.

China probably will never adopt the West's political structures, nor will it become an entirely free-market, small-government economy. At least in the medium term, it will likely remain a single-party state, where the economy preserves a major role for both the state and state-owned enterprises. Nor will China assimilate entirely to a Western culture.

Yet the aspirations of China's people are similar to those who live in the West. To borrow a Chinese phrase, the current goal is "[Western] modernity with Chinese characteristics." To grow and prosper, China has to buy into the current economic model that, together with the forces of globalization, will mean more Westernization in practice.

The growth of China's aspirations will have a massive impact on the world's resource consumption. China is already the world's largest consumer of most of the world's commodities—coal, oil, iron ore, copper, aluminum, rare earth metals, and agricultural products (such as soybean, rice, and wheat).[18] As China's middle class continues to grow—estimated to reach 270 million people by 2022—the world's common resources will be put under even more strain.

We have already seen economies focused on primary resources shift their destinations from the US and Europe to China. The external costs of this growth in demand are wide reaching, from overfishing and extinction in the Eastern Pacific to deforestation, pollution, and poor working conditions in Central Africa.

This brings up an important final caveat in regard to China's model of strong state governance. China, and Chinese companies, have been accused of treating developing countries poorly. According to these accusations, China aggressively pursues natural resources in Africa, often supporting corrupt officials and governments in exchange for access. The projects are often staffed entirely with migrant Chinese labor, providing little benefit to the surrounding economy. In Southeast Asia, China's dam-building projects have threatened severe repercussions for countries further downriver. The most fiery critics deem China to be acting like a "neocolonialist," akin to the European and American colonial powers of old.

I do not believe that the Chinese attitude toward these countries goes anywhere near that far. But the Chinese are the latest in a series of large economies exploiting smaller, resource-rich countries for the benefit of their own economy. Yet the issue is not states relying on large economic powers: after all, Canada and Mexico's economies are tied closely to the United States, yet no one would seriously argue that either is subject to American "neocolonialism." The issue is state strength: Canada and Mexico are, in general, stronger states. The response to claims of Chinese neocolonialism may not be to criticize China but rather to find a way to strengthen these poorer, smaller states so that they will no longer be at the bottom of the global economic supply chain.

• • •

Despite these issues, China is still well placed for the twenty-first century, especially compared to countries that have let their governance capacity wither over time. China may not yet have the right objectives and goals for a resource-constrained future, but as noted earlier, when Beijing does decide to pursue a true sustainability agenda, it will already have in place the tools and mechanisms to intervene in the economy. Other countries, developed and developing, will need to build these tools from scratch or recapture them from the vested interests that have already taken control.

To its credit, Beijing does seem to have realized that a true sustainability agenda will be vital to the future of the country, and has thus begun taking steps in that direction.

Beijing has launched the world's largest reforestation program to hold back growing desertification, by growing a "green belt" around Beijing and other major northern provinces, and has also tried to get a handle on urban air pollution.

Early in 2017, Beijing announced plans to invest over US$360 billion in renewable power generation, and Chinese industry has succeeded in dropping the costs of solar power almost to the level of fossil fuels. This is not an entirely selfless act: growing investment in wind and solar energy both allows China to reduce its reliance on fossil fuels from abroad and also helps the country corner the market in clean energy. But it does show how these state investments can have real economic benefits.

Beijing is also willing to set aggressive targets to address certain kinds of polluting consumption. In September 2017, Beijing announced that it was considering a ban on the sale of gas-powered cars "in the near future." China's consumption of electric vehicles has skyrocketed in recent years: over five hundred thousand electric cars were sold in China in 2016, which was 50 percent more than the year before. (Admittedly, this is a small proportion of the twenty-eight million cars sold in China in the same period.)

Finally, China is willing to sanction both its own officials and those in large companies for poor environmental protection. The Environmental Protection Law, amended in 2015, gave the government greater power to throw senior managers into administrative detention if their companies continued to break environmental regulations. And, before one thinks that the law only allowed for "authoritarian" measures, the law also allowed NGOs to bring lawsuits concerning environmental protection.[19]

This shift in attitude goes further: Beijing now considers environmental protection as a "key performance indicator" when it comes to deciding which officials to promote and which to discipline.

But just as important is the attempt to define a different path for China that does not rely on the West as its frame of reference. One initiative by President Xi Jinping was the "China Dream": the individual aspirations for China's people.

At the most recent National People's Congress in November 2017, Xi redefined the "principal contradiction" of China. The principal contradiction is a Maoist idea, whereby forward progress is driven by the conflict between two contradictory principles. Before Xi, the principal contradiction was defined by Deng Xiaoping as the contradiction between the needs of China's population and the country's backwardness vis-à-vis the rest of the world. Given the state of China's economy at the time, a firm focus on China's development was understandable. But President Xi has updated the principal contradiction for China's new circumstances, now defining it as the tension between "unbalanced and inadequate development and the people's ever-growing needs for a better life." This is an admission that China's development has not been perfect and that, more important, it needs to be altered to allow for a more balanced (and, one hopes, more sustainable) outcome.

China can still do much more in defining a new path. For example, Beijing has yet to fully flesh out what the China Dream actually means, which has unfortunately allowed people to fill in the gaps themselves. To many Chinese people, the China Dream is equivalent to more consumption, thus making it little different from its American counterpart. Beijing may try to discuss the China Dream in more spiritual and constrained terms, but until the state more explicitly defines what it considers to be a moderately prosperous society, the Chinese society and economy will continue down its consumerist and thus wasteful and unsustainable path.

Defining the China Dream is therefore also an opportunity to build a whole socioeconomic and political philosophy around resource constraints and sustainable development.

What does China still need to do?

One pressing need is for a broader and much more progressive rural development approach. This will take pressure off the cities and allow for a more sustainable distribution of people across the entire country. It will also reduce the disparity in incomes between urban and rural areas, perhaps encouraging more people to stay in rural areas and help those areas develop.

China must also recognize that sustainability efforts go beyond just investment in green and renewable energy. It is about creating a less resource-intensive way of life, which would not be alien to Chinese people or their past traditions. Older ideas about what standard of living is appropriate need to be resurrected, and built into a new emerging socioeconomic and political narrative. Solar panels may make the headlines, but China also needs to ensure that all parts of its economy do not overuse resources, because even renewable energy can be put to unsustainable growth practices.

Focusing on creating a more sustainable agricultural sector will be a good way to combine these two imperatives, at least in the beginning. China still needs to feed its population, who will start to demand more food as their incomes increase; for example, China already imports five million tons of rice per year, and started to import rice from the US for the first time in 2017.[20] How China guides its people's appetites will thus be critical to developing both a more sustainable economy and a more sustainable lifestyle, not to mention addressing the national security issues linked to being self-sufficient in staples such as rice.

There is already a move to create this sustainable agricultural sector among local farmers. On several occasions, I have had the opportunity to work with farmers and cooperatives led by visionary local leaders trying to create more environmentally responsible and thus sustainable ways to grow more food. In both the northeastern province of Jilin and the central province of Shanxi, extremely well informed cooperatives are trying to implement a system of "natural farming" that combines crop and livestock production to produce more yields with far less waste and chemical pollution. These cooperatives have taken upon themselves a secondary social responsibility as well: creating a vibrant rural community that helps the elderly and encourages people to stay.

• • •

China is arguably quite lucky when it comes to defining and walking a new path in a resource-constrained twenty-first century. Its large population may increase its resource needs, but it is also an asset: Chinese economist Justin Lin, claiming to be paraphrasing former premier Wen Jiabao, stated that "when you multiply any problem by China's population, it is a very big problem. But when you divide it by China's population, it becomes very small."[21] It is very politically stable, being one of the few single-party states (along with Vietnam) to have seen multiple peaceful transitions of power. It has the twin benefits of becoming very recently successful in following a different economic model yet also having a very long cultural history to draw upon when it comes time to define a new path forward.

China also benefits from being ethnically and linguistically homogenous (though some of this was a matter of government policy, rather than a natural condition of China). Homogeneity can make it easier for a government—democratic or nondemocratic—to claim to be a unifying presence.

Most other developing countries are not so lucky. With a few exceptions (e.g., India, Indonesia, Nigeria), they are not as large as China, and so do not have the same manpower and resources to drive solutions. As noted earlier, their governing infrastructure is not as well developed as China's, which means they do not have the tools to consistently intervene in the economy as Beijing can. And, finally, many of these countries are much more linguistically, ethnically, and religiously diverse than China. Both India and Indonesia, for example, have multiple official languages, numerous ethnicities, and significant populations of religious minorities. Thus the need to ensure legitimacy and accountability is much more pressing for New Delhi and Jakarta than it is for Beijing.

Although China can be a role model for other developing countries, it is by no means a perfect one. Chapter 12 will try to lay out an ideal transition path for countries to build their own state strength and develop a new economic model for the twenty-first century.

12

TRANSITION

From Business as Usual
to the Sustainable State

This chapter will portray some of the issues countries will need to deal with as they work toward becoming sustainable states. This is not meant to be a fixed recipe that all states should follow, but rather some ideas that functioning states aware of sustainability challenges and committed to sustainability goals should consider. I refer to them in this chapter as sustainability "pillars," which must be critical elements of the economic policy framework, such that they lay the foundations for building a moderate and shared prosperity. But, most important, large developing nations—the front line of our collective global challenge—will need to move away from many misguided and blatantly wrong approaches.

• • •

This discussion of transitions will not deal with the world's more advanced economies, whether they are large (e.g., the US and Japan) or small (e.g., Singapore and Hong Kong). This is not to deny their need to act or their place in reshaping their economies to attain some level of sustainability. These economies will need to become more sustainable, one hopes becoming strong, sustainable states. However, that shift will be different for advanced economies, primarily because of the nature of their governments and the expectations of their populations accustomed to a "good life."

These countries have promised, and most have delivered, a certain standard of living for their people for over a generation, if not more. This standard of living is clearly impossible to sustain in a resource-constrained future, yet changing it would mean that the government is "breaking a promise." This affects political stability. Many of these economies are already seeing rising tensions as younger generations realize that they are unlikely to achieve the same standard of living as that of their parents and grandparents (which perhaps explains the growing popularity of populist movements, good and bad, among the young). And this is even before advanced economies have undertaken any kind of reckoning about what standards of living are truly sustainable (in line with their global moralizing on these issues to the developing world).

To complicate matters, some larger advanced economies have wedded their economic heft to geopolitical power and, oftentimes, their own self-image. Limiting that economic heft thus has a security and cultural dimension that complicates matters. It adds another set of vested interests—not just companies and economic elites that benefit from the free-market model but also security interests that see these economic factors as a path to geopolitical strength, and cultural groups that see them as integral to the national identity.

This does not mean that change is impossible. In fact, for the good of the planet, we must hope that these advanced economies can change their populations' expectations. However, progress will inevitably be slow. Advanced economies will need to deconstruct their institutions, push back against vested interests, change the political discourse, and manage their populations' expectations. They will need to compromise, which will slow them down even further. The truth is that mature democracies do not do this quickly.

This chapter will also not talk about the "failed state," such as Somalia, Venezuela, Libya, or any state that does not have the fundamental institutions of governance. At this point, these states have much more fundamental issues than worrying about sustainability and resource management.

• • •

Instead, the chapter will focus on the following three types of state.

The first type is the large poor country, such as China, India, Nigeria, Pakistan, and Brazil. These are the countries that will drive resource consumption over the coming decades. As their populations grow and get richer over time, they will start to consume more and therefore use more resources. We are already seeing how China's development is impacting the consumption of primary commodities around the world; the rise of India, Indonesia, Nigeria, and others will do the same.

But these countries also have the most resources to solve problems if they can foster the political will. Their large populations and economies give them the capacity to solve large problems. Solutions that would be extremely difficult for a smaller country to institute would be much easier for an economy the size of India's. Achieving scale—which would be vital for some of the state-backed investments in infrastructure described in chapter 8— would also be easier for a larger economy than for a smaller one.

Then there are the smaller middle-income countries, such as Malaysia, Thailand, South Africa, and even Iran. These countries have populations that are doing reasonably well, especially compared to other countries in the developing world. Their populations have achieved the basic rights of life and are therefore focused on achieving a higher level of prosperity. However, these countries cannot and should not seek a development model that strives to provide a Western standard of living, due to resource constraints.

These countries also have issues with vested interests. As these countries have undergone some level of development, an economic and political elite has been created, who will defend the privileges they have earned or been granted and will resist attempts to curb overconsumption. These interests will need to be managed or even overcome if these middle-income countries are to move onto a sustainable path of development.

The final set of countries comprises smaller poor countries, such as Laos, Cambodia, Sri Lanka, Jamaica, Lesotho, and Zambia. These countries can be quite poor and may have fewer economic and natural resources than their larger counterparts. They do, however, have the means and potential to achieve a more sustainable development path. They at least have a functioning state, yet it can be tougher for them to solve social problems. They will be restricted in the level of investment and "power" they can offer.

However, smaller countries may also have more flexibility than larger countries. As countries like China and India grow, their economic size will bring along many of the geopolitical concerns that have plagued larger advanced economies. These larger countries will run the risk of getting distracted by their new status as great powers—much as the currently advanced economies did when they were growing.

What joins all these countries together is that they have not yet completed—and, in some cases, not even started—their journey toward fully replicating the Western economic model. This means they can change to a more sustainable version of the state more easily than can Western countries. They do not need to worry about contradicting vested interests, as they are not yet rich enough to have enough of them to make a difference. They do not need to worry about how to sell a more moderate version of prosperity, because it would still be better than what their people have now.

This is similar to the idea of "leapfrogging" common in discussions about technological development, where a less developed country skips over the middle stages of technology to adopt the latest and greatest, such as skipping over landlines and broadband to go straight to mobile phones and cellular data. Countries can leap from a poor and unsustainable economy to a moderately prosperous and sustainable economy, skipping the free-market, unsustainable, and unequal stage in between. Developing countries do not have the legacy issues within the unsustainable economy, which have often been hardwired into a difficult-to-change political model.

Think about how much work it would take for the US to return to the more activist version of government it had before the 1980s (which itself would not be enough to be truly sustainable). Each new program, new government institution, and new regulation would be fought tooth and nail by lobbyists, vested interests, and those concerned with preserving a free-market small-government ideology. The inevitable compromises involved would yield changes smaller than hoped for. The only way large changes could be made rapidly would be if they were to occur during a time of great crisis (along the lines of the Great Depression)—something we should hope would never come.

Developing countries, starting from a lower base, will not have this problem.

● ● ●

The first and most fundamental task for governments is to frame a clear political philosophy about what a sustainable state and society would look like, particular to their time and context. This philosophy, with well-defined sustainability "pillars" (as described in the next section), should drive policy and decision-making. President Xi's attempt to define a more environmentally friendly vision for China's future development is an example of what I am referring to. Beijing has decided that it must adopt a more sustainable outlook and is changing how it governs and regulates to suit that new objective. As this book goes to print, Beijing has announced a radical restructuring of its Environmental Ministry with far-reaching implications for embedding its sustainability goals as key sectors of the economy.

This is the difference between *policy* and *politics*. Politics is a discussion about philosophy, values, and concepts—setting out a long-term vision for society. One should be conscious of what is actually possible or feasible, but such a philosophy should be bold. Policy, or the actual decisions by the government, follows from that; it seeks the best way to achieve that objective.

However, some leaders choose to let policy drive their decisions. They see governance as statistics to be maximized, whether that is in terms of foreign investment, economic growth, or other economic metrics. Their vision of the world, insofar as they have one, is derived from what policies are possible within the status quo.

For example, many countries have altered their governing and economic philosophies according to the whims of foreign investors and donors. Investors demand certain changes to policies and priorities to further their interests, and governments oblige, apparently convinced that they have no choice in the matter. This is the dreaded "race to the bottom" that many antiglobalization activists fear.

But a stronger state will set its own agenda and accept donor aid and investment if—and only if—they align with the state's long-term objectives. This is at the same time a test of whether aid is genuine or tied to other agendas. But to do all this, these countries need that most critical ingredient: capacity in basic policymaking, or what I have referred to as competence.

This is not to say that the political philosophy should not be aligned with realities on the ground. States emerging from violent conflict, such as Cambodia and Rwanda, will need a governing philosophy that recognizes the massive amount of work that needs to be done to repair the damage. It can be easy to decry the authoritarian actions of someone like Cambodian president Hun Sen or Rwandan president Paul Kagame in their attempts to rebuild their countries after violent conflict. But it can be hard to think what alternative was possible at the time they came to power.

Democracies, too, present their own political realities, in that the governing philosophy needs to be able to withstand electoral scrutiny. It should be tailored to preserve important democratic principles and concepts, yet clearly outline the hard trade-offs, the consequences of certain policies, and the price of inaction.

The creation of this philosophy is central to the political stability of societies in the twenty-first century. The lack of such a philosophy could lead to growing inequality: not just income or wealth inequality, but also inequality in terms of consumption and access to resources. Long-standing inequality has pernicious effects on stability for any kind of society, democratic or nondemocratic, rich or poor.

•••

Underneath this political philosophy are several pillars that should guide government activity and act as standards against which to judge the efforts of the sustainable state. These are not the big and flashy "projects" that are designed to grab public and international attention yet have little long-term effect. Instead, these are broad-based initiatives designed to directly improve living conditions across a whole population.

The first pillar concerns land. States in large developing countries should focus on their large rural population, ensuring that these people are stable and well fed. States should not recklessly encourage urban migration in some mad rush to "modernize." They should support a viable food production system that is stable and locally owned, farmed, and managed, one that in turn provides enough surplus to feed an urban population. Although the government should undertake efforts to directly provide basic needs to a rural population, a vibrant agricultural sector will also provide farmers with more opportunities to earn an income and thus improve their own economic position, thereby becoming self-sufficient within the context of a moderately prosperous society.

An immediate step is land reform and redistribution: breaking up land owned by agribusinesses and large farms, which are too big to support sustainability, and distributing them among small households. This is not calling for an ill-conceived notion about nationalizing land. *The Economist*—not normally a supporter of these kinds of interventions—compared countries that pursued land reform and countries that did not. Maoist China saw its grain output jump by 70 percent in the decade after World War II; Japan and Taiwan also saw rice and sugar yields increase after their own reforms. Southeast Asian countries, which largely did not implement land reform (or, in the case of the Philippines, implemented it badly) have seen persistent inequality between cities and the countryside as "the state favours agribusiness and plantations over small farmers."[1]

The second pillar is education. Giving people important skills and training is clearly necessary for both urban and rural development. But too often education is focused on the very top of the income scale: CEOs, doctors, lawyers, and tech programmers, as opposed to the whole range of careers and skills needed for any country and especially large developing nations. Education is not just the world-class university but also the agricultural centers that train thousands of farmers on the latest farming and supply-chain management techniques, and the institutes that create a whole class of skilled professionals.

What is missing is the huge middle ground between a basic school education and the college degree focused on the top end of the income scale. This is more than just vocational training, which often focuses on providing workers with the skills to work in factories or low-end service jobs. There also needs to be training for skilled professionals: carpenters, electricians, plumbers, technicians, and the like. This requires a change in our culture and how it understands education.

The third pillar is mobility. People and goods need to be able to travel from one place to another with a certain level of ease and speed, whether that is within a single community (i.e., public transportation within a city) or across the whole country (i.e., a rail network connecting towns and secondary cities).

Infrastructure is typically invested in so as to foster economic growth, as opposed to promoting sustainable wealth creation and distribution. Investment tends to focus on those places that already have a great deal of economic activity, which widens regional inequality. We should instead see investments in mobility as a mechanism for economic empowerment and a way to redistribute wealth across a country. Wealth generated in one area of the country can be spread across a wider area through investments in mobility, which would in turn unlock more paths to economic development in worse-off areas.

In the city, investments in mobility will focus on good public transportation and must be accompanied by restrictions on private cars. There are some simple and straightforward controls cities can place on cars, such as limits on private vehicle registrations. Cities can also invest in cheap public transportation, such as buses or electric trolleys.

More broadly, states should invest in a network that connects secondary towns, and develop these regional economic hubs as part of a wider economy that includes the immediate hinterland. This would help distribute economic activity away from major metropolitan areas. This may even lead to a more sustainable balance between different urban areas: citizens will no longer need to live in the major metropolitan area to be where "things happen," as they can easily travel back and forth.

The fourth pillar is health care. Most important is starting with disease and infection prevention. This means improving sanitation and the quality of water, food, nutrition, and shelter, as well as cleaning up and reducing pollution.

The issue facing investments in health care is similar to the problem facing investments in education. Heath care investments usually focus on the high-income end of the scale. This leads to a focus on doctors, surgeons, hospitals, and cutting-edge medical and pharmaceutical technology.

For example, India's education system and investments in higher-end health care institutions mean that the country can compete on high-end medical treatment (i.e., surgeries) on a quality comparable to developed countries. On its own, this is a remarkable achievement, and one that India can legitimately be proud of. However, India's reputation as a center for medical tourism sits oddly with the poor quality of public health throughout most of the country.

It is far more useful to focus on less flashy public health initiatives. Some of these interventions are low cost and can be installed, managed, and monitored by local communities if they are given the right training. However, without a public health system to provide these interventions systematically, it can be hard to improve health on a regional or national scale. Creating a team of trained public health workers—who require less training and resources than doctors or nurses—can provide that community-based health care across an entire country.

For example, Cuba has long been credited with creating a high-quality health care system that vastly exceeds what its economic resources would suggest. This proves it can be done when a government is competent and committed to social welfare and protecting public good. Cuba's cradle-to-grave approach focuses on prevention, which has helped the country achieve high health standards on par with the developed world. The health care system can focus on simple and straightforward interventions, such as providing free eyeglasses and contact lenses to people with impaired vision.

The fifth pillar is housing. This is especially important in urban areas of the developing world, where the combination of a growing population and government neglect can lead to serious housing unaffordability crises. Governments must treat providing low-cost housing as a top priority.

Public housing can also be a vehicle through which to develop a more sustainable lifestyle, both on the individual and the community levels. Public homes could be designed to rely less on artificial cooling and heating, thus reducing energy use in hot summers and cold winters. They might be integrated with public transportation systems, thus reducing the need for a private car.

On the communal level, public housing can be a vehicle for urban planning. Rather than creating a sprawling suburbia, relying on cars, big-box retail stores, and massive backyards, the state can create dense clusters of public housing, surrounded by green space. This can help control the spread of urbanization and suburbanization.

Governments in the developing world should also develop innovative social financing programs to fund the construction of these homes. Interestingly enough, there is no global effort to find direct solutions to this, as market solutions (with some NGO activity) are seen as the only way forward. Governments should be willing to borrow and spend money to provide universal access to shelter; such a project would be a much more worthwhile investment than other proposed infrastructure projects. In fact, lifting people out of drudgery will free the poor to engage in more economic activity on a more secure basis.

The sixth pillar comprises energy and the environment—two things that, in our hot future, are closely connected. The government needs to ensure that everyone has equal access to some minimum level of energy (though not necessarily beyond that). But it must do so in a way that does not threaten common resources and a population's access to them.

This will likely include some focus on renewables, similar to what China has done in its aggressive push toward solar energy. But the government should also tackle the underpricing and subsidies that currently distort energy markets. States must ensure that people—typically urban free riders—pay the true cost of their energy usage. Any measures must balance sustainability objectives. For example, the state could implement a system of electronic road pricing and increased petrol taxes thereby reducing urban congestion and improving air quality.

From there, the state can look to resource and environmental management, with the eventual goal of creating a system that properly prices consumption.

Environmental management would include the creation of "no-go zones" supporting biodiversity and preserving flora and fauna. It would also include ameliorating pollution, reducing its harms, and controlling its emission. Finally, it would mean managing the rural-urban divide to ensure a more sustainable balance between city and countryside, through smarter urban planning, investment in good national public transportation, and rural development.

Any of these steps would require an expansion of the state and changes to how it enforces rules. Thus states should also work to build competence in their governing institutions. This is admittedly a much longer process than the other steps—after all, it took Singapore decades to build the efficient city-state we see today. But competent institutions will carry the decisions of the sustainable state to future generations as leaders change. States should look to policies that build the four elements of institutional competence discussed in chapter 7: administrative expertise, public policymaking, leadership, and meritocracy.

● ● ●

What about other actors in society? How do they fit into this system, and how can they aid this transition?

Businesses, for their part, have the data that helps a government map out where exactly resources are underpriced. An examination of a business's supply chain would present the points where costs are being externalized. Businesses can also be good partners in determining what specific things a community could use to develop, especially when it comes to devising the kinds of infrastructure a location may need to improve the vibrancy of the local economy.

Civil society will play a role as well. Civil society groups provide a mechanism to help communicate ideas and conditions to the government. They help bolster accountability by ensuring that local needs and problems are not neglected and by working with governments to find solutions.

This is different from how the West sees NGOs. Western observers tend to see NGOs either as activist organizations that try to openly pressure the government to change or as alternatives to state action if the government is unwilling or unable to help.

Activism has its uses, especially in democratic contexts. But activism sometimes positions the state as an enemy that can never be trusted and that will only work with the NGO under duress. This can lead to an aggressive attitude toward the government, which, understandably, will not endear the NGO's views to those in authority.

Just as prevalent is the view that NGO work can be a good replacement for state activity. Several developing countries use NGO activity as justification for ignoring a problem, as they assume the problem on the ground is "handled." But civil society groups just do not have the resources to solve problems on a national or sometimes even a regional scale over an extended period.

Most NGOs would admit that they are too small to solve any particular social issue on their own. Yet many are also wary of working with state governments, especially in the developing world. A closer relationship between NGOs and the state could instead allow solutions to be nationalized and bolstered with public support.

• • •

This chapter is not trying to lay out a path forward for any specific country. Each country faces its own set of economic, environmental, and political conditions, so the specifics of each country's transition to a sustainable state will be different. Every country needs to create an overarching political philosophy, but this philosophy, and the pillars beneath it, will be different as circumstances change.

As a large country with a state-driven economy, China will take a different path than India, a raucous democracy, which in turn will be on a different journey than Cambodia—a much smaller, much less developed country.

However, I hope this chapter has laid out some general principles that could be adapted to numerous different kinds of state.

CONCLUSION
Either States Act, or Doom Looms

M uch has happened between when this book was conceived and when it was finished. After the election of Donald Trump, the success of Britain's Leave campaign, and the near-victories of far-right populists across Europe, the prescription of free markets and globalization now seems ill-suited not just for the developing world but for the developed world as well. The "populist" movements in the developed world are reactions against an economic system that appears to have failed to provide long-term social gains. Different populist movements apportion the blame differently: some movements blame large businesses and economic elites; others have chosen to denigrate immigrants and other countries (especially after the rise of the rest makes it seem as though these mature economies have been "left behind").

Some of these developments have accelerated what was already happening. President Trump's decision to pursue a more muscular foreign policy around the world has removed even the pretense of universal values. Asian countries, no longer sure that the US will pay attention forever, are starting to talk among themselves about how to best manage the region's security. A key aspect of security will, in my view, be driven by the challenge of sustainability I've described in this book, even if many policymakers have yet to connect the dots and see the linkages. The hope is that they are beginning to.

The old order is changing in the realm of sustainability as well. After President Trump pulled out of the Paris Climate Accord, China and Europe both pledged to work together to continue the fight against climate change. Around the world, the fight against the scourge of plastic is being taken seriously. In March 2018, the city of Mumbai decided to ban plastics from all its civil markets. This is a big deal.

But the main result of these changes is that the world seems more open to new ideas. Even those who support Western democracies are wondering how their systems could have led to such clearly bad results as Trump's election or the Brexit decision. In this part of the world, there is suddenly much less willingness to treat Western ideas as automatically superior to non-Western ones. This shift is long overdue. Even Asian elites, who may have been trained in Western schools and work in Western companies, are less prone to automatically support Western ideas, and at least question them.

This opens more possibilities. A critique of the Western free-market model, especially when it comes to sustainability, has a better chance of being more widely accepted now than even five years ago, when I wrote *Consumptionomics*. And it may be accepted not just in the developing world but in advanced economies, where people may be wondering how their high living standards were unable to prevent instability.

• • •

This book is intended to challenge the vision of sustainable development presented at business and global policy conferences and forums and endorsed by well-established institutions. I have made these arguments before at these conferences and institutions, and am thus familiar with some of the responses. In this conclusion, I will take some time to respond to some of the likely criticisms and, I hope, provide some additional clarity.

Response 1: This book is based on an idealistic assumption that the state will always do the right thing with its strength, when past history shows that the state has often made inefficient and harmful economic decisions.

This book does not necessarily assume—or hope—that the state will do the right thing. Instead, it starts from the argument that, if the sustainability crisis is to be solved, the state *must* take the lead, and must ultimately do the right things. The state may be a flawed mechanism, but state action is at least capable of solving the problem of sustainable development. The alternatives—markets or technology—are not capable of solving the crisis by themselves.

It is certainly possible that the state will use its strength toward the wrong ends, whether that is a drift toward authoritarianism and violent coercion, or to encourage environmentally damaging and unsustainable economic practices. But the answer when faced with suboptimal state behavior is not to argue that the state is thus bad in all cases, but rather to think of ways to improve it. In a resource-constrained twenty-first century, we do not have the luxury of believing we can live without a strong state.

That is partly why *The Sustainable State* has tried to define the "right" things a strong state can focus on, to ensure that its strength is oriented toward socially optimal outcomes.

Response 2: This book is anti-Western and anti-Western values. In arguing that the West's vision of the world is incorrect and harmful, the book is stating its belief that the West must be punished.

I admit that this book is not taking a Western position, but a non-Western view is not the same as an anti-Western one. My views are rooted in the experience gained in the non-Western world, which faces a different challenge than the Western world (where I have also lived and worked) when it comes to sustainable development. The Western world is richer and relatively smaller, and has largely achieved universal access to basic needs. Western countries have also had time to develop stronger institutions that (apart from some recent high-profile missteps) have allowed their democracies to run smoothly.

The non-Western world does not have that luxury. Its population is large and growing. Most of these people are still poor; even those out of poverty are still living lives with unstable access to basic needs and with a great deal of drudgery. That their standard of living must improve is a moral imperative.

The Western model may have been "right" at the time of the West's development (though it cannot ignore the negative effects of colonization in its search for resources to enrich itself), but it is certainly not appropriate now. Trying to push the Western economic and political model, even with minor cosmetic tweaks, would be inappropriate for the developing world, which needs an economic model better suited to its conditions.

The West has its own challenge: how to manage the expectations of its populations, which have been promised a lifestyle that is unsustainable and resource intensive. This will be a difficult adjustment, but one that we must hope these countries will make—and in a way that preserves people's trust in their government. No one will be made better off if the

West is forced to make these adjustments chaotically, or in a way that harms its own people.

It is not up to this book to determine how best for Western states to become their own version of sustainable states. Nor, if I'm being realistic, will suggestions from a non-Western perspective necessarily be that helpful. Best to leave that to Western thinkers, economists, policymakers, and leaders.

Response 3: The book is antidemocratic, as the strong state is inherently oppressive.

I think that this book has made the point that there is nothing in state strength that is incompatible with democratic values or systems. A strong state is merely one that is willing to take firm action to protect the public good, and in the interest of the majority rather than vested interests.

Democracies are clearly capable of that. Representative democracies also can contribute to a government's legitimacy and accountability, and they certainly can deepen the connection between a government and its people, leading to a stronger state.

But democracies are not *automatically* capable of this. Elections by themselves do not lead to good outcomes, nor are representative democracies by themselves evidence of a strong connection between a government and the people. Democracies also add their own complicating factors when it comes to achieving sustainable development, such as when they must ask people to suffer sacrifices in the short term in the hope of reducing some future harm.

I am not saying that democracies can *never* be sustainable states. Instead, I merely argue that democracies, as currently defined in the West, are not inherently better placed to become such states and may not be best suited to large developing nations faced with the conundrum of growth and sustainable development. Democracies can just as easily be weak states as strong ones and will face their own unique obstacles as they transform their economies. Nondemocratic states are the same.

Response 4: This book apologizes for authoritarian leaders, excusing the oppression of their people so long as they "make the trains run on time."

It is worth asking why the nondemocratic states cited in this book have had such good outcomes when it comes to improving living standards. It wasn't that long ago that people argued that democratic governance was necessary to develop the economy and improve living standards, believing that nondemocratic governments were incapable of truly understanding or caring about people's living standards.

Many of these nondemocratic leaders are genuinely popular in their countries, to an extent that is too difficult to explain away with claims of "brainwashing" or "indoctrination." These leaders have tried to provide real benefits to their populations, combined with appeals to national pride.

A recent example is the difference between Hugo Chávez and his successor, Nicolás Maduro. Both were accused of being authoritarians in waiting. Yet Hugo Chávez distributed benefits to the population and championed the poor, winning him genuine support among Venezuelans. This support was fleeting: Maduro quickly squandered his people's trust in the government through severe economic mismanagement, thus forcing him to turn to outright political oppression.

For those who sincerely believe that democratic systems are the best form of government (not in a practical sense, but in a moral one), these better outcomes, and the trust the people now have in these governments, need to be taken seriously. Saying that China's growth and success "don't matter" because the country is not democratic means blinding yourself to important lessons.

I am not saying that India needs to become a dictatorship or authoritarian government to become a strong state, or a sustainable state. But India (or, more accurately, outside observers) should not excuse India's massive failings vis-à-vis China on the basis of its democratic nature.

Rather than dismiss the successes of nondemocratic leaders, supporters of democracies should try to learn something from them. Is there anything democracies can learn from the experience of these nondemocratic states? Why are these leaders popular, while making tough decisions, despite the lack of popular elections? And are there ways to strengthen democracies so that they can achieve the same outcomes?

Response 5: This book is antitechnology. It rejects entirely the idea that technology can play a positive role in improving sustainability outcomes.

The book does takes issue not with technology but with how the idea of technological development has been applied to the sustainability issue. We often talk about technology in a vacuum, without any consideration of how said technology will improve the situation. We rarely talk about technology with any specificity, instead throwing around buzzwords like "the sharing economy" and "3D printing."

When promoted in this way, technology is merely a means of avoiding talking in any detail about uncomfortable decisions about lifestyles and standards of living. This sort of talk about technology is a method for avoiding sacrifices.

A more serious approach to using technology to solve the sustainability crisis would first require defining the problem by rejecting collective denial, next developing a tailored solution to the issue, then creating a mechanism to disseminate it to the wider populace. This has been done before—except in these cases it was often the government that helped guide the development of the appropriate technology. It also requires an acknowledgment of where technology works against sustainability goals (of which the book provides examples).

Technology will play a long-term role in improving our management of resources. We may develop more resource- and energy-efficient methods of consumption, allowing us to improve our living standards without affecting common resources. But the free market, by underpricing resources and encouraging consumption, does not encourage the creation of technologies that enable us to consume less, using fewer resources. And even if these technologies are invented, there still need to be mechanisms to get them into the hands of ordinary people. After all, toilets are an old technology, yet billions around the world still lack good access to them.

I am not calling for us to stop using our smartphones, rip up internet cables, or halt investments in R&D to improve energy systems. This book merely makes the honest argument that digital technology will not provide us with the solution to the sustainability crisis and that technology development must specifically target the challenges. The world needs water treatment plants, distribution systems, sewers, and wastewater plants much more than it does increasing numbers of fiber-optic networks, apps, and server farms.

Response 6: This book is antibusiness. In criticizing corporate social responsibility, it argues that businesses will always be inherently harmful and can never strive for anything other than profit.

There is a grain of truth in this response—namely, I do not believe that corporate social responsibility (CSR) will have a transformative impact on how businesses conduct their operations. Companies are just not built that way. In fact, from my very close encounters with, and intimate knowledge of, these operations, it is clear that most CSR strategies are simply PR campaigns. In fact, they reflect both a lack of understanding on the part of companies and how low a priority the issues are in what drives the core business. This does not mean that corporations are evil, but we should be honest in understanding that companies are just not designed to handle these sorts of issues given their business models. They would thus be ill-suited to take on this sort of responsibility. Even corporate leaders who are sincere about sustainability would likely do the job poorly given the pressure to maximize profits and appease shareholders, and how their incentives are structured. There are few Mahatmas and Mandelas in the corporate world; they tend not to last long.

We often focus on companies because we are think they are easier than governments to influence. When this pressure works, it tends to work quickly, such as when customers pressure retailers to drop suppliers with poor working conditions. Thus people push for CSR initiatives because they have given up on states exerting their social responsibility. Or, in some cases, they look to businesses providing these social values because they are concerned that states are too dangerous or corrupt.

I would rather free companies from the responsibility of managing society. It's a job they are poorly suited for, and to expect otherwise is to set oneself up for disappointment. I instead want to focus on where that responsibility truly lies—the state—and ensure that its power to protect the public good and promote sustainable development is not usurped by vested interests.

$$\bullet \; \bullet \; \bullet$$

I end this book by painting a hypothetical future for one large developing country in particular: Indonesia. There are several reasons to focus on Indonesia. It has a large, growing population, projected to be the world's fifth largest by 2050 at 320 million. It is also a fast-growing economy: analysts have included it in such groupings as the Next Eleven and the MINT, and have even (jokingly) suggested that it could replace India as the *I* in the BRICs.[1]

Population growth and economic development will strain resources in Indonesia much as they have in China and will in India. And, as chapter 9 explained, Indonesia has its own unique challenges when it comes to resource management, as shown by the connection between its poor forestry management and the annual Southeast Asian haze crisis.

Just as important, Indonesia is a democracy—one that is still maturing, to be sure, but with the concurrent transfers of power, it is increasingly unlikely that Indonesia will undergo significant democratic backslide. If state strength is to be combined with democratic values and systems of governance, Indonesia will be the place to do it.

Over the next several decades, Indonesia, like India and China, will need to develop a new political philosophy with sustainability as the backbone. What should Indonesia do over the next thirty years? And what should the country look like by 2050?

It is probably best to start at the end and work backward from there. One thing we would probably want to see is each of Indonesia's major islands becoming "self-sufficient." This would not mean that their economies would actually be able to provide all the materials and commodities that people need, but rather that each island would have an economy vibrant enough to provide adequate opportunities for its growing population, such that people could decide to stay and improve their local region rather than feeling that they needed to move elsewhere, especially overcrowded Java.

This would mean a program of investment both in Indonesia's less developed islands (e.g., Sumatra, Sulawesi, Kalimantan, and the Indonesian part of Papua New Guinea) and in its secondary cities, to avoid too much economic centralization in Jakarta and the island of Java.

Indonesia could take advantage of its bounty of natural resources. By taking greater control of commodities, it can ensure that they are harvested and exploited in a sustainable manner—firstly for local populations—while ensuring that revenues are turned toward providing basic needs. For example, Indonesia can take the revenues from oil and gas exploitation and funnel them toward investments in renewable energy across the archipelago. This investment would be backed by the state, rather than purely by private sector entities or NGOs.

Indonesia's government would also play a greater role in management of agricultural commodities, such as palm oil and wood pulp. Much as with energy and mining, Indonesia could ensure that these commodities are managed sustainably, with the long-term goal of reducing the size of the industry. The Indonesian government can embark on a program of land reform and redistribution, splitting up the large plantations into smaller farms growing higher-value produce. Money can also be funneled into investments in rural development: not just roads and ports, but cold chains, hospitals, local universities, financial institutions, and training centers.

Indonesia would also need to deepen the social contract between the people and the government, strengthening the relationship between the two.

People need to see themselves reflected in the government, not just because they have a "representative" but because the government is willing to tackle living conditions and social problems on the ground. As noted earlier in the book, most Indonesians do not think it important to get involved in Parliament or to think too deeply about their representative. One assumes this is because the relationship between the people and the government is still weak: because the government is not seen as actively working to improve living conditions on the ground, people do not believe that their choice of representative makes much of a difference. This allows representatives to win on narrow bases of support and to be susceptible to corruption.

In a stronger Indonesian state, the government would actively work to solve social issues on the ground. That may require more government intervention in the economy and more direct provision of basic needs than what the free-market model would suggest, but it would lead to a deeper relationship between the people and the government. People would trust in the government and thus take a greater role in political discussions. This requires an immediate acknowledgment of and investment in building competency across the institutions of the state, not just in the center. The Chinese example is one to look at.

Greater trust in the government would help Jakarta in its other task: being honest about resource constraints and risk. This would prevent the government from overpromising what it could do, which would breed disappointment among the population. A trusted and competent government has the room to be honest; when Jakarta says, for example, that allowing unlimited car ownership would significantly worsen traffic, its arguments would be believed by the population. By extension, if a demagogue tried to gain political support by promising a standard of living that would be impossible in a resource-constrained twenty-first century, the people could reject those arguments due to their greater awareness of resource constraints. That, at least, would be the hope.

If Indonesia succeeded in crafting an appealing political philosophy, it might encourage the country's elites to see themselves as part of the majority. Elites might therefore be more willing to accept the conditions and regulations of the government, rather than fighting against them or (more likely) working behind the scenes to sabotage them or continue to degrade the institutions through corrupt practices. They might, for example, be part of the solution to cleaning the highly polluted Ci Liwung River that runs through Jakarta and affects millions of people.

Finally, Indonesia would have found a way to preserve traditional cultures. Indonesia is one of the world's most ethnically, culturally, and linguistically diverse countries. It is the world's largest Muslim country, with significant populations of Christians, Buddhists, Confucians, and Hindus. Finding some way to preserve different cultures within Indonesia will be important if the country is to remain stable in the coming decades.

Outside observers are justifiably concerned about the fates of Indonesia's ethnic minorities in the face of the rise of political Islam. The blasphemy case brought against the former governor of Jakarta and ethnic Chinese Basuki Tjahaja Purnama, more commonly known as Ahok, is a case in point. Conservative Islamist movements called for Ahok's conviction after he quoted a verse from the Quran in a way they deemed to be derogatory. Cases like these are clearly harmful to social harmony in Indonesia.

But one should also think about where the Muslim majority is coming from. Political scientists often state that the most intractable conflicts are "paired-minority conflicts," where both sides believe they are a minority and thus under threat. One can easily understand how ethnic minorities in Indonesia believe they are minorities. But Muslims in Indonesia may believe the same—that they are a minority of Indonesian Muslims in a global culture dominated by Western values. Regardless of what you may think of the social changes happening in Indonesia due to globalization, you can understand how people might be unnerved by them.

Balancing openness to the global economy, preservation of the traditional Indonesian culture, and protections for ethnic and cultural minorities will be a major challenge for Indonesia—and an important one, given the internal and external effects of social division. But a state that has built a strong social contract with its population may be more able than a weak state to achieve these three objectives.

Then there is the underlying threat of Islamic extremism. As the world's largest Muslim-majority democracy, Indonesia has been quite fortunate in avoiding the problems of violent Islamic extremism. But it remains a threat, and perhaps a growing one if resource constraints become stricter. Limited access to basic needs can feed social unrest and extremism; revolutions and uprisings have often been correlated with the price (and, by extension, the supply) of food. As land, water, and other resources become scarce as well, the causes of conflict could multiply.

Investing in basic needs universally across a population will reduce feelings of insecurity among both ethnic minorities and the Muslim majority. By aligning with sustainability principles, this investment will also deepen trust in the government among both populations, meaning that the Indonesian government could act as a trusted arbitrator in disputes.

I am not naïve enough to think that all ethnic and cultural divisions could be solved by getting rid of poverty, drudgery, and destitution and framing that around sustainability, the challenge of our times. All diverse communities have issues with preserving social harmony. But a national development program that tackles basic needs would at least facilitate the job of the state in achieving social harmony and protecting traditional cultures.

This is a version of Indonesia that would achieve all the objectives of the sustainable state. It would manage resources—whether they are oil, minerals, the rainforest, major rivers, or clean air—for the public good. It would invest heavily in providing basic needs across the whole population, while also investing in paths upward to provide higher-quality basic needs as Indonesia continues to develop.

This would be a stronger Indonesia, more able to achieve its social objectives. It would be a more sustainable Indonesia, as it moves away from a growth-at-all-costs economic model toward one that respects hard resource constraints and seeks to define what moderate prosperity looks like for a large and diverse nation spread across hundreds of islands. And it would be a more democratic Indonesia, as its work toward providing basic needs will deepen the relationship between the government and ordinary Indonesians, bolstering the government's legitimacy and accountability, while ensuring that the population sees itself reflected in the government.

Let us hope that Indonesia—and other major developing economies—rise to the challenge by building a sustainable state.

Introduction

1. Xuemin Liu et al., "Green Development and Resource Support" in *China Green Development Index Report 2011,* edited by Xiaoxi Li and Jiancheng Pan (Berlin, Germany: Springer-Verlag, 2012), 205.

2. Ibid.

3. Gurcharan Das, *India Grows At Night: A Liberal Case for a Strong State* (New Delhi, India: Penguin Books India, 2012), 3.

Chapter 1

1. Donella H. Meadows et al., *The Limits to Growth* (New York, NY: Universe Books, 1972), 23.

2. Ronald Reagan, "Remarks at Convocation Ceremonies at the University of South Carolina in Columbia," September 20, 1983, American Presidency Project, http://www.presidency.ucsb.edu/ws/index.php?pid=40486.

3. Graham Turner, "Is Global Collapse Imminent?" MSSI Research Paper No. 4, Melbourne Sustainable Society Institute, University of Melbourne, August 4, 2014, http://sustainable.unimelb.edu.au/sites/default/files/docs/MSSI-ResearchPaper-4_Turner_2014.pdf.

4. United Nations, *Report of the World Commission on Environment and Development: Our Common Future,* 1987, http://www.un-documents.net/our-common-future.pdf.

5. Mathis Wackernagel, Laurel Hanscom, and David Lin, "Making the Sustainable Development Goals Consistent with Sustainability," *Frontiers in Energy Research,* July 11, 2017, https://www.frontiersin.org/articles/10.3389/fenrg.2017.00018/full.

6. Greenpeace, *Who's Holding Us Back? How Carbon-Intensive Industry Is Preventing Effective Climate Legislation*, November 2011, http://www .greenpeace.org/international/Global/international/publications/climate /2011/391%20-%20WhosHoldingUsBack.pdf.

7. Shashi Tharoor, *An Era of Darkness: The British Empire in India* (New Delhi, India: Aleph Book Company, 2016).

8. Walter Rodney, *How Europe Underdeveloped Africa* (Baltimore, MD: Black Classic Press, 2011).

9. Claude Alvares, "Resisting the West's Intellectual Discourse," in *Dominance of the West over the Rest* (Penang, Malaysia: Just World Trust, 1995), 12–13.

10. Joe Studwell, *How Asia Works: Success and Failure in the World's Most Dynamic Region* (New York, NY: Grove Press, 2013).

11. Kalim Siddiqui, "The Political Economy of Development in Singapore," *Research in Applied Economics* 2, no. 2 (2010), http://www.macrothink.org /journal/index.php/rae/article/view/524/367.

12. Studwell, *How Asia Works*.

13. Trucost, *Natural Capital at Risk: The Top 100 Externalities of Business*, April 2013, http://naturalcapitalcoalition.org/wp-content/uploads/2016/07 /Trucost-Nat-Cap-at-Risk-Final-Report-web.pdf.

Chapter 2

1. Tiffany Hsu, "Alibaba's Singles Day Sales Hit New Record of $25.3 Billion," *New York Times*, November 10, 2017, https://www.nytimes.com/2017/11 /10/business/alibaba-singles-day.html?_r=0.

2. "Adobe Data Shows Cyber Monday Is Largest Online Sales Day in History with $6.59 Billion," *Adobe*, November 27, 2017, http://news.adobe.com /press-release/experience-cloud/adobe-data-shows-cyber-monday-largest -online-sales-day-history-659.

3. Kevin J. Delaney, "Bill Gates and Investors Worth $170 Billion Are Launching a Fund to Fight Climate Change through Energy Innovation," *Quartz*, December 11, 2016, https://qz.com/859860/bill-gates-is-leading-a -new-1-billion-fund-focused-on-combatting-climate-change-through -innovation/.

4. Adnan Al-Daini, "The March of Renewable Energy Is Unstoppable Even by President Trump," *HuffPost*, May 4, 2017, http://www.huffingtonpost.co.uk /adnan-aldaini/renewable-energy_b_15799310.html.

5. Coral Davenport, "Clean Energy 'Moving Forward' Despite Trump's E.P.A. Pick, Experts Say," *New York Times*, December 8, 2016, https:// www.nytimes.com/2016/12/08/us/politics/trump-climate-epa-coal-jobs .html.

6. Pilita Clark, "The Big Green Bang: How Renewable Energy Became Unstoppable," *Financial Times*, May 18, 2017, https://www.ft.com/content/44ed7e90-3960-11e7-ac89-b01cc67cfeec.

7. Barack Obama, "The Irreversible Momentum of Clean Energy," *Science* 355, no. 6321, January 13, 2017, http://science.sciencemag.org/content/355/6321/126.

8. "Government of the United Kingdom," *The Stern Review Report on the Economics of Climate Change*, October 30, 2006, 1, http://webarchive.nationalarchives.gov.uk/20100407172811/http://www.hm-treasury.gov.uk/stern_review_report.htm.

9. Christopher Meyer and Julia Kirby, "The Big Idea: Leadership in the Age of Transparency," *Harvard Business Review*, April 2010, https://hbr.org/2010/04/the-big-idea-leadership-in-the-age-of-transparency.

10. Michael Schrage, "Embracing Externalities Is the Road to Hell," *Harvard Business Review*, April 21, 2010, https://hbr.org/2010/04/the-road-to-hell.html.

11. Haruka Yanagisawa, ed., *Community, Commons and Natural Resource Management in Asia* (Singapore: National University of Singapore Press, 2015): Wooyoun Lee, "Deforestation and Agricultural Productivity in Choson Korea in the 18th and 19th Century," 25–60; Shinichi Shigetomi, "Communal Land Formation and Local Society in Rural Thailand," 61–81; Minoti Chakravarty-Kaul, "Village Communities and 'Publicness' in Northern India: Self-Governance of Common Property Resources and the Environment, 1803–2008," 82–112; Yutaka Suga, "Historical Changes in Communal Fisheries in Japan," 113–135.

12. WWF Nature Greater Mekong, *Ecosystems in the Greater Mekong: Past Trends, Current Status, Possible Futures*, May 2013, 7, http://d2ouvy59p0dg6k.cloudfront.net/downloads/greater_mekong_ecosystems_report_020513.pdf.

13. Jill Petzinger, "Performance Anxiety Is Putting Car-Crazy Germans off Buying Electric Vehicles," *Quartz*, April 9, 2017, https://qz.com/953748/why-germans-dont-want-electric-cars/.

14. Centre for Public Impact, *Renewable Energy in Germany: Energiewende*, April 1, 2016, https://www.centreforpublicimpact.org/case-study/renewable-energy-germany/.

Chapter 3

1. "Xi Skips Old Growth Pledge as China Seeks Quality, Not Quantity," *Bloomberg*, October 18, 2017, https://www.bloomberg.com/news/articles/2017-10-18/xi-skips-old-growth-pledge-as-china-seeks-quality-not-quantity.

2. Jorgen Randers, *2052: A Global Forecast for the Next Forty Years* (White River Junction, VT: Chelsea Green Publishing, 2012).

3. Erik Bichard, "Fracking Boom Could Mean up to 12% More Carbon Emissions," *Conversation,* October 16, 2014, https://theconversation.com /fracking-boom-could-mean-up-to-12-more-carbon-emissions-33050.

4. Sarah Gibbens, "How Humans Are Causing Deadly Earthquakes," *National Geographic,* October 2, 2017, https://news.nationalgeographic.com /2017/10/human-induced-earthquakes-fracking-mining-video-spd/.

5. Gayathri Vaidyanathan, "Fracking Can Contaminate Drinking Water," *Scientific American,* April 4, 2016, https://www.scientificamerican.com /article/fracking-can-contaminate-drinking-water/.

6. Herman E. Daly. *Steady-State Economics: Second Edition with New Essays.* (Washington, DC: Island Press, 2012), 17.

7. Ibid, 99.

8. Herman E. Daly, "Sustainable Growth: An Impossibility Theorem," in Herman E. Daly and Kenneth Townsend, eds., *Valuing the Earth: Economics, Ecology, Ethics* (Cambridge, MA: MIT Press, 1993), 269–270.

9. Food and Agriculture Organization of the United Nations, *Food Wastage Footprint and Climate Change,* 2015, http://www.fao.org/fileadmin/templates /nr/sustainability_pathways/docs/FWF_and_climate_change.pdf.

10. Milton Friedman, *Capitalism and Freedom* (Chicago, IL: The University of Chicago Press, 1962), 112.

11. Max Chafkin and Jing Cao, "The Barbarians Are at Etsy's Hand-Hewn, Responsibly Sourced Gates," *Bloomberg Businessweek,* May 18, 2017, https:// www.bloomberg.com/news/features/2017-05-18/the-barbarians-are-at -etsy-s-hand-hewn-responsibly-sourced-gates.

12. David Dayen, "Unfriendly Skies," *American Prospect,* November 3, 2017, http://prospect.org/article/unfriendly-skies.

13. Thomas Buckley and Matthew Campbell, "If Unilever Can't Make Feel-Good Capitalism Work, Who Can?" *Bloomberg Businessweek,* August 31, 2017, https://www.bloomberg.com/news/features/2017-08-31/if-unilever -can-t-make-feel-good-capitalism-work-who-can.

14. This play on words has been widely used, but this particular instance was drawn from Jacob Hecker and Paul Pierson, *American Amnesia: How the War on Government Led Us to Forget What Made America Prosper* (New York, NY: Simon & Schuster, 2016), 4.

Chapter 4

1. Michael Bloomberg and Carl Pope, *Climate of Hope: How Cities, Businesses, and Citizens Can Save the Planet* (New York, NY: St. Martin's Press, 2017), 3.

2. Jeffrey M. Jones, "U.S. Preference for Stricter Gun Law Highest Since 1993," *Gallup,* March 14, 2018. http://news.gallup.com/poll/229562/preference-stricter-gun-laws-highest-1993.aspx.

3. "Release: Gun Owners Overwhelmingly Support Background Checks, See NRA as Out of Touch, New Poll Finds," *The Center for American Progress,* November 17, 2015, https://www.americanprogress.org/press/release/2015/11/17/125618/release-gun-owners-overwhelmingly-support-background-checks-see-nra-as-out-of-touch-new-poll-finds/.

4. Nurith Aizenman, "A Little-Known Climate Fund Is Suddenly in the Spotlight," *goats and soda,* National Public Radio, June 9, 2017, http://www.npr.org/sections/goatsandsoda/2017/06/09/532106567/a-little-known-climate-fund-is-suddenly-in-the-spotlight.

5. Matt Rivers, "Xi's Meeting with California Governor: A Message to Trump on Climate?" *CNN,* June 7, 2017, http://edition.cnn.com/2017/06/07/asia/xi-brown-meeting-climate-china/index.html.

6. We should be clear that supporting action against climate change is not the same as embracing sustainable development. For people like Governor Brown, sustainable development would only come through challenging the American Dream of consumption-led economic growth.

7. International Coffee Organization, "Coffee Market Report," February 2016, http://www.ico.org/documents/cy2015-16/cmr-0216-e.pdf.

8. Richard Florida, "Is Life Better in America's Red States?" *New York Times,* January 3, 2015, https://www.nytimes.com/2015/01/04/opinion/sunday/is-life-better-in-americas-red-states.html?_r=0.

9. "Delhi Faces Water Crisis after Canal Sabotaged in Deadly Protests," *Guardian,* February 22, 2016, https://www.theguardian.com/world/2016/feb/22/india-caste-protesters-accept-offer-to-end-riots-and-water-crisis.

Chapter 5

1. Jacob Hecker and Paul Pierson, *American Amnesia: How the War on Government Led Us to Forget What Made America Prosper* (New York, NY: Simon & Schuster, 2016).

2. Stephen Metcalf, "Neoliberalism: The Idea That Swallowed the World," *Guardian,* August 18, 2017, https://www.theguardian.com/news/2017/aug/18/neoliberalism-the-idea-that-changed-the-world.

3. "Rwanda's Economy: An Unlikely Success Story," National Public Radio, September 16, 2012, http://www.npr.org/2012/09/17/161222794/rwandan-economy-makes-unlikely-climb-in-rank.

4. David Pilling and Lionel Barber, "Interview: Kagame Insists 'Rwandans Understand the Greater Goal,'" *Financial Times,* August 27, 2017, https://www.ft.com/content/a2838936-88c6-11e7-bf50-e1c239b45787.

5.   Hiroko Tabuchi and Eric Lipton, "How Rollbacks at Scott Pruitt's E.P.A. Are a Boon to Oil and Gas," *New York Times,* May 20, 2017, https://www.nytimes.com/2017/05/20/business/energy-environment/devon-energy.html; Alec MacGillis, "Is Anyone Home at HUD?" *ProPublica,* August 22, 2017, https://www.propublica.org/article/is-anybody-home-at-hud-secretary-ben-carson.

6.   Lee Drutman and Steven Teles, "Why Congress Relies on Lobbyists Instead of Thinking for Itself," *Atlantic,* March 10, 2015, https://www.theatlantic.com/politics/archive/2015/03/when-congress-cant-think-for-itself-it-turns-to-lobbyists/387295/.

7.   Simon Cartledge, *A System Apart: Hong Kong's Political Economy from 1997 until Now* (Hawthorn, Australia: Penguin Books, 2017).

8.   Julia Lurie, "Here's How Much Water Golf Courses, Ski Resorts, and Pools Are Using in California," *Mother Jones* (August 2015), http://www.motherjones.com/environment/2015/08/golf-pools-water-drought-california/.

Chapter 6

1.   Joshua Kurlantzick, *Democracy in Retreat: The Revolt of the Middle Class and the Worldwide Decline of Representative Government* (New Haven, CT: Yale University Press, 2013), 128.

2.   Kishore Mahbubani, *Can Asians Think? Understanding the Divide between East and West* (Singapore: Marshall Cavendish, 2004).

Chapter 7

1.   Thomas Fuller, "Myanmar Backs Down, Suspending Dam Project," *New York Times,* September 30, 2011, http://www.nytimes.com/2011/10/01/world/asia/myanmar-suspends-construction-of-controversial-dam.html.

2.   Michael Vatikiotis, *Blood and Silk: Power and Conflict in Modern Southeast Asia* (London, UK: Weidenfeld & Nicolson, 2017), 9.

3.   Brian Kennedy, "Most Americans Trust the Military and Scientists to Act in the Public's Interest," *Pew Research Center,* October 18, 2016, http://www.pewresearch.org/fact-tank/2016/10/18/most-americans-trust-the-military-and-scientists-to-act-in-the-publics-interest/.

4.   Lianne Chia, "Bursting at the Seams: Singapore's Cast-Off Clothing," *Channel NewsAsia,* November 18, 2016. http://www.channelnewsasia.com/news/singapore/bursting-at-the-seams-singapore-s-cast-off-clothing-7682044

5.   Raymond Yeung, "Bad Fashion? Hongkongers Found to Spend HK$3.9 Billion on Clothes They Never or Seldom Wear," *The South China Morning Post,* June 2, 2016. http://www.scmp.com/news/hong-kong/health-environment/article/1979362/bad-fashion-hongkongers-found-spend-hk39-billion.

Chapter 9

1. "Haze from Indonesian Fires May Have Killed More Than 100,000 People—Study," *Guardian* September 19, 2016, https://www.theguardian.com/world/2016/sep/19/haze-indonesia-forest-fires-killed-100000-people-harvard-study.

2. Gecko Project, "The Palm Oil Fiefdom," *Mongabay,* October 10, 2017, https://news.mongabay.com/2017/10/the-palm-oil-fiefdom/.

3. Novianti Setuningsih, "VP Kalla Slams Neighboring Countries over Haze Complaints," *Jakarta Globe,* March 3, 2015, http://jakartaglobe.id/news/vp-kalla-slams-neighboring-countries-over-haze-complaints/.

4. Fergus Jensen, "Less Haze This Year, Indonesia Promises Southeast Asia," *Reuters,* August 29, 2016, https://www.reuters.com/article/us-indonesia-haze/less-haze-this-year-indonesia-promises-idUSKCN1141NZ.

5. Hans Nicholas Jong, "First Real Test for Jokowi on Haze as Annual Fires Return to Indonesia," *Mongabay,* August 8, 2017, https://news.mongabay.com/2017/08/indonesian-president-jokowis-first-real-test-begins-as-annual-fires-return/.

6. Joe Sandler Clark, "Forest Fires Rage across Indonesia as Dry Season Begins," *Unearthed,* March 8, 2017, https://unearthed.greenpeace.org/2017/08/03/indonesia-forest-fires-begin/.

7. Michael Vatikiotis, *Blood and Silk: Power and Conflict in Modern Southeast Asia* (London, UK: Weidenfeld & Nicolson, 2017). 160.

8. Sandra Hamid, "Indonesia's Election Activists Fight to End Money Politics," *InAsia,* Asia Foundation, January 22, 2014, https://asiafoundation.org/2014/01/22/indonesias-election-activists-fight-to-end-money-politics/.

Chapter 10

1. Cahyandito Martha-Fani, "Air Pollution in Jakarta, Indonesia," February 2001, http://www.stadtklima.de/cities/asia/id/djakarta/AirPollution.pdf.

2. Karen Kaplan, "Policy Change in Jakarta Accidentally Teaches Drivers the Value of Carpool Lanes," *Los Angeles Times,* July 6, 2017, http://www.latimes.com/science/sciencenow/la-sci-sn-carpool-lane-policy-20170706-story.html.

3. Agnes Anya, "Jakarta Optimistic about Odd-Even License Plate Policy," *Jakarta Post,* May 16, 2016, http://www.thejakartapost.com/news/2016/05/16/jakarta-optimistic-about-odd-even-license-plate-policy.html.

4. "Jakartans Spend 400 Hours a Year in Traffic, Says Survey," *Jakarta Post,* February 9, 2015, http://www.thejakartapost.com/news/2015/02/09/jakartans-spend-400-hours-a-year-traffic-says-survey.html.

5. Michael Tatarski, "Vietnam's Tale of Two Metros, One Built by the Japanese and the Other by the Chinese," *This Week in Asia,* July 30, 2017, http://www

.scmp.com/week-asia/business/article/2104149/vietnams-tale-two -metros-one-built-japanese-and-other-chinese.

6. Aparajita Rayi, "10 Million Bengalureans Lose 60 Crore Hours, Rs 3,700 Crore a Year to Road Congestion," *Times of India,* January 6, 2017, https:// timesofindia.indiatimes.com/city/bengaluru/10-million-bengalureans -lose-60-crore-hours-rs-3700-crore-a-year-to-road-congestion/articleshow /56368901.cms.

7. World Health Organization, *Global Status Report on Road Safety 2015,* http://www.who.int/violence_injury_prevention/road_safety_status/2015 /en/.

8. "20 Per Cent of Emergency Patient Deaths Blamed on Traffic Jam Delays," *Nation,* January 17, 2017, http://www.nationmultimedia.com/news/national /30304268.

9. World Health Organization, "WHO Releases Country Estimates on Air Pollution Exposure and Health Impact," September 27, 2016, http:// www.who.int/mediacentre/news/releases/2016/air-pollution-estimates /en/.

10. Anuradha Mascarenhas, "At 2.5 Million, India Tops List of Pollution-Linked Deaths: Study," *Indian Express,* October 20, 2017, http://indianexpress .com/article/india/at-2-5-million-india-tops-list-of-pollution-linked -deaths-study-4898337/.

11. Krishnadas Rajagopal, "8 People Die in Delhi Every Day Due to Pollution: SC," *Hindu,* February 7, 2017, http://www.thehindu.com/news/cities/Delhi /8-people-die-in-Delhi-every-day-due-to-pollution-SC/article17205973 .ece.

12. United Nations Department of Economic and Social Affairs, *Urban and Rural Areas 2009,* http://www.un.org/en/development/desa/population /publications/pdf/urbanization/urbanization-wallchart2009.pdf.

13. *Demographia World Urban Areas* (14th annual ed.) (Bellevue, IL: Demo-graphia, April 2018), 22.

14. Wendell Cox, "How Much of the World Is Covered in Cities?" *New Geogra-phy,* July 23, 2010, http://www.newgeography.com/content/001689-how -much-world-covered-cities.

15. United Nations Department of Economic and Social Affairs, *World Urban-ization Prospects: The 2014 Revision* (2014), http://www.un.org/en /development/desa/population/publications/pdf/urbanization/the_worlds _cities_in_2016_data_booklet.pdf; Richard Dobbs et al., *Urban World: Map-ping the Economic Power of Cities* (San Francisco, CA: McKinsey Global Institute, 2011), 9.

16. Mingxing Chen, Hua Zhang, Weidong Liu, and Wenzhong Zhang, "The Global Pattern of Urbanization and Economic Growth: Evidence from the

Last Three Decades," *PLoS One* 9, no. 8 (August 6, 2014), doi:10.1371/jour-nal.pone.0103799.

17. *Demographia World Urban Areas* (13th annual ed.) (Bellevue, IL: Demographia, April 2017), 17.

18. OECD Glossary of Statistical Terms, "Informal Settlements." November 14, 2001, https://stats.oecd.org/glossary/detail.asp?ID=1351.

19. "Rio Slum Landslide Leaves Hundreds Dead," *Guardian,* April 8, 2010, https://www.theguardian.com/world/2010/apr/08/rio-landslide-brazil.

20. Tolu Ogunlesi, "Inside Makoko: Danger and Ingenuity in the World's Biggest Floating Slum," *Guardian,* February 23, 2016, https://www.theguardian.com/cities/2016/feb/23/makoko-lagos-danger-ingenuity-floating-slum.

21. United Nations Economic and Social Commission for Asia and the Pacific, *Urbanization Trends in Asia and the Pacific,* November 2013, http://www.unescapsdd.org/files/documents/SPPS-Factsheet-urbanization-v5.pdf.

22. United Nations Department of Economic and Social Affairs, *World Economic and Social Survey 2013: Sustainable Development Challenges,* http://www.un.org/en/development/desa/policy/wess/wess_current/wess2013/WESS2013.pdf.

23. AsianCitiesAdapt, *Responding to Urban Heat Island Effects,* Policy Pointer No. 2, http://asian-cities-adapt.iclei-europe.org/fileadmin/files/Policy_Pointer/Policy_Pointer_UHI_Final.pdf; Manjula Ranagalage, Ronald C. Estoque, and Yuji Murayama, "An Urban Heat Island Study of the Colombo Metropolitan Area, Sri Lanka, Based on Landsat Data (1997–2017)," *International Journal of Geo-Information* 6:7, May 2, 2017, https://doi.org/10.3390/ijgi6070189; Sigit D. Arifwidodoa and Takahiro Tanaka, "The Characteristics of Urban Heat Island in Bangkok, Thailand," *Procedia* 195 (July 3, 2015), https://www.sciencedirect.com/science/article/pii/S1877042815039634.

24. Francisco Estrada, "A Global Economic Assessment of City Policies to Reduce Climate Change Impacts," *Nature Climate Change,* no. 7 (2017).

25. Chaitanya Mallapur, "61% Rise in Heat-Stroke Deaths over Decade across India," *Hindustan Times,* May 28, 2015, http://www.hindustantimes.com/india/61-rise-in-heat-stroke-deaths-over-decade-across-india/story-UPCxZAVYZXjJ1xyjdwtxQL.html.

26. Stephen Leahy, "Parts of Asia May Be Too Hot for People by 2100," *National Geographic,* August 2, 2017, http://news.nationalgeographic.com/2017/08/south-asia-heat-waves-temperature-rise-global-warming-climate-change/.

27. Asit K. Biswas and Cecilia Tortajada, "Urbanization and Migration in Developing Asia," *Diplomat,* September 11, 2015, http://thediplomat.com/2015/09/urbanization-and-migration-in-developing-asia/.

28. Jeanne Batalova, Andriy Shymonyak, Guntur Sugiyarto, *Firing Up Regional Brain Networks: The Promise of Brain Circulation in the ASEAN Economic Community,* Asian Development Bank, 2017, https://www.adb .org/publications/regional-brain-networks-asean

Chapter 11

1. Maggie Zhang, "New Environment Tax Will Hit Businesses in China Hard, Say Experts," *South China Morning Post,* October 3, 2017, http://www.scmp .com/business/china-business/article/2113650/new-environment-tax-will -hit-businesses-china-hard-say.

2. "China Sets Out Scaled-Back Vision for Biggest Carbon Market," *Bloomberg,* December 19, 2017, https://www.bloomberg.com/news/articles /2017-12-19/china-unveils-plan-for-world-s-biggest-carbon-trading -market.

3. Nectar Yan, "Will China's Carbon Trading Scheme Work without an Emissions Cap?" *South China Morning Post,* January 3, 2018, http://www .scmp.com/news/china/policies-politics/article/2125896/big-black-hole -chinas-carbon-market-ambitions.

4. Arthur Kroeber, *China's Economy: What Everyone Needs to Know*® (New York, NY: Oxford University Press, 2016).

5. Alister Doyle, "China Says One-Child Policy Helps Protect Climate," *Reuters,* August 30, 2007, https://www.reuters.com/article/us-climate -population-correction/corrected-china-says-one-child-policy-helps -protect-climate-idUSL3047203920070830; Wang Feng, Yong Cai, and Baochang Gu, "Population, Policy, and Politics: How Will History Judge China's One-Child Policy?" *Population and Development Review,* no. 38, Issue Supplement (2012), 115–129.

6. Matthew E. Kahn and Siqi Zheng, *Blue Skies over Beijing: Economic Growth and the Environment in China* (Princeton, NJ: Princeton University Press, 2016).

7. Zhuang Pinghui, "China Could Prevent 3 Million Deaths a Year If Air Quality Standards Tightened, Study Suggests," *South China Morning Post,* March 15, 2017, http://www.scmp.com/news/china/society/article/2078999 /china-could-prevent-3-million-deaths-year-if-air-quality.

8. "Four-Fifths of China's Water from Wells 'Unsafe Because of Pollution,'" *Guardian,* April 16, 2016, https://www.theguardian.com/environment/2016 /apr/12/four-fifths-of-chinas-water-from-wells-unsafe-because-of -pollution.

9. Nadya Ivanova, "Toxic Water: Across Much of China, Huge Harvests Irrigated with Industrial and Agricultural Runoff," *Circle of Blue,* January 18, 2013, http://www.circleofblue.org/2013/world/toxic-water-across-much

-of-china-huge-harvests-irrigated-with-industrial-and-agricultural
-runoff/.

10. Kroeber, *China's Economy.*

11. Dominique Patton, "More Than 40 Percent of China's Arable Land Degraded: Xinhua," *Reuters,* November 4, 2014, https://www.reuters.com
/article/us-china-soil/more-than-40-percent-of-chinas-arable-land
-degraded-xinhua-idUSKBN0IO0Y720141104.

12. "All Dried Up," *Economist,* October 10, 2013, https://www.economist
.com/news/china/21587813-northern-china-running-out-water
-governments-remedies-are-potentially-disastrous-all.

13. Chris Luo, "New Study Shows Dramatic Fall in Number of Rivers in China,"
South China Morning Post, March 27, 2013, http://www.scmp.com/news
/china/article/1200961/new-study-shows-dramatic-fall-number-rivers-china.

14. Kroeber, *China's Economy.*

15. Hannah Ryder, "The End of Poverty in China?" *Project Syndicate,*
March 28, 2017, https://www.project-syndicate.org/commentary/china
-end-rural-poverty-by-2020-by-hannah-ryder-1-2017-03?barrier= accessreg.

16. The World Bank Development Research Group, "Poverty Headcount Ratio at $3.20 a Day (2011 PPP) (% of Population)," https://data.worldbank
.org/indicator/SI.POV.LMIC?locations= CN.

17. The World Bank Development Research Group, "Poverty Headcount Ratio at $5.50 a Day (2011 PPP) (% of Population)," https://data.worldbank
.org/indicator/SI.POV.UMIC?locations= CN.

18. Brendan Coates and Nghi Luu, "China's Emergence in Global Commodity
Markets," June 1, 2017, https://static.treasury.gov.au/uploads/sites/1/2017
/06/01-China-Commodity-demand.pdf.

19. Peter Corne and Johnny Browaeys, "China Cleans Up Its Act on Environmental Enforcement," *Diplomat,* December 9, 2017, https://thediplomat
.com/2017/12/china-cleans-up-its-act-on-environmental-enforcement/.

20. Michael Hirtzer, "China Agrees to Allow Imports of U.S. Rice for First
Time: USDA," *Reuters,* July 20, 2017, http://www.scmp.com/business
/global-economy/article/2103518/china-allows-imports-us-rice-first-time
-ever.

21. Kroeber, *China's Economy,* 456.

Chapter 12

1. "For Asia, the Path to Prosperity Starts with Land Reform," *Economist,* October 12, 2017, https://www.economist.com/news/asia/21730184-countries
-did-it-properly-have-grown-fastest-asia-path-prosperity-starts-land.

Chapter 13

1.   Jim O'Neill, "Who You Calling a BRIC?" *Bloomberg View,* November 13, 2013, https://www.bloomberg.com/view/articles/2013-11-12/who-you -calling-a-bric-; Jim O'Neill, "The 'Next Eleven' and the World Economy," *Bloomberg View,* April 18, 2018, https://www.project-syndicate.org /commentary/n-11-global-economy-by-jim-o-neill-2018-04.

BIBLIOGRAPHY

Books and Book Chapters

Alvares, Claude. "Resisting the West's Intellectual Discourse." In *Dominance of the West over the Rest*. Penang, Malaysia: Just World Trust, 1995, 1–21.

Bloomberg, Michael, and Carl Pope. *Climate of Hope: How Cities, Businesses, and Citizens Can Save the Planet*. New York, NY: St. Martin's Press, 2017.

Cartledge, Simon. *A System Apart: Hong Kong's Political Economy from 1997 until Now*. Hawthorn, Australia: Penguin Books, 2017.

Chakravarty-Kaul, Minoti. "Village Communities and 'Publicness' in Northern India: Self-Governance of Common Property Resources and the Environment, 1803–2008." In Haruka Yanagisawa (ed.), *Community, Commons and Natural Resource Management in Asia*. Singapore: National University of Singapore Press, 2015, 82–112.

Daly, Herman E. *Steady-State Economics: Second Edition with New Essays*. Washington, DC: Island Press, 2012.

Daly, Herman E., "Sustainable Growth: An Impossibility Theorem." In Herman E. Daly and Kenneth Townsend, eds., *Valuing the Earth: Economics, Ecology, Ethics*. Cambridge, MA: MIT Press, 1992, 267–275.

Das, Gurcharan. *India Grows At Night: A Liberal Case for a Strong State*. New Delhi, India: Penguin Books, 2012.

Friedman, Milton. *Capitalism and Freedom*. Chicago, IL: The University of Chicago Press, 1962.

Hecker, Jacob, and Paul Pierson. *American Amnesia: How the War on Government Led Us to Forget What Made America Prosper*. New York, NY: Simon & Schuster, 2016.

Kahn, Matthew E., and Siqi Zheng. *Blue Skies over Beijing: Economic Growth and the Environment in China*. Princeton, NJ: Princeton University Press, 2016.

Kroeber, Arthur. *China's Economy: What Everyone Needs to Know®* New York, NY: Oxford University Press, 2016.

Kurlantzick, Joshua. *Democracy in Retreat: The Revolt of the Middle Class and the Worldwide Decline of Representative Government*. New Haven, CT: Yale University Press, 2013.

Lee, Wooyoun. "Deforestation and Agricultural Productivity in Choson Korea in the 18th and 19th Century." In Haruka Yanagisawa (ed.), *Community, Commons and Natural Resource Management in Asia*. Singapore: National University of Singapore Press, 2015, 25–60.

Liu, Xuemin, et al., "Green Development and Resource Support." In Xiaoxi Li and Jiancheng Pan (eds.), *China Green Development Index Report 2011*. Berlin, Germany: Springer-Verlag, 2012, 205.

Mahbubani, Kishore. *Can Asians Think? Understanding the Divide between East and West*. Singapore: Marshall Cavendish, 2004.

Meadows, Donella H., et al., *The Limits to Growth*. New York, NY: Universe Books, 1972.

Randers, Jorgen. *2052: A Global Forecast for the Next Forty Years*. White River Junction, VT: Chelsea Green Publishing, 2012.

Rodney, Walter. *How Europe Underdeveloped Africa*. Baltimore, MD: Black Classic Press, 2011.

Shigetomi, Shinichi. "Communal Land Formation and Local Society in Rural Thailand." In Haruka Yanagisawa (ed.), *Community, Commons and Natural Resource Management in Asia*. Singapore: National University of Singapore Press, 2015, 61–81.

Studwell, Joe. *How Asia Works: Success and Failure in the World's Most Dynamic Region*. New York, NY: Grove Press, 2014.

Suga, Yutaka. "Historical Changes in Communal Fisheries in Japan." In Haruka Yanagisawa (ed.), *Community, Commons and Natural Resource Management in Asia*. Singapore: National University of Singapore Press, 2015, 113–135.

Tharoor, Shashi. *An Era of Darkness: The British Empire in India*. New Delhi, India: Aleph Book Company, 2016.

Vatikiotis, Michael. *Blood and Silk: Power and Conflict in Modern Southeast Asia*. London, UK: Weidenfeld & Nicolson, 2017.

Yanagisawa, Haruka, ed. *Community, Commons and Natural Resource Management in Asia*. Singapore: National University of Singapore Press, 2015.

Scientific Papers and Journal Articles

Arifwidodoa, Sigit D., and Takahiro Tanaka. "The Characteristics of Urban Heat Island in Bangkok, Thailand." *Procedia* 195 (July 3, 2015). http://ac.els-cdn

.com/S1877042815039634/1-s2.0-S1877042815039634-main.pdf?_tid
=0e58c03e-7758–11e7–84f0–00000aab0f27&acdnat=1501660754_e550af
d15e9409e599c33f286ac435f0.

Chen, Mingxing, Hua Zhang, Weidong Liu, and Wenzhong Zhang. "The Global Pattern of Urbanization and Economic Growth: Evidence from the Last Three Decades." *PLoS One* 9, no. 8 (August 6, 2014). doi:10.1371/journal .pone.0103799.

Coates, Brendan, and Nghi Luu. "China's Emergence in Global Commodity Markets," June 1, 2017. https://static.treasury.gov.au/uploads/sites/1/2017 /06/01-China-Commodity-demand.pdf.

Estrada, Francisco. "A Global Economic Assessment of City Policies to Reduce Climate Change Impacts," *Nature Climate Change*, no. 7 (2017), 403–406. https://www.nature.com/articles/nclimate3301

Feng, Wang, Yong Cai, and Baochang Gu, "Population, Policy, and Politics: How Will History Judge China's One-Child Policy?" *Population and Development Review* 38 Issue Supplement (2012), 115–129.

Obama, Barack. "The Irreversible Momentum of Clean Energy." *Science* 355, no. 6321. (January 13, 2017). http://science.sciencemag.org/content/355 /6321/126.

Ranagalage, Manjula, Ronald C. Estoque, and Yuji Murayama. "An Urban Heat Island Study of the Colombo Metropolitan Area, Sri Lanka, Based on Landsat Data (1997–2017)." *International Journal of Geo-Information* 6, no. 7 (May 2, 2017). https://doi.org/10.3390/ijgi6070189.

Siddiqui, Kalim. "The Political Economy of Development in Singapore." *Research in Applied Economics* 2, no. 2 (2010). http://www.macrothink.org /journal/index.php/rae/article/view/524/367.

Turner, Graham. "Is Global Collapse Imminent?" MSSI Research Paper No. 4. Melbourne Sustainable Society Institute, University of Melbourne, August 4, 2014. http://sustainable.unimelb.edu.au/sites/default/files/docs /MSSI-ResearchPaper-4_Turner_2014.pdf.

Wackernagel, Mathis, Laurel Hanscom, and David Lin, "Making the Sustainable Development Goals Consistent with Sustainability." *Frontiers in Energy Research,* July 11, 2017. https://www.frontiersin.org/articles/10.3389 /fenrg.2017.00018/full.

Reports

AsianCitiesAdapt. *Responding to Urban Heat Island Effects.* Policy Pointer No. 2, n.d. http://asian-cities-adapt.iclei-europe.org/fileadmin/files/Policy_Pointer /Policy_Pointer_UHI_Final.pdf.

Asian Development Bank. *Firing Up Regional Brain Networks: The Promise of Brain Circulation in the ASEAN Economic Community,* 2017. https://www

.adb.org/publications/regional-brain-networks-asean FINAL.pdf&usg=AFQ jCNHJ48TKpgrIukM23U26ih5UhDxE0w.

Centre for Public Impact. *Renewable Energy in Germany: Energiewende,* April 1, 2016. https://www.centreforpublicimpact.org/case-study/renewable-energy -germany/.

Demographia World Urban Areas (14th annual ed.) (Bellevue, IL: Demographia, April 2018).

Dobbs, Richard, et al., *Urban World: Mapping the Economic Power of Cities* (San Francisco, CA: McKinsey Global Institute, 2011), 9.

Food and Agriculture Organization of the United Nations. *Food Wastage Foot- print and Climate Change,* 2015. http://www.fao.org/fileadmin/templates /nr/sustainability_pathways/docs/FWF_and_climate_change.pdf.

Government of the United Kingdom. *The Stern Review Report on the Economics of Climate Change,* October 30, 2006. http://webarchive.nationalarchives .gov.uk/20100407172811/http://www.hm-treasury.gov.uk/stern_review _report.htm.

Greenpeace. *Who's Holding Us Back? How Carbon-Intensive Industry Is Prevent- ing Effective Climate Legislation,* November 2011. http://www.greenpeace .org/international/Global/international/publications/climate/2011 /391%20-%20WhosHoldingUsBack.pdf.

International Coffee Organization. "Coffee Market Report," February 2016. http://www.ico.org/documents/cy2015-16/cmr-0216-e.pdf.

Trucost. *Natural Capital at Risk: The Top 100 Externalities of Business,* April 2013. http://naturalcapitalcoalition.org/wp-content/uploads/2016/07/Trucost -Nat-Cap-at-Risk-Final-Report-web.pdf.

United Nations. *Report of the World Commission on Environment and Develop- ment: Our Common Future,* 1987. http://www.un-documents.net/our-common -future.pdf.

United Nations Department of Economic and Social Affairs. *Urban and Rural Areas 2009.* http://www.un.org/en/development/desa/population/publications /pdf/urbanization/urbanization-wallchart2009.pdf.

United Nations Department of Economic and Social Affairs. *World Economic and Social Survey 2013: Sustainable Development Challenges.* http://www.un .org/en/development/desa/policy/wess/wess_current/wess2013 /WESS2013.pdf.

United Nations Department of Economic and Social Affairs. *World Urbaniza- tion Prospects: The 2014 Revision,* 2014. http://www.un.org/en/development /desa/population/publications/pdf/urbanization/the_worlds_cities_in _2016_data_booklet.pdf.

United Nations Economic and Social Commission for Asia and the Pacific. *Ur- banization Trends in Asia and the Pacific,* November 2013. http://www .unescapsdd.org/files/documents/SPPS-Factsheet-urbanization-v5.pdf.

World Health Organization. *Global Status Report on Road Safety 2015.* http://
www.who.int/violence_injury_prevention/road_safety_status/2015/en/.

WWF Nature Greater Mekong. *Ecosystems in the Greater Mekong: Past Trends, Current Status, Possible Futures,* May 2013, 7. http://d2ouvy59p0dg6k.cloudfront
.net/downloads/greater_mekong_ecosystems_report_020513.pdf.

Newspaper Articles and Press Releases

Adobe Digital Insights. "Adobe Data Shows Cyber Monday Is Largest Online Sales Day in History with $6.59 Billion," November 27, 2017. http://news
.adobe.com/press-release/experience-cloud/adobe-data-shows-cyber
-monday-largest-online-sales-day-history-659.

Aizenman, Nurith. "A Little-Known Climate Fund Is Suddenly in the Spotlight." National Public Radio, June 9, 2017. http://www.npr.org/sections
/goatsandsoda/2017/06/09/532106567/a-little-known-climate-fund-is
-suddenly-in-the-spotlight.

Al-Daini, Adnan. "The March of Renewable Energy Is Unstoppable Even by President Trump." *HuffPost,* May 4, 2017. http://www.huffingtonpost.co.uk
/adnan-aldaini/renewable-energy_b_15799310.html.

"All Dried Up." *Economist,* October 10, 2013. https://www.economist.com
/news/china/21587813-northern-china-running-out-water-governments
-remedies-are-potentially-disastrous-all.

Anya, Agnes. "Jakarta Optimistic About Odd-Even License Plate Policy." *Jakarta Post,* May 16, 2016. http://www.thejakartapost.com/news/2016/05/16
/jakarta-optimistic-about-odd-even-license-plate-policy.html.

Bichard, Erik. "Fracking Boom Could Mean up to 12% More Carbon Emissions." *Conversation,* October 16, 2014. https://theconversation.com/fracking
-boom-could-mean-up-to-12-more-carbon-emissions-33050.

Biswas, Asit K., and Cecilia Tortajada. "Urbanization and Migration in Developing Asia." *Diplomat,* September 11, 2015. http://thediplomat.com/2015/09
/urbanization-and-migration-in-developing-asia/.

Buckley, Thomas, and Matthew Campbell. "If Unilever Can't Make Feel-Good Capitalism Work, Who Can?" *Bloomberg Businessweek,* August 31, 2017. https://www.bloomberg.com/news/features/2017–08–31/if-unilever-can-t
-make-feel-good-capitalism-work-who-can.

Chafkin, Max, and Jing Cao. "The Barbarians Are at Etsy's Hand-Hewn, Responsibly Sourced Gates." *Bloomberg Businessweek,* May 18, 2017. https://
www.bloomberg.com/news/features/2017–05–18/the-barbarians-are-at
-etsy-s-hand-hewn-responsibly-sourced-gates.

Chia, Lianne. "Bursting at the seams: Singapore's cast-off clothing," *Channel NewsAsia,* November 18, 2016. http://www.channelnewsasia.com/news
/singapore/bursting-at-the-seams-singapore-s-cast-off-clothing-7682044.

"China Sets Out Scaled-Back Vision for Biggest Carbon Market." *Bloomberg,* December 19, 2017. https://www.bloomberg.com/news/articles/2017–12–19/china-unveils-plan-for-world-s-biggest-carbon-trading-market.

Clark, Joe Sandler. "Forest Fires Rage across Indonesia as Dry Season Begins," *Unearthed,* March 8, 2017. https://unearthed.greenpeace.org/2017/08/03/indonesia-forest-fires-begin/.

Clark, Pilita. "The Big Green Bang: How Renewable Energy Became Unstoppable." *Financial Times,* May 18, 2017. https://www.ft.com/content/44ed7e90–3960–11e7-ac89-b01cc67cfeec.

Corne, Peter, and Johnny Browaeys. "China Cleans Up Its Act on Environmental Enforcement." *Diplomat,* December 9, 2017. https://thediplomat.com/2017/12/china-cleans-up-its-act-on-environmental-enforcement/.

Cox, Wendell. "How Much of the World Is Covered in Cities?" *New Geography,* July 23, 2010. http://www.newgeography.com/content/001689-how-much-world-covered-cities.

Davenport, Coral. "Clean Energy 'Moving Forward' Despite Trump's E.P.A. Pick, Experts Say." *New York Times,* December 8, 2016. https://www.nytimes.com/2016/12/08/us/politics/trump-climate-epa-coal-jobs.html.

Dayen, David. "Unfriendly Skies." *American Prospect,* November 3, 2017. http://prospect.org/article/unfriendly-skies.

Delaney, Kevin J. "Bill Gates and Investors Worth $170 Billion Are Launching a Fund to Fight Climate Change through Energy Innovation." *Quartz,* December 11, 2016. https://qz.com/859860/bill-gates-is-leading-a-new-1-billion-fund-focused-on-combatting-climate-change-through-innovation/.

"Delhi Faces Water Crisis after Canal Sabotaged in Deadly Protests." *Guardian,* February 22, 2016. https://www.theguardian.com/world/2016/feb/22/india-caste-protesters-accept-offer-to-end-riots-and-water-crisis.

Doyle, Alister. "China says One-Child Policy Helps Protect Climate," *Reuters,* August 30, 2007. https://www.reuters.com/article/us-climate-population-correction/corrected-china-says-one-child-policy-helps-protect-climate-idUSL3047203920070830.

Drutman, Lee, and Steven Teles. "Why Congress Relies on Lobbyists Instead of Thinking for Itself." *Atlantic,* March 10, 2015. https://www.theatlantic.com/politics/archive/2015/03/when-congress-cant-think-for-itself-it-turns-to-lobbyists/387295/.

Florida, Richard. "Is Life Better in America's Red States?" *New York Times,* January 3, 2015. https://www.nytimes.com/2015/01/04/opinion/sunday/is-life-better-in-americas-red-states.html?_r=0.

"For Asia, the Path to Prosperity Starts with Land Reform." *Economist,* October 12, 2017. https://www.economist.com/news/asia/21730184-countries-did-it-properly-have-grown-fastest-asia-path-prosperity-starts-land.

"Four-Fifths of China's Water from Wells 'Unsafe Because of Pollution.'" *Guardian,* April 16, 2016. https://www.theguardian.com/environment/2016/apr/12/four-fifths-of-chinas-water-from-wells-unsafe-because-of-pollution.

Fuller, Thomas. "Myanmar Backs Down, Suspending Dam Project." *New York Times,* September 30, 2011. http://www.nytimes.com/2011/10/01/world/asia/myanmar-suspends-construction-of-controversial-dam.html.

Gecko Project. "The Palm Oil Fiefdom." *Mongabay,* October 10, 2017. https://news.mongabay.com/2017/10/the-palm-oil-fiefdom/.

Gibbens, Sarah. "How Humans Are Causing Deadly Earthquakes." *National Geographic,* October 2, 20917. https://news.nationalgeographic.com/2017/10/human-induced-earthquakes-fracking-mining-video-spd/.

Hamid, Sandra. "Indonesia's Election Activists Fight to End Money Politics." *InAsia.* Asia Foundation, January 22, 2014. https://asiafoundation.org/2014/01/22/indonesias-election-activists-fight-to-end-money-politics/.

"Haze from Indonesian Fires May Have Killed More Than 100,000 People—Study." *Guardian,* September 19, 2016. https://www.theguardian.com/world/2016/sep/19/haze-indonesia-forest-fires-killed-100000-people-harvard-study.

Hirtzer, Michael. "China Agrees to Allow Imports of U.S. Rice for First Time: USDA." *Reuters,* July 20, 2017. http://www.scmp.com/business/global-economy/article/2103518/china-allows-imports-us-rice-first-time-ever.

Hsu, Tiffany. "Alibaba's Singles Day Sales Hit New Record of $25.3 Billion." *New York Times,* November 10, 2017. https://www.nytimes.com/2017/11/10/business/alibaba-singles-day.html?_r=0.

Ivanova, Nadya. "Toxic Water: Across Much of China, Huge Harvests Irrigated with Industrial and Agricultural Runoff." *Circle of Blue,* January 18, 2013. http://www.circleofblue.org/2013/world/toxic-water-across-much-of-china-huge-harvests-irrigated-with-industrial-and-agricultural-runoff/.

"Jakartans Spend 400 Hours a Year in Traffic, Says Survey." *Jakarta Post,* February 9, 2015. http://www.thejakartapost.com/news/2015/02/09/jakartans-spend-400-hours-a-year-traffic-says-survey.html.

Jensen, Fergus. "Less Haze This Year, Indonesia Promises Southeast Asia." *Reuters,* August 29, 2016. https://www.reuters.com/article/us-indonesia-haze/less-haze-this-year-indonesia-promises-idUSKCN1141NZ.

Jones, Jeffrey M. "U.S. Preference for Stricter Gun Law Highest Since 1993." *Gallup,* March 14, 2018. http://news.gallup.com/poll/229562/preference-stricter-gun-laws-highest-1993.aspx.

Jong, Hans Nicholas. "First Real Test for Jokowi on Haze as Annual Fires Return to Indonesia." *Mongabay,* August 8, 2017. https://news.mongabay.com/2017/08/indonesian-president-jokowis-first-real-test-begins-as-annual-fires-return/.

Kaplan, Karen. "Policy Change in Jakarta Accidentally Teaches Drivers the Value of Carpool Lanes." *Los Angeles Times,* July 6, 2017. http://www .latimes.com/science/sciencenow/la-sci-sn-carpool-lane-policy-20170706 -story.html.

Katz, Josh. "Drug Deaths in America Are Rising Faster Than Ever." *New York Times,* June 5, 2017. https://www.nytimes.com/interactive/2017/06/05 /upshot/opioid-epidemic-drug-overdose-deaths-are-rising-faster-than -ever.html.

Kennedy, Brian. "Most Americans Trust the Military and Scientists to Act in the Public's Interest." Pew Research Center, October 18, 2016. http://www .pewresearch.org/fact-tank/2016/10/18/most-americans-trust-the -military-and-scientists-to-act-in-the-publics-interest/.

Leahy, Stephen. "Parts of Asia May Be Too Hot for People by 2100." *National Geographic,* August 2, 2017. http://news.nationalgeographic.com/2017/08 /south-asia-heat-waves-temperature-rise-global-warming-climate-change/.

Luo, Chris. "New Study Shows Dramatic Fall in Number of Rivers in China." *South China Morning Post,* March 27, 2013. http://www.scmp.com/news /china/article/1200961/new-study-shows-dramatic-fall-number-rivers -china.

Lurie, Julia. "Here's How Much Water Golf Courses, Ski Resorts, and Pools Are Using in California." *Mother Jones,* August 2015. http://www.motherjones .com/environment/2015/08/golf-pools-water-drought-california/.

MacGillis, Alec. "Is Anyone Home at HUD?" *ProPublica,* August 22, 2017. https://www.propublica.org/article/is-anybody-home-at-hud-secretary -ben-carson.

Mallapur, Chaitanya. "61% Rise in Heat-Stroke Deaths Over Decade Across India." *Hindustan Times,* May 28, 2015. http://www.hindustantimes.com /india/61-rise-in-heat-stroke-deaths-over-decade-across-india/story -UPCxZAVYZXjJ1xyjdwtxQL.html.

Martha-Fani, Cahyandito. "Air Pollution in Jakarta Indonesia," February 2001. http://www.stadtklima.de/cities/asia/id/djakarta/AirPollution.pdf.

Mascarenhas, Anuradha. "At 2.5 Million, India Tops List of Pollution-Linked Deaths: Study." *Indian Express,* October 20, 2017. http://indianexpress.com /article/india/at-2-5-million-india-tops-list-of-pollution-linked-deaths -study-4898337/.

Metcalf, Stephen. "Neoliberalism: The Idea That Swallowed the World." *Guardian,* August 18, 2017. https://www.theguardian.com/news/2017/aug/18 /neoliberalism-the-idea-that-changed-the-world.

Meyer, Christopher, and Julia Kirby. "The Big Idea: Leadership in the Age of Transparency," *Harvard Business Review,* April 2010, https://hbr.org/2010 /04/the-big-idea-leadership-in-the-age-of-transparency.

Ogunlesi, Tolu. "Inside Makoko: Danger and Ingenuity in the World's Biggest Floating Slum." *Guardian,* February 23, 2016. https://www.theguardian.com/cities/2016/feb/23/makoko-lagos-danger-ingenuity-floating-slum.

O'Neill, Jim. "The 'Next Eleven' and the World Economy," *Bloomberg View,* April 18, 2018. https://www.project-syndicate.org/commentary/n-11-global-economy-by-jim-o-neill-2018-04.

O'Neill, Jim. "Who You Calling a BRIC?" *Bloomberg View,* November 13, 2013. https://www.bloomberg.com/view/articles/2013-11-12/who-you-calling-a-bric-.

Patton, Dominique. "More Than 40 Percent of China's Arable Land Degraded: Xinhua." *Reuters,* November 4, 2014. https://www.reuters.com/article/us-china-soil/more-than-40-percent-of-chinas-arable-land-degraded-xinhua-idUSKBN0IO0Y720141104.

Petzinger, Jill. "Performance Anxiety Is Putting Car-Crazy Germans off Buying Electric Vehicles." *Quartz,* April 9, 2017. https://qz.com/953748/why-germans-dont-want-electric-cars/.

Pilling, David, and Lionel Barber, "Interview: Kagame Insists 'Rwandans Understand the Greater Goal.'" *Financial Times,* August 27, 2017. https://www.ft.com/content/a2838936–88c6–11e7-bf50-e1c239b45787

Pinghui, Zhuang. "China Could Prevent 3 Million Deaths a Year If Air Quality Standards Tightened, Study Suggests." *South China Morning Post,* March 15, 2017. http://www.scmp.com/news/china/society/article/2078999/china-could-prevent-3-million-deaths-year-if-air-quality.

Rajagopal, Krishnadas. "8 People Die in Delhi Every Day Due to Pollution: SC." *Hindu,* February 7, 2017. http://www.thehindu.com/news/cities/Delhi/8-people-die-in-Delhi-every-day-due-to-pollution-SC/article17205973.ece.

Rayi, Aparajita. "10 Million Bengalureans Lose 60 Crore Hours, Rs 3,700 Crore a Year to Road Congestion." *Times of India,* January 6, 2017. https://timesofindia.indiatimes.com/city/bengaluru/10-million-bengalureans-lose-60-crore-hours-rs-3700-crore-a-year-to-road-congestion/articleshow/56368901.cms.

"Release: Gun Owners Overwhelmingly Support Background Checks, See NRA as Out of Touch, New Poll Finds." The Center for American Progress, November 17, 2015. https://www.americanprogress.org/press/release/2015/11/17/125618/release-gun-owners-overwhelmingly-support-background-checks-see-nra-as-out-of-touch-new-poll-finds/.

"Rio Slum Landslide Leaves Hundreds Dead." *Guardian,* April 8, 2010. https://www.theguardian.com/world/2010/apr/08/rio-landslide-brazil.

Rivers, Matt. "Xi's Meeting with California Governor: A Message to Trump on Climate?" CNN, June 7, 2017. http://edition.cnn.com/2017/06/07/asia/xi-brown-meeting-climate-china/index.html.

"Rwanda's Economy: An Unlikely Success Story." National Public Radio, September 16, 2012. http://www.npr.org/2012/09/17/161222794/rwandan -economy-makes-unlikely-climb-in-rank.

Ryder, Hannah. "The End of Poverty in China?" *Project Syndicate,* March 28, 2017. https://www.project-syndicate.org/commentary/china-end-rural -poverty-by-2020-by-hannah-ryder-1–2017–03?barrier= accessreg.

Schrage, Michael. "Embracing Externalities Is the Road to Hell." *Harvard Business Review,* April 21, 2010. https://hbr.org/2010/04/the-road-to-hell.html.

Setuningsih, Novianti. "VP Kalla Slams Neighboring Countries over Haze Complaints." *Jakarta Globe,* March 3, 2015. http://jakartaglobe.id/news/vp -kalla-slams-neighboring-countries-over-haze-complaints/.

Tabuchi, Hiroko, and Eric Lipton. "How Rollbacks at Scott Pruitt's E.P.A. Are a Boon to Oil and Gas." *New York Times,* May 20, 2017. https://www.nytimes .com/2017/05/20/business/energy-environment/devon-energy.html.

Tatarski, Michael. "Vietnam's Tale of Two Metros, One Built by the Japanese and the Other by the Chinese." *This Week in Asia,* July 30, 2017. http://www .scmp.com/week-asia/business/article/2104149/vietnams-tale-two -metros-one-built-japanese-and-other-chinese.

"20 Per Cent of Emergency Patient Deaths Blamed on Traffic Jam Delays." *Nation,* January 17, 2017. http://www.nationmultimedia.com/news/national /30304268.

Vaidyanathan, Gayathri. "Fracking Can Contaminate Drinking Water." *Scientific American,* April 4, 2016. https://www.scientificamerican.com/article /fracking-can-contaminate-drinking-water/.

World Health Organization. "WHO Releases Country Estimates on Air Pollution Exposure and Health Impact," September 27, 2016. http://www.who.int /mediacentre/news/releases/2016/air-pollution-estimates/en/.

"Xi Skips Old Growth Pledge as China Seeks Quality, Not Quantity." *Bloomberg,* October 18, 2017. https://www.bloomberg.com/news/articles/2017–10–18 /xi-skips-old-growth-pledge-as-china-seeks-quality-not-quantity.

Yan, Nectar. "Will China's Carbon Trading Scheme Work without an Emissions Cap?" *South China Morning Post,* January 3, 2018. http://www.scmp.com /news/china/policies-politics/article/2125896/big-black-hole-chinas -carbon-market-ambitions.

Yeung, Raymond. "Bad Fashion? Hongkongers Found to Spend HK$3.9 Billion on Clothes They Never or Seldom Wear," *The South China Morning Post,* June 23, 2016. http://www.scmp.com/news/hong-kong/health-environment /article/1979362/bad-fashion-hongkongers-found-spend-hk39-billion.

Zhang, Maggie "New Environment Tax Will Hit Businesses in China Hard, Say Experts." *South China Morning Post,* October 3, 2017. http://www.scmp .com/business/china-business/article/2113650/new-environment-tax-will -hit-businesses-china-hard-say.

Other

OECD, "Informal Settlements," *Glossary of Environment Statistics, Studies in Methods,* Series F, No. 67. New York, NY: United Nations, 1997, https://stats.oecd.org/glossary/detail.asp?ID=1351.

Reagan, Ronald. "Remarks at Convocation Ceremonies at the University of South Carolina in Columbia," September 20, 1983. American Presidency Project, http://www.presidency.ucsb.edu/ws/index.php?pid=40486.

The World Bank Development Research Group. "Poverty Headcount Ratio at $3.20 a Day (2011 PPP) (% of Population)." https://data.worldbank.org/indicator/SI.POV.LMIC?locations= CN.

The World Bank Development Research Group. "Poverty Headcount Ratio at $5.50 a day (2011 PPP) (% of Population)." https://data.worldbank.org/indicator/SI.POV.UMIC?locations= CN.

ACKNOWLEDGMENTS

Writing this book while holding a full-time job running the Global Institute for Tomorrow (GIFT) in Hong Kong, especially during a period when it is expanding into Southeast Asia and Japan, meant that I needed the support, help, patience, and tolerance of many. They are far too numerous to mention here, but I must acknowledge a few.

First, I thank all my colleagues at GIFT who tolerated my constant interruptions in the office with ideas for the book. I also thank them for carrying the load when I was distracted by the book. In particular, I thank Mei Cheung for taking so much off my plate and making sure I met my various commitments. Eric Stryson, Karim Rushdy, Helena Lim, Caroline Ngai, Yuxin Hou, Rachita Mehrotra, Pial Khadilla, Synna Ong, Rafiqah Ghany, Olivia Lai, and Steven Yuen, thank you for your support.

Two colleagues, Feini Tuang and Nicholas Gordon, spent a good deal of time helping me write the book, and to them I am extremely indebted.

Feini helped with research, fact checking, and developing diagrams. She is a stickler for details and passionate about the topic, particularly the issues related to rural development and agriculture, and I relied on her to check that I was on firm ground. She helped keep me honest.

Nicholas helped flesh out my thoughts with details from research. Given my constant travels, I relied on him to turn my emails, scribbled notes, and short discussions into initial drafts that I could develop further while on the road. He was also an invaluable source of counterarguments and a check on any tendency to be too polemical. I am grateful for his repeated "I do not think you should say that."

Then there are others who by just being there and providing encouragement gave me the strength to take on these issues in the manner I have.

For this I first thank my dear friend and mentor Professor Hideh Takahashi from Japan, who has been an inspiration and constant source of ideas and support with his samurai spirit. He may be surprised, but David Eldon, a member of GIFT's Advisory Council, is another I thank for always being available to offer advice and encouragement. Then there is Ronnie Chan, well known as the "godfather" of the Asia Society, who never failed to support me and who constantly encouraged me to write more.

Others I must mention because they have all encouraged me or shown great interest over the years are Dr. Edgar Cheng, Fred Tsao, Tai Sook Yee, Thierry Malleret, Bernard Pouliot, Ravi Chidambaram, Priti Devi, Zoher Abdoolcarim, Yonden Lhatoo, Annie Cheng, Yuichi Nishigori, Simon Cartledge, and Marius Van Huijstee. I must also acknowledge the late Professor Jean Pierre Lehman who had been a staunch supporter and who always had constructive things to say even when I tested out my most radical ideas in discussions with him.

A special mention must be made of Dr. David Victor of UCSD, who chaired the Global Agenda Council on Governance for Sustainability at the World Economic Forum, of which I was a member. It was David who urged me to turn a paper I wrote for the GAC about sustainability and the pivotal role of the state in the developing world into a book to initiate a wider debate. Even though these were ideas I had been developing for years, it was David's suggestion that made me realize that now was the time to turn them into a book.

Finally, I thank Steve Piersanti of Berrett-Koehler for his faith in me. I met Steve about ten years ago, and he encouraged me to get in touch with him if I needed a publisher. In early 2017, when I felt I needed a publisher with a global reach and who would understand the topic, appreciate its urgency, and not run scared from its controversial nature, the first person who came to mind was Steve.

I sent the outline expecting not to hear back or, at best, to receive a gentle rejection. What I received instead is what I now know to expect from Steve: encouragement, great interest, superb editing insights, coaching, noninterference in the author's independence, a deep respect for writers, and, most important, warm friendship. In this he is ably supported by a great team, of whom I got to know Jeevan Sivasubramaniam, Lasell Whipple, and Michael Crowley.

I also thank all those who participated in the book survey to pick a title and cover. This was a great idea by Berrett-Koehler, and those who responded with their picks and comments were of immense help. I am very grateful for their interest. I hope you like the title and the cover.

INDEX

Page references followed by *fig* indicate an illustrated figure; followed by *t* indicate a table.

About thirty years ago, soon after returning to Asia from a few years volunteering in Africa on development issues, Chandran Nair became very interested in the nature of economic development and the resultant impacts on the environment and natural resources of the world. He was particularly interested in the question of what would happen if the poor countries of the developing world, which account for the majority of the global population, aspired to rich lifestyles.

This led him to a career in environmental consulting, during which he built Asia's largest environmental consulting group. Fifteen years in consulting offered him an opportunity to work with many from all parts of the world, both in government and the private sector, and gain deep insights into the impacts of a fast-rising Asia. His experience led to an acute appreciation of the untenable tension between growth and what by then had become known as sustainable development.

Because of his belief that the developing world needs fresh ideas and that these should not simply be imported from the rich world, he left consulting to start the Global Institute for Tomorrow, which he labels a pan-Asian think "and do" tank. His views on issues in Asia and the developing world have been featured in the print media ranging from the *Financial Times,* the *Wall Street Journal,* and the *New York Times* to the *Huff Post, Guardian,* and *China Daily.* His opinions have been sought by an array of media outlets including the BBC, CNN, NHK, Al Jazeera, CCTV, Bloomberg, and Channel New Asia, among others.

He is a member of the Club of Rome and a fellow of the Royal Society of Arts. He is a keen sportsman and managed the Hong Kong field hockey team to two Asian Games. He plays the saxophone and used to be a member of an Afro-Jazz-Reggae band during his time in Africa.